LOST

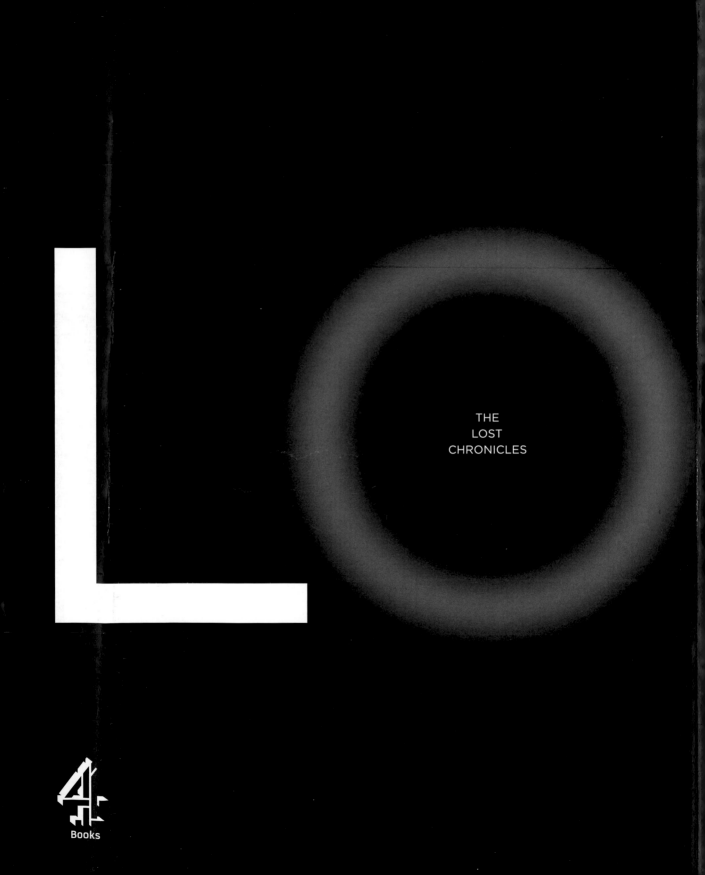

THE
LOST
CHRONICLES

4
Books

S T

BY
MARK COTTA
VAZ

TRANSWORLD PUBLISHERS
61-63 Uxbridge Road, London W5 5SA
a division of The Random House Group Ltd

RANDOM HOUSE AUSTRALIA (PTY) LTD
20 Alfred Street, Milsons Point, Sydney,
New South Wales 2061, Australia

RANDOM HOUSE NEW ZEALAND LTD
18 Poland Road, Glenfield, Auckland 10, New Zealand

RANDOM HOUSE SOUTH AFRICA (PTY) LTD
Isle of Houghton, Corner of Boundary Road and Carse O'Gowrie, Houghton 2198,
South Africa

Published in the UK in 2005 by Channel 4 Books a division of Transworld Publishers in
association with Hyperion.

A catalogue record for this book is available from the British Library.
Cased Edition ISBN 1905 026102 / 9781905 026104
Trade paperback ISBN 1905 026129 / 9781905 026128

Printed in Germany

 5 7 9 10 8 6 4

Papers used by Transworld Publishers are natural, recyclable products made from
wood grown in sustainable forests. The manufacturing processes conform to the
environmental regulations of the country of origin.

TO

J.J. ABRAMS,

DAMON
LINDELOF,

AND
THE CAST
AND CREW
OF *LOST*.

– M.C.V.

3

LET'S GET
LOST

The word "lost" is heavy with meaning and mystery. It defines both physical disorientation and psychological states of defeat and despair. And who hasn't absorbed at least a bit of lost lore? In fiction there are primordial lands that time forgot, in archeology the mystery of "lost" civilizations, in history and legend the tales of sailing ships gone off course in strange seas, intrepid explorers venturing dangerously far afield, airmen who fly into the blue and are never seen again.

Lost, the new ABC–TV weekly drama series released in the USA during the 2004–05 season, features the classic lost scenario of people stranded on an uncharted island. But the premise is about more than struggling to survive in a strange, wild place. As series co–creators J.J. Abrams and Damon Lindelof put it: "The show is about lost people on a lost island." Produced by Disney's Touchstone division (Disney also owns ABC), each hour–long episode chronicles a day or two in the ongoing ordeal of the survivors of Oceanic Airline Flight #815, which was bound from Sydney to Los Angeles when the plane strayed off course, broke up in mid–air, and crashed on a very mysterious island.

THE WORD "LOST" IS HEAVY WITH MEANING AND MYSTERY. IT DEFINES BOTH PHYSICAL DISORIENTATION AND PSYCHOLOGICAL STATES OF DEFEAT AND DESPAIR.

This book is a behind–the–scenes look at the making of the first *Lost* season, the creative challenges of producing a weekly drama, a look back at *Lost* mysteries and the emerging series mythology—we'll even spend a week with the cast and crew to witness the making of an episode.

This book is also a record of a phenomenon of popular culture. *Lost*, along with another new ABC series, *Desperate Housewives*, which follows the suburban intrigues of a group of sexy housewives, is credited with raising formerly beleaguered ABC to the top of the

FOR SAFETY REASONS, A CRANE AND CABLE SUPPORTED THE WING AT THE *LOST* CRASH SET. DURING POST–PRODUCTION, VISUAL EFFECTS SUPERVISOR KEVIN BLANK DIGITALLY ERASED ANY EVIDENCE OF THE SUPPORTING RIG, PROVIDING THE ILLUSION OF A FREE-STANDING WING.

US network ratings chart. "Fourth–place nose–diver ABC has pulled a Lazarus act," *San Francisco Chronicle* television columnist Tim Goodman noted enthusiastically in a January 5, 2005 column, " … That the entire country swooned for *Desperate Housewives* and *Lost* is this season's biggest stunner. Both shows are terrifically entertaining and smart and have pro-pelled ABC to the ratings stratosphere."

Entertainment Weekly, in a December 24, 2004 report, also noted that ABC had pulled a "stunner of a comeback," moving into second place in total viewer-ship. *Lost* itself was solidly in the top ten in the USA, with an estimated 17.7 million weekly viewers—"Surprise hit!" the *EW* article trumpeted. The success ran contrary to typical network programming of recent years, which has counted on live events and low–cost "reality" shows to deliver ratings, not big–budget episodic productions. *Lost* was even an unlikely network drama, a world apart from traditional "procedural" shows featuring cops, courtrooms and hospital emergency rooms.

And while the typical tele-vision production was shot on soundstages and backlots in places like Los Angeles or Vancouver, the logistics of *Lost* were complex. The main *Lost* production office (along with J.J. Abrams' own office and that of his other ABC show, *Alias*), are at storied Walt Disney Studios in Burbank, located at the far end of the lot near a pedestrian bridge connecting Disney to ABC headquarters. The filming of each episode is entirely set on the Hawaiian island of Oahu, a setup far from *Gilligan's Island*, that whacky TV comedy from the 1960s in which tour boat castaways regularly faced the chal-lenges of surviving on a Hollywood soundstage.

The success of *Lost* was not preordained. Although championed by a few true believers, skeptics rightfully wondered how the premise of strangers stranded on a deserted island could possibly sustain a weekly series. Indeed, the initial pilot script that made its way to producer–director Abrams had plot points hinging on such matters as survivors learning how to spearfish—

hardly enough to keep a worldwide audience riveted to their sets.

That the initial, sketchy premise was developed into a hit was due to the creative energy of co–creators Abrams and Lindelof (who also serves as a series writer and executive producer), the team of producers and writers, and the cast and crew. Abrams, who also cre-ated the long–running *Felicity* and whose *Alias* was heading into its fourth season, brought to his work a love of B–genre material, the stuff of comic book super-hero action, hard–boiled crime, creepy horror, science fiction, 1970s disaster movies—anything in the pop pantheon that might instinctively register as "Totally Cool." It was a kind of mantra for Abrams to take B–genre material and do it "A" with top–flight writing, casting and production values. For Abrams, Lindelof and their collaborators, the creative possibilities for the lost island scenario would not be limiting but liberating.

As they developed the lost island premise, the island itself emerged as a character. Outwardly, the island is

THE SUCCESS RAN CONTRARY TO TYPICAL NETWORK PROGRAMMING OF RECENT YEARS, WHICH HAS COUNTED ON LIVE EVENTS AND LOW-COST "REALITY" SHOWS TO DELIVER RATINGS, NOT BIG-BUDGET EPISODIC PRODUCTIONS.

tropical, gets plenty of rain and provides the survivors with an abundance of fish, fruit trees and wild game. The terrain ranges from vast beachfronts to jungles and a valley with soaring mountains and caves and waterfalls. But the island also embodies the mysteries and terrors of the Unknown (and a lot of those cool B–genre elements). Most of the island remains unexplored and mysterious, but it's more than that—strange, even supernatural, phenomena occupy the survivors as much as basic issues of food, shelter and security. *Lost*

stunt coordinator Michael Vendrell evokes a popular reality show and a classic TV thriller when he describes *Lost* as "*Survivor* meets *The Twilight Zone*."

The strange happenings include a gigantic "thing" lurking in the jungle, polar bears normally found in the Arctic, a radio message transmitted on the island sixteen years ago that is still broadcasting, the possible existence of a tribe of "Others" inhabiting the interior, puzzling evidence of past human habitations (notably two skeletons dubbed "Adam and Eve") and a sealed, man-made hatch in the jungle that may hold the secrets of the island.

The *Lost* mysteries have inspired spirited workplace watercooler talk and Internet chatter. Arguably, part of the show's popularity is that it keeps fans guessing. "The writers are all working hard to keep the mystery and mythology of the show alive on a kind of *Twilight Zone* level," noted Jack Bender, an executive producer and one of the series' episode directors and creative masterminds. "There's this tweaky aspect—what *is* this island? The Internet people think they're all dead and it's Purgatory. But the audience cares about these people and their secrets, all of which falls into classic drama. I think that's why J.J.'s shows work, whether it's *Felicity*, which was a character-driven show, or *Alias*, which is a spy show—you care about the characters. Ultimately, that's the heart of this show: What are these people going to face every week?"

Indeed, the survivors have brought some heavy baggage to the island, and not just the suitcases, backpacks and boxes strewn along their beach crash-site

(although some of that luggage holds the deepest secrets of some characters). All of the fourteen featured passengers are burdened with painful emotional baggage, with each character's often tortured past revealed in flashbacks.

Matthew Fox, who plays the successful surgeon who emerges as a leader of the lost colony, has pointed to the fully–realized characters as one of the show's compelling aspects, echoing Abrams and Lindelof's concept, as producer Jean Higgins recalls: "Matthew

did an interview where he was really articulate about the show. He said, 'When all is said and done, it's not about the people being physically lost but that the people are psychologically lost and finding themselves.' To me, that's really the key, that you're so involved in the characters."

CHARLIE (DOMINIC MONAGHAN) FEELS THE CRASH OF OCEANIC AIRWAYS FLIGHT 815 WAS AN ACT OF FATE. SHANNON (MAGGIE GRACE) SCREAMS AMID THE CHAOS OF THE PLANE CRASH.

"We're seeing moments of it in the short term, but overriding this series will be a big, epic feel and answers to questions like, 'What's the true nature of the human species?'" Matthew Fox mused. "You drop fifty people in the middle of nowhere, strip away all of society's rules that we take for granted every day and which guide us in a behavioral manner, and suddenly it's survival of the fittest. And on top of all that, you add this mystery and sci–fi element. You know they're going to be battling amongst themselves but there are also many moments when they'll have to band together to battle something bigger than themselves and that's when I feel the series will feel hopeful and positive, almost operatic."

Lost is also a show with serious consequences for its characters. Early in the series the creators declared that one of the main characters would die and they kept that grim promise with the passing of Boone (Ian Somerhalder), a young former lifeguard and head of a division of a matrimony business owned by his mother. The death would have a ripple effect on the dynamic of the show, given that Boone had become an acolyte of John Locke (Terry O'Quinn), the hunter and seeming mystic among the survivors, and that Boone had a complex relationship with his stepsister Shannon and disapproved of her attraction to Sayid (Naveen Andrews), a former member of the Iraqi Republican Guard.

"There was an episode where Boone complained to Locke about Sayid hitting on his sister," observed executive producer Bryan Burk. "And Locke says something to the effect, 'We need him on our side.' And the question is: When did we start having sides? There's this idea that there's going to be different

Burk's last point touches on the little miracle of episodic television, wherein a premise gets rolling, generates its own inexorable forward momentum, and series creators sprint ahead of their creation to make production deadlines and keep an emerging storyline fresh and intriguing, all the while aiming for the iconic

JACK, KATE AND SAWYER SHARE A DRAMATIC MOMENT.
SERIES CO-CREATOR DAMON LINDELOF.
JOHN LOCKE PREPARES DINNER.

story arcs that loom like landmarks on the creative journey. In this case, it's a creative journey that is projected to unfold over a number of seasons to come.

groups, that things will fracture. At its core, that's what's so exciting about *Lost*—these are real people in extraordinary situations. If [fans] are sticking around, hoping to find out what this crazy monster thing is that's running through the jungle then, fine, stick around. But that's not what this show is about. For me, the show doesn't really kick in until our second or third season."

But at the beginning, when the idea was being dreamed up and developed, *Lost* had been all "blue sky," full of unlimited potential and possibilities. In the ensuing creative process the creators broke the usual rules by which a network series is created. "It was a weird and amazing process," Bryan Burk recalled.

THE LOST

HISTORY

A closed eyelid opens, the pupil dilated as if shocked back into consciousness from some hallucinatory nightmare. Above, tall trees sway in the breeze. A young man dressed in a suit, his face bloodied and tie askew, is flat on his back and breathing hard. He hears a sound—out of a thicket of bamboo a dog appears and skips past him into the forest. The man struggles to his feet in pain. He reaches into a jacket pocket and pulls out a little bottle of liquor, the kind used for airline cocktails. As if he suddenly remembers something, he begins to run through the forest, passes a white tennis shoe caught on a thin tree, bursts out of the brush into the open—a tranquil scene of pristine beach and frothy surf, blue sky and ocean. But he hears a scream and a mechanical whining coming from around a bend of trees. He follows the noise and is back in his nightmare, a crash site where burning airplane wreckage lines the beach, the turbines of an engine are still dangerously spinning and survivors are staggering, screaming, falling down on the sand in shock. A cry for help snaps Jack out of his daze and into action. Jack calls for assistance to help pull off a piece of wreckage that has pinned one survivor, he pulls off his tie to use as a tourniquet for the man's bloodied leg …

Thus opened the pilot for *Lost*. No elaborate plot setup, no introduction of passengers boarding a plane, no protracted buildup to a mechanical malfunction and crash—suddenly, *wham*! Along with Jack, the audience was dropped into a full–blown, disorienting disaster zone of smoking metal and bloodied victims. It was an opener that aired almost exactly as imagined by series creators. In those few opening minutes the lost island theme was presented, a continuing motif introduced (an eye suddenly opening), the central character and heroic personality of Jack established and at least a glimpse provided of most of the principal characters.

The origins of *Lost* are about network executives pushing an idea that ran counter to predictable programming and a production team that dreamed up a compelling story arc and brought a bare–bones premise to life. By all accounts, once J.J. Abrams was sent the idea of plane crash survivors stranded on a deserted island, a creative whirlwind was unleashed.

Bryan Burk, a young producer who had made a career move from feature film production to television, had gotten involved with *Alias* halfway through its first season. Burk had missed the genesis and development of that TV show, so getting caught up in the *Lost* whirlwind was a new experience. But so it would be for everyone involved. *Lost*, in practically every respect, was an anomaly in the business of launching a TV series.

LEFT: **PRODUCER BRYAN BURK AND J.J. ABRAMS ON SET.** RIGHT: **JACK (MATTHEW FOX), THROWN INTO THE JUNGLE WHEN THE PLANE CRASHED, RETURNS TO THE NIGHTMARE OF THE CRASH SITE.**

It had all begun quite innocently, Burk recalled, around 11:00 p.m. on Thursday, January 8, 2004. He had arrived to meet J.J. Abrams at Kate Mantilini, a restaurant on Wilshire Boulevard in Beverly Hills, favored for such comfort food offerings as macaroni and cheese and Snicker's–bar cake. Abrams was at a table, working on a script for a pilot he would also direct, called *The Catch*. The proposed series about private investigators was expected to fill a remaining slot in ABC's 2004–2005 schedule and Abrams was focused on getting his script to the network for approval and then, hopefully, beginning preproduction on the pilot. When Burk joined him, Abrams pulled out something the network had sent him that very day, a pilot script Burk recalls as being titled *Nowhere*.

Abrams recalls the network had always referred to the project as *Lost* and all he knew at the outset was

that it was about people stuck on a deserted island. The project carried a special urgency, having been sent over by Lloyd Braun, then ABC's entertainment chairman, who had personally proposed the idea at a summer 2003 network retreat. A writer had been attached to Braun's idea, but the resulting *Nowhere* script seemed to be going the way of its title. Braun still loved the concept and while resigned to it not making that year's schedule, had called on J.J. Abrams, one of the network's star producers, to see what he could make of it.

When Burk sat down with Abrams at the restaurant, Abrams handed him the script and asked him to take a look at it right then and there. "To this day, J.J. has never read that original script," Burk recalled. "I got halfway

DIRECTOR J.J. ABRAMS WITH MATTHEW FOX AT THE BEACH CRASH-SITE SET.

discuss the elements he felt were necessary to feed the premise. The inevitable aspects would be man against man, man against nature. But the biggest element would be man against the Unknown. The island, Abrams proposed, would be a place of mystery and secrets.

"Lloyd's response was, 'Great—let's do it!'" Burk recalled. "And J.J. was like, 'Uh, what? I'm in the middle of writing *The Catch*, I can't possibly take on another thing right now.' And Lloyd said, 'Don't worry, we'll find you a writer, we'll find you someone to work with.'"

The writer, contacted that very day, was Damon Lindelof, who had developed a pilot for ABC that hadn't been picked up, and was working on the series *Crossing Jordan*. Although Lindelof was an *Alias* fan, he had met neither Abrams nor Burk when he walked into Abrams' office the following Monday, having had only the weekend to ponder the castaway idea.

through it and could see why it wasn't working. Act One begins and you meet everybody on a plane and by the end of the opening act you know everything about them and then the plane starts to go down. Act Two, they learn to survive and by the end of that act they've learned how to spearfish. Basically, that script summed up all the fears people in general had about the show, which was how can we make a series out of this? It was just about people stuck on an island and, from what I read, seemed very generic. You'd definitely run out of steam."

Halfway through, Burk put down the script and started talking with Abrams about a show he always wanted to do that would be a unique blending of various science fiction elements. "And then, J.J. just said, 'Well, why can't we do that on a deserted island?' I said, 'I suppose we could.' And that was the end of the conversation for that night."

The next day, Abrams floated the deserted island idea and the notion of a sci–fi element to *Alias* writers and co–executive producers Jesse Alexander and Jeff Pinker. Later that Friday, Abrams called Braun to

DAMON SITS DOWN AND SAYS, "I'VE BEEN THINKING ABOUT IT AND LET'S CALL [THE MAIN CHARACTER] JACK. THE WAY IT WOULD BEGIN IS HE'S WEARING AN ARMANI SUIT AND HE'S KIND OF DISCOMBOBULATED AND HE WAKES UP ON A BEACH ... "

"In walks this guy who was about our age and wearing a *Star Wars* fan–club T–shirt and we're like, 'Hey, how come we're not best friends already?'" Burk laughed. "Damon sits down and says, 'I've been thinking about it and let's call [the main character] Jack.

PILOT DIRECTOR J.J. ABRAMS PREPARES A SHOT WITH MAGGIE GRACE AND DOMINIC MONAGHAN, WITH BOOM OPERATOR ROBERT JOE MICHALSKI IN BACKGROUND.

LOST VISUAL EFFECTS SUPERVISOR KEVIN BLANK (WITH FIANCÉE JANICE BARNES), ONE OF THE CO–RECIPIENTS OF THE VISUAL EFFECTS SOCIETY'S AWARD FOR BEST SUPPORTING VISUAL EFFECTS IN A BROADCAST PROGRAM, HONORING THE *LOST* PILOT.

"We thought that was a cool way to begin the show," Burk noted. "And then J.J.'s wheels started going and you could see he and Damon were instantly the best of friends and bouncing ideas off each other. Suffice to say, we had all these things we love, like a great mystery, with this idea about these mysterious radio transmissions at the end [of the pilot episode]. I'm also pretty sure that in that first pitch we killed Jack at the end of the third act."

Abrams' office was still in "the height of all the craziness," Burk recalled, with J.J. finishing his pilot script for *The Catch*, and Jesse Alexander and Jeff Pinker deep into the new season of *Alias*. Still, after that Monday pitch session, time was carved out during the rest of the week for Alexander, Pinker, Burk and Lindelof to meet in Alexander's office to dream up a lost island pilot and story arc for a potential series. At the end of each day, Abrams would hear the ideas, then huddle with Lindelof to further develop the emerging story.

Meanwhile, by Thursday Abrams had turned in his pilot script for *The Catch*. The next day, Abrams got the

The way it would begin is he's wearing an Armani suit and he's kind of discombobulated and he wakes up on a beach.'"

The opening scenario Lindelof outlined would, in almost every particular, make it into the pilot episode, with the crash having thrown Jack into a nearby jungle, then a golden retriever (later changed to a labrador) runs past like the white rabbit out of *Alice in Wonderland*, Jack follows, and comes to the wreckage of a 747.

A tour de force visual effects sequence for the *Lost* pilot was the breakup of the Oceanic airplane, particularly the tail section ripping apart. "For the final breakup we added camera shake and digital plane pieces breaking apart," explained visual effects supervisor Kevin Blank (who shared supervisory duties on the pilot with Mitch Suskin). "We shot several passes of the plane set with a locked–off camera before we removed the back of the airplane interior and put up a forty–foot greenscreen. The next day we brought in stunt people and ratcheted them into the air, so it would look like they're flying back into the empty sky for the final image."

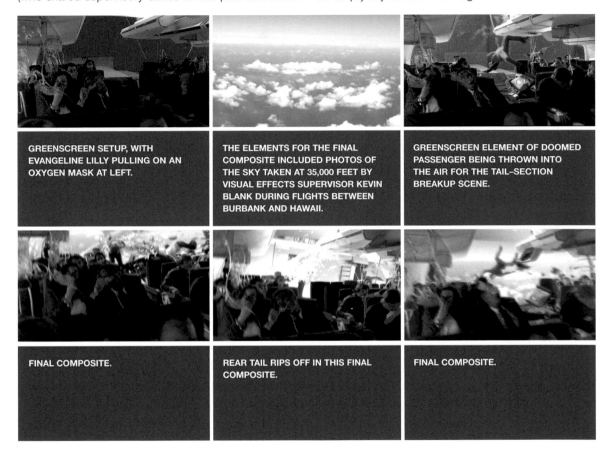

GREENSCREEN SETUP, WITH EVANGELINE LILLY PULLING ON AN OXYGEN MASK AT LEFT.

THE ELEMENTS FOR THE FINAL COMPOSITE INCLUDED PHOTOS OF THE SKY TAKEN AT 35,000 FEET BY VISUAL EFFECTS SUPERVISOR KEVIN BLANK DURING FLIGHTS BETWEEN BURBANK AND HAWAII.

GREENSCREEN ELEMENT OF DOOMED PASSENGER BEING THROWN INTO THE AIR FOR THE TAIL–SECTION BREAKUP SCENE.

FINAL COMPOSITE.

REAR TAIL RIPS OFF IN THIS FINAL COMPOSITE.

FINAL COMPOSITE.

call from the network—they loved it. *The Catch* seemed destined to fill a slot in the schedule. That Friday, Abrams and Lindelof also turned in a fifteen–page outline. By Saturday morning, J.J. Abrams got a call from Lloyd Braun and, in turn, Abrams called Bryan Burk with the news—based on the outline, ABC had greenlit the pilot for *Lost*.

The swiftness with which the *Lost* pilot was greenlit—with only a treatment, not a full script—was stunning. Typically, a potential series is presented to a network and once a pilot script is submitted, the creators and production company receive creative notes from the network and rewrite accordingly. By January, prospective pilots are greenlit for production, triggering a mad dash to assemble a cast and crew and shoot the pilot, delivery deadlines usually dictating the production wrap within fourteen days or less. Another winnowing process then takes place, as network executives screen the pilots and make final selections. Finally, in come schedulers to determine time slots for the new lineup. By May, the new shows are ready for "up–fronts," industry lingo for the airtime bought by advertisers for the season,

IN THE STORY, A LIVE ENGINE SUCKS IN A BYSTANDER AND EXPLODES. HERE THE PYROTECHNIC EFFECT IS BEING FILMED.

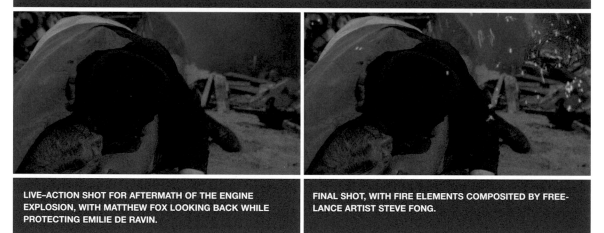

LIVE–ACTION SHOT FOR AFTERMATH OF THE ENGINE EXPLOSION, WITH MATTHEW FOX LOOKING BACK WHILE PROTECTING EMILIE DE RAVIN.

FINAL SHOT, WITH FIRE ELEMENTS COMPOSITED BY FREE-LANCE ARTIST STEVE FONG.

followed by marketing. In June each network's development team begins the creative cycle all over again.

Lost had bypassed that normally six–to–eight–month process, with all its inherent pitfalls and attrition. An idea that had been creatively stalled and briefly discussed at a midnight meeting in a restaurant had become, in slightly over a week, a real deal. Meanwhile, Abrams was still proceeding with *The Catch*.

There was still a major creative issue that had to be settled. Abrams and Lindelof had initially planned to make Jack a noble, heroic figure and then kill him off at the end of act two of a seven–act pilot. Steven McPherson, then head of Touchstone, was adamant— *You can't kill Jack*, Burk recalled. "He said, 'How can you ask your audience to put their faith in this doctor, in the one person who's leading the survivors, and then kill him?' That was actually the thing that had been exciting to us, but he just made this great argument."

The concerns about Jack's death had been expressed from a number of quarters. On Monday,

January 26, a major meeting was scheduled on the greenlit lost island pilot. Abrams' team would sit down with a group that included Braun, Steven McPherson, then head of Touchstone, Susan Lyne, then president of ABC Entertainment, and Thom Sherman, who would become head of Bad Robot, Abrams' production company. It was a mere two weeks before shooting the pilot that a final meeting decided Jack's fate. "The one note we kept getting back from many different avenues was to let Jack live," Damon Lindelof recalled. "Before

one person who could direct it and that was J.J. But he was locked up to do *The Catch*, which was also proceeding simultaneously."

But it never got to the point where another director had to be selected for what would be a feature–length two–hour pilot. Abrams decided to push *The Catch* pilot

SAWYER (JOSH HOLLOWAY) BEING RESTRAINED AFTER ATTACKING SAYID (NAVEEN ANDREWS). "JOSH WAS SO IMPOSSIBLY *ON*, HE JUST GOT IT," PILOT DIRECTOR J.J. ABRAMS RECALLED OF THE FIGHT SCENE.

we went into this meeting, J.J. said, 'Stop, wait!' And for about twenty minutes we talked about what it would mean if we let Jack live."

By the time casting began, the production demands for the pilot had gotten bigger and bigger, although the big–ticket project had the advantage of having come from ABC. "At our first big production meeting with Damon and I and everyone from Touchstone and ABC, we realized this pilot was going to take a lot of days to shoot and be very expensive," Burk recalled. "It was such a freight train going forward with so little prepro-duction time that Damon and I realized there was only to the following season. He would concentrate on *Lost* and direct the pilot.

Reportedly, the biggest pilot episode ABC had previously done was an estimated twenty–two–day shoot for Abrams' *Alias* opener. *Lost* was more than a month of shooting for a two–hour show and rumored to be the most expensive pilot ever made.

But back when the production start–date loomed, they still had to write the script, cast the actors, assemble the crew, scout and secure locations. Sarah Caplan, an *Alias* producer who took on production duties for the pilot, recalls that it was the narrowest of preproduction windows—six weeks of prep. In retrospect,

Caplan coolly understates the challenge: "The lack of time was an interesting factor."

J.J. Abrams wanted the production to be big in every way. He had tapped Sarah Caplan as his producer because he felt she was the only one who could meet the daunting challenge. "I learned you can do anything," Caplan summed up.

At the start, Caplan had one major, overriding decision—*where* were they going to shoot? There was no time to recreate a lost island jungle setting on

THE L–10 11 BEING CUT UP IN THE MOJAVE AIRPLANE GRAVEYARD FOR TRANSPORT TO THE SAN FRANCISCO BAY AREA. PHOTOS BY SARAH CAPLAN.

Caplan went to Hawaii with only the *Lost* treatment in hand but got a warm reception in Oahu, with special help from Walea L. Constantinau of the Honolulu Film Office. The beach crash–site set that was decided upon was at Mokuleia, a public beach with a road that would actually cut through the set. But other than traffic concerns, Mokuleia was ideal, with a beautiful beach big enough to hold the plane wreckage, along with a picturesque mountain backdrop and nearby jungle.

It was "full steam ahead" when Caplan returned to Burbank where the script and casting were still in the works. Meanwhile, in addition to Caplan producing and Abrams directing, the rest of the production team was taking form, including Mark Worthington as production designer and Larry Fong as director of photography. The studio had reservations about whether Fong, who had mostly done commercials and rock videos, could handle a project of the scope envisioned for *Lost*, but Fong was Abrams' choice and won the assignment.

Except for a few days to shoot soundstage scenes of the airplane interior in Los Angeles, the entire production would be filmed on Oahu. The plane for the crash–site set was always envisioned as a real plane that would be broken into pieces. Abrams wanted a 747 but the production settled for an L–10 11, one of the early wide–body jets. The *Lost* production found its mythical Oceanic Airways jet in an airplane graveyard on the outskirts of Lancaster and Palmdale in the Mojave Desert. It was a "weird, bizarre" place, Caplan recalled, including jumbo jets literally kept under wraps, which had been grounded after the "9/11" terrorist attack caused a drop in air travel.

They had their plane, but all the barges out of Los Angeles to Hawaii were booked. The only alternative was to get a ship that was in dry dock up north in Oakland. The entire L–10 11 would have to be cut up in the airplane graveyard and driven up to the Bay Area.

"The cutting was done in the Mojave, with an amazing piece of equipment," Caplan explained. "It looks like a big digger but has a giant clipper at the end and it just starts slicing into the plane. The fuselage is like a big tube and this cuts it in half and then in quarters, just slices through. Quite amazing. When we were

an elaborate soundstage, *Gilligan's Island* style. Regardless, the ambitions were to make it big and make it real. Caplan knew they needed a pristine beach, a nearby jungle and a plane. The "studio"— shorthand for both the ABC network and Touchstone— proposed Australia. But the best possibility for a deserted beach was in Brisbane, with the nearest jungle a plane ride away. The other problem was that the pilot and ensuing series would require actors to relocate to Australia, a tough sell given its distance from Los Angeles, the heart of the entertainment industry. The morning Caplan was to head out to scout sites in Australia she canceled that trip and asked to be sent to Hawaii.

having this work done, there were a number of men, airplane builders, who came by to watch. This airplane graveyard is near Lancaster and Palm, this whole area for aerospace and where they built jets and planes. Some of the men who had built the old L–10 11's stood and watched this with tears in their eyes. When the cutter clipped off the tail, everyone cheered. A lot of the plane pieces were put into containers, some of the engines were kept intact, the seventy–foot wings were chopped up. It was all taken up by truck. It was touch and go about whether it would arrive in Hawaii in time. A day later would have screwed things up."

By then, the set locations had already been visited by Abrams and Mark Worthington, the necessary permits obtained through the Hawaiian Film Board. Worthington had made a scale model of what the plane wreck set at Mokuleia beach would look like and had shown it to the state people. The challenges on the beach included Abrams' directive that they were not going to have the seventy–plus–foot wing as a computer generated image—it was going to be the real wing dangerously sticking up in the air. "I got a great special effect guy to be our consultant, Tommy Fisher," Caplan explained. "He did *Titanic*, for instance. A very savvy character."

Caplan recalls that one of the signature bits of *Lost*

mythology happened when she and J.J. Abrams were on Oahu, driving along a bumpy road. "J.J. wanted something odd on the island and at first it was going to be a wild boar. But he didn't think that was weird enough. He wanted something unusual—a rhinoceros came up. Then, as a joke, I said a polar bear would be unusual.

"I didn't propose the polar bear seriously," Caplan laughed. "But J.J. went, '*Polar bear*! That's it! That's what it should be.' I created a monster."

ACTOR DOMINIC MONAGHAN WALKS IN FRONT OF A HOLLOW ENGINE ON THE CRASH-SITE SET.

THE LIVE–ACTION IMAGE DIGITALLY ENHANCED WITH THE ILLUSION OF A STILL SPINNING ENGINE. COMPUTER–GENERATED IMAGERY WAS CREATED BY ARTIST SPENCER LEVY OF KAIA, INC., AN EFFECTS HOUSE BASED IN NEW MEXICO.

THE DRAMATIC STANDING WING OF THE OCEANIC WRECK. THIS PHOTO BY BRYAN BURK CAPTURES A MOMENT DURING ABRAMS' LONG–DISTANCE DEBATE WITH ABC ABOUT THE PILOT ENDING.

At the beach location, the production also had to contend with squatters, a group of largely indigenous Hawaiians who traditionally camped out on the beaches. "The squatters are also a nationalist movement, it was a complex setup [dealing with the issue], something a film crew cannot get involved in," Caplan noted. "But we needed this beach and everything was ironed out. Some of the squatters were moved further down the beach, others stayed in our encampment. I think they were bemused by our production."

All through the process, Caplan just kept focused on the mantra: "We'll get it done."

To disassemble the plane at the beach set required two construction coordinators who wouldn't be able to work with their normal crews back in L.A., but with a team of people from Hawaii. Caplan got Bill Gideon and Dale Destefani. "I needed two coordinators who would think it was fun and want to get it done. I think film crews, especially American film crews, are good in a crisis, they're very resourceful. It's a point of pride. It's an American thing, I think, to like a challenge."

The beach became a scene of controlled chaos as earth movers and fork lifts began laying down the wreckage. Caplan noted that because of the hotel construction in Oahu they thankfully could get a hundred–foot crane to keep the signature standing wing secured and up in the air.

The disaster scene was so realistic that there were frantic phone calls to the authorities about a crashed plane and rescue operation on Mokuleia. "For a while we tried to keep the production under wraps," Caplan recalled. "But I remember we were in our hotel elevator and people were talking about a plane crash. In the end, we had to put out a press release [about the production]."

Lost visual effects supervisor Kevin Blank recalls the beach was essentially extended with a covering of sand over the public road which, although not a major

EVANGELINE LILLY AND IAN SOMERHALDER POSE AT THE *LOST* PREMIERE PARTY AT QUEEN'S SURF BEACH IN WAIKIKI. THE PILOT BEING SHOWN TO PARTYGOERS ON A BIG SCREEN. MAGGIE GRACE, JOSH HOLLOWAY AND MALCOLM DAVID KELLEY AT THE PREMIERE.

DIRECTED BY
J.J. ABRAMS

thoroughfare and literally the end of the road, still required "an army of PA's [production assistants]" to hold up traffic, usually at least three cars, when the cameras were rolling.

"We had three weeks of shooting at the beach and it was fantastic," Caplan recalled. "We'd swim at lunchtime. There would be turtles in the water and it was gorgeous. Every night the wing was lowered and raised back up the next day. J.J. was very well prepared about how he was going to shoot. He's very smart and, I would say, ballsy. A great combination."

Abrams and Lindelof sum up the difficulties of the pilot by describing how, in the midst of shooting, the network called and asked if they could shoot an alternate ending and make the show a standalone TV movie. "We said, 'How can we possibly do that?'" Lindelof recalled. "The pilot was designed so people would want to see more, everything was based on making this a series. The analogy was like being asked to build a car and coming back to ask, 'Can it also be a boat?' 'No, it can't be a boat, you told us to build a car and if you make it a boat it'll sink!'"

"This happened literally while we were shooting the pilot," Abrams nodded, with a wan smile. "I have a picture Bryan Burk took of me pacing on the wing of the plane, talking on my cell phone back with ABC, having this impassioned argument of how it was impossible to do a closed ending for the show. Luckily, we weren't required to do that."

Although the *Lost* series itself would emphasize physical effects, the pilot was a major visual effects effort, with close to 200 shots, Kevin Blank estimated. There were twenty–five to thirty shots alone required for the digital removal of the crane and wires holding up an airplane wing. A dramatic scene in which a live engine

dumbfounded that Sarah Caplan put the pilot together," Burk concluded. "It was amazing the network and studio took a chance and decided that if they were going to do it, they were going to do it right, regardless of the expense. Everyone made a leap of faith with an immense project, before there was even a script. They had complete faith in J.J. and Damon."

"What's great about this show is it's not supposed to work, it sort of defies the laws of television in a very

THE CAST ASSEMBLES! **PERRINEAU AND O'QUINN CHILL OUT.**

sucked in a bystander and explodes was a heavily visual effects number.

The final schedule, Caplan notes, saw the preproduction period starting on January 26, 2004, with the interior plane shoot in Los Angeles on March 9 and the Hawaii work beginning on March 17 and the pilot finished on May 1.

Bryan Burk would note the entire process—from that Thursday when Lloyd Braun contacted J.J. Abrams to the production delivering an eighty–two–minute pilot to ABC—was less than four months. "It's amazing how April [Webster, casting director] was able to assemble this cast in such a short amount of time, I'm

exciting way," Lindelof smiled. "But the thing J.J. has always strived to do is to take TV and *not* do the boilerplate procedural but ask how to make something exciting, how can it look and feel different?"

Bryan Burk added that the feedback he gets from people in the industry is that no one had ever heard of a show getting on the air so quickly, and that they were surprised that such a complicated production had kept moving forward.

"Who could have dreamt that, even a year ago, we'd have this show?" Burk smiled. "That people are watching is the most rewarding, crazy thing in the world."

SURVIVOR

STORIES

In the *Lost* storyline, the chain of events
leading to the plane crash would be replayed
in the memories of the survivors. These
are the known facts: Oceanic Flight 815 was
six hours out from Sydney and bound for
Los Angeles when the plane's radio went out
and the pilot turned back to make an
emergency landing at Fiji. The plane was a
thousand miles off course and flying at
40,000 feet when turbulence began shaking
the plane and it broke apart, beginning with
the tail section. Some forty-eight passengers
are known to have survived the crash. Of
the survivors, the following are the main figures
whose stories are explored in *Lost*.

JACK SHEPHARD (MATTHEW FOX)

Why he was on the plane: Jack, a young spinal surgeon, had come to Australia seeking his estranged father, a formerly respected and successful head of surgery, and found him—in a morgue. Jack was bringing his father's body back to Los Angeles on the Oceanic flight.

On the island: As the only known doctor among the survivors, Jack emerged as designated healer and de facto leader of the lost colony. He was one of the discoverers of the caves in the valley and an advocate for moving there because of its natural shelter and fresh water. A level–headed guy, he cannot explain why he's seen the apparition of his father.

Flashback: Had a life–long schism with his successful father, who felt his son was emotionally weak and would never measure up. While a rising young surgeon working at the same hospital as his father, Jack revealed it was his father's negligence that resulted in a pregnant woman's death. The revelation destroyed his father's career and accelerated his downward spiral.

A RUNNING SUBPLOT IN THE UNFOLDING *LOST* SAGA IS THE TRIANGLE OF JACK, SAWYER AND KATE.
JOHN LOCKE IN A TYPICALLY INTENSE MOMENT.

KATE RYAN (EVANGELINE LILLY)

Why she was on the plane: Kate, a criminal on the run, had been arrested in Australia and was in handcuffs under the custody of a U.S. marshal.

On the island: Resourceful and an experienced tracker, independent but well–liked, capable of manipulating men to get what she wants. The object of Jack and Sawyer's affections. Used both Sawyer and Jack to recover and open a silver case the marshal had carried, which held a key icon of her mysterious past—a model airplane.

Flashback: Pulled a bank robbery in New Mexico, the purpose of which was to get into the safe–deposit box holding the model plane, which she recovered from the silver case on the island. Secretive about her past, enigmatically confessed to Jack that she once killed the man she loved.

SAWYER (JOSH HOLLOWAY)

Why he was on the plane: Was returning from Australia, where he had gone to settle an old score.

On the island: Scavenger, hoarder, packrat supreme. If someone wants anything of real or personal value from the airplane wreckage—from a laptop computer to a diary—chances are Sawyer has it. Seems to enjoy the role of outcast and troublemaker. Was the victim of torture at the hands of Sayid while Jack watched. Has a thing for Kate and has nicknamed her "Freckles." Along with Sayid, has heard the eerie "whispers" in the jungle.

Flashback: Hails from Tennessee, once answered to the name James Ford. His father had killed his mother and then himself, a tragedy he witnessed as a young boy. The killings were the brutal aftermath of a disastrous deal with a con artist named Sawyer. Many years later, still burning for revenge, had been told the whereabouts of Sawyer and had gone to Sydney where he shot the man to death, only to realize he killed an innocent man and had been used by another con artist to settle a debt. In his self-loathing adopted the name Sawyer.

JOHN LOCKE (TERRY O'QUINN)

Why he was on the plane: Had come to Australia to participate in an organized walkabout, the ancient aboriginal rite of survival in the wilderness. Was returning home because he was rejected from the walkabout when he showed up in a wheelchair.

On the island: Immediately after the crash, discovered he had miraculously regained the full use of his legs. Had on board a case of hunting knives, which he recovered from the wreckage and uses as the colony's designated hunter. Is seemingly in tune with the island's mysterious forces and the only survivor to gaze upon the gigantic "thing" lurking in the jungle. He attracted his first disciple in Boone, with whom he discovered a mysterious sealed hatch deep in the jungle.

Flashback: No one on the island, except the late Boone Carlyle, knows Locke was a paraplegic. Back home, was a regional collection supervisor for a box company before shucking it all for his walkabout dream. Nicknamed the "colonel" for his fascination with war games. Had been seeing a therapist and had a platonic phone–in friendship with a phone–sex woman until she rejected his invitation to join him in Australia. Felt the walkabout was his destiny; now feels the island is where he will work out his purpose.

SUN KWON (YUNJIN KIM)

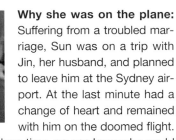

Why she was on the plane: Suffering from a troubled marriage, Sun was on a trip with Jin, her husband, and planned to leave him at the Sydney airport. At the last minute had a change of heart and remained with him on the doomed flight.

On the island: For a long time, no one knew she could speak English, not even her husband (Michael first learned her secret, then Kate). Has asserted her independence from her husband, notably in the casual dress he considers immodest and her use of English. A natural horticulturist, Sun started a fruit and herb garden and has collected medicinal plants from the jungle—some eucalyptus she provided helped Shannon overcome a severe asthma attack.

Flashback: The daughter of a wealthy and powerful Korean businessman, she had fallen in love with Jin, a waiter who seemed below her station. But in exchange for her daughter's hand, Jin agreed to work for her father. Sun has grown apart from her husband but still loves him.

JIN-SOO KWON (DANIEL DAE KIM)

Why he was on the plane: Had flown to Sydney and was bound for Los Angeles with his wife to deliver expensive watches as gifts to associates of his powerful boss.

On the island: Frustrated by his marital problems, bound by a strict code of honor, a non–English speaking Korean—Jin has had a tough time adjusting to life on the island. Had to be forcibly restrained after tackling Michael when he saw him wearing one of the watches he had been delivering on behalf of his boss, which Michael had innocently picked out of the wreckage. Jin was falsely accused of burning a raft Michael had been constructing. Language barrier remains a problem, but Jin has made attempts at becoming part of the community, including helping Michael rebuild his raft. A superb fisherman, he presented fresh fish to Hurley as an overture of friendship.

Flashback: Was so ashamed of his humble background and his fisherman father that he falsely told everyone, even Sun, that his father was dead. To win Sun's hand in marriage agreed to work for her powerful father, Mr. Paik. His stressful work, with its long hours, had already strained their marriage when Sun discovered Jin had done some violent enforcing for her father.

SAYID FACES OFF AGAINST THE MYSTERIOUS FRENCH WOMAN IN THE JUNGLE. **THE VOLATILE JIN BEING SEPARATED FROM SAYID.**

SAYID (NAVEEN ANDREWS)

Why he was on the plane: Had heard that Nadia, the love from his past, was alive and living in America. Was on his way to the U.S. to find her when he took the fateful flight.

On the island: A former Iraqi soldier trained in torture, his martial bearing and confidence make him a natural leader. When Jack wanted to establish a settlement at the caves, Sayid was a strong advocate for remaining on the beach to watch for passing ships or planes and keep signal fires going. Attempted to set up a radio distress signal and intercepted a strange, sixteen–year–old transmission from a mysterious French woman. To get asthma inhalers for Shannon, tortured Sawyer in the mistaken assumption Sawyer was with-holding them. Ashamed for breaking a personal vow to renounce torture he left the camp alone, ostensibly to map the island. Was captured by Danielle Rousseau, the mysterious French woman and the last of a scien-tific expedition that had been stranded on the island. From Rousseau learned of the "Others" and escaped her lair with papers and maps that may hold secrets of the island.

Flashback: Fought in the first Persian Gulf War as a member of the Iraqi Republican Guard. Was a torturer who rejected his military career when his old sweet-heart, Nadia, was delivered into his hands as an enemy of the government. Engineered her escape but did not know if she was still alive until seven years later.

MICHAEL DAWSON (HAROLD PERRINEAU)

Why he was on the plane: Had gone to Sydney to bring his ten–year–old son, Walt, back home to the States after his estranged lover, the boy's mother, suddenly died.

On the island: Michael last saw his son when Walt was one year old and Susan, the boy's mother, left with their child for a career opportunity in Amsterdam. As a virtual stranger, Michael struggles with being a role model and authority figure for his son. Has had run–ins with Jin, Locke and one of the polar bears that inexplicably inhabit the island. Determined to escape, has spearheaded the building of a raft.

Flashback: Put his art career on hold to work construction jobs to pay the bills during Susan's pregnancy and help her through law school. Separated from his out–of–wedlock child when Susan moved to Amsterdam and lost her when she married her boss, Brian, who subsequently adopted Walt. Michael first heard about Susan's death when Brian unexpectedly visited him, confessing he wasn't capable of being a single dad, and asked Michael to take Walt back.

WALT (MALCOLM DAVID KELLEY)

Why he was on the plane: Heading from his home in Australia to the United States with his blood father and his adopted father's dog, Vincent.

On the island: Adjusting to life without his mother and struggling to accept the blood father he never knew. The ten–year–old has gravitated towards Locke as a father figure, triggering jealousy in Michael. After Michael and Locke rescued Walt from a polar bear, formed a bond with his father. Locke taught him backgammon and Walt's a superb player (Hurley owes him tens of thousands in lost game I.O.U.'s). Loves to explore the island with Vincent and has fallen under its spell—Walt burned his father's first raft because he didn't want to leave.

Flashback: Walt doesn't know this, but Brian had become afraid of him since strange things were always happening around the boy. The day his mother became sick, Brian saw a bird fly to its death when it hit a window at their home, as if Walt had mentally called it to its death. Walt seems to have the power to think of things and make them happen.

JACK RESUSCITATES CHARLIE. IN WILDER TIMES, CHARLIE, AN ASPIRING ROCK GOD, FRONTS FOR DRIVE SHAFT.

CHARLIE PACE (DOMINIC MONAGHAN)

Why he was on the plane: Returning from Sydney where he had gone to convince his older brother, Ian, to restart their old punk–rock band, Drive Shaft. His brother, who has retired from the rock–and–roll life and is raising a family, declined, to Charlie's chagrin.

On the island: In the beginning, felt self–conscious and underappreciated—only Locke recognized him from his Drive Shaft days. Locke inspired Charlie to kick his secret heroin habit and Jack quietly provided medication to ease withdrawal pains. Proved his worth to his fellow survivors when he helped rescue Jack from a cave–in. Has developed a strong attachment to Claire, a pregnant young Aussie, and was with her when they were both kidnapped by Ethan, possibly one of the mysterious "Others." Charlie was hung and left for dead by Ethan but was found by Jack and Kate, with Jack miraculously resuscitating him. When Ethan reappeared to reclaim Claire, Charlie shot him to death with one of the guns the U.S. marshal had checked on to the plane.

Flashback: The rock–and–roll life provoked a crisis of conscience for this good Catholic boy. Felt betrayed by his brother who urged him to stay with the band— *you'll be a rock god*—but then usurped Charlie's front–man role. Followed his brother into heroin addiction, but long after Ian kicked the habit and retired from the music scene, Charlie was still using and dreaming of rock–god glory.

CLAIRE LITTLETON (EMILIE DE RAVIN)

Why she was on the plane: Unmarried and very pregnant, had been heading from her home in Australia to Los Angeles on the advice of a psychic who had ostensibly arranged for an L.A. couple to adopt her baby upon its birth.

On the island: Self–conscious that her impending birth represents yet another challenge for the embattled community. Has had vivid nightmares about being attacked and her unborn baby stolen. Became the object of Charlie's affections and initially resisted his gentle advances, but has grown closer to him. She and Charlie were kidnapped by Ethan. Claire somehow escaped, still healthy and pregnant, but with no memory of her ordeal. The amnesia has forced Claire to learn to trust Charlie all over again. Was the bait when Ethan reappeared to kidnap her back, with Charlie killing Ethan to protect Claire.

Flashback: Had been abandoned by her young lover who couldn't face the responsibility of being a parent. As a lark, visited a psychic for a reading but the psychic was so shocked by what he saw in her future he stopped the session. The psychic later revealed to Claire that she alone had to raise the child but ultimately recommended a couple in Los Angeles as the only option for adoption. Claire is convinced there was no couple, that the psychic knew her plane would go down and she would be stranded on an island and forced to raise the child.

HUGO "HURLEY" REYES (JORGE GARCIA)

Why he was on the plane: Had gone to Australia to meet someone he hoped had the answers to a sequence of numbers he's certain have magical, destructive powers.

On the island: A stoutly–built young man, Hurley has had trouble adjusting to the uneven diet (at one point, got upset when Locke and Boone kept coming back empty–handed from their hunting expeditions). But Hurley has kept his sense of humor. Secretly built a two–hole golf course and then hosted the first Island Open. Has made gestures of friendship with Jin, despite their language barrier.

Flashback: Has had a troubled life, including being a patient in a mental hospital. His luck seemed to change when he won a $156–million lottery using a sequence of numbers he had heard from a friend in the mental hospital, but nothing but bad luck has come with the winnings. The mental patient declared the numbers were cursed and Hurley had gone to Australia to solve the mystery of the numbers, but failed. He remains convinced he's cursed and that his bad luck actually caused the crash.

SHANNON RUTHERFORD (MAGGIE GRACE)

Why she was on the plane: Boone was taking her home after another wild fling gone sour.

On the island: Self–conscious, constantly bickered with her stepbrother before his death. Revealed to have an asthmatic condition, which led to the torture of Sawyer who was believed to be hoarding her inhalers, but a eucalyptus mixture prepared by Sun has helped her condition. She used her rudimentary knowledge of French to help Sayid translate maps and documents he'd taken from the French woman's lair. Has become romantically attached to Sayid. Has learned a number of valuable skills, thanks to a variety of old boyfriends.

Flashback: As a stepsister, and feeling on the outs with Boone's mother, concocted a scheme in which her call for help would lead Boone to fly to her rescue and write a big check to buy off her new boyfriend, enabling Shannon and her lover to start a life together. When dumped by her Aussie lover, had come to Boone's hotel room and initiated their sexual fling.

BOONE CARLYLE (IAN SOMERHALDER)

Why he was on the plane: Had gone to Sydney to bring home Shannon, his sexy, wild stepsister, who had gotten into her usual boy trouble.

On the island: Frustrated at feeling useless and disrespected by his fellow survivors, desperately wanted to contribute to their mutual survival. Attracted to Locke's rugged, mystical, back–to–nature persona and became his virtual disciple. In the jungle with Locke, while helping search for Charlie and Claire when they were kidnapped, discovered the sealed hatch. Later died in a tragic accident.

Flashback: A former lifeguard and executive in a lucrative wedding business owned by his mother (whom he calls "the Martha Stewart of Matrimony"). Had come to Sydney to rescue his stepsister, discovered Shannon and her lover were setting him up to get the big check Boone always wrote to make a problem go away. When Shannon was double–crossed, she came to Boone's hotel and they made love. Boone struggled with the emotional aftermath of this on the island.

When the *Lost* treatment was greenlit, the hard work began of making the vision come to life. But the key to the entire enterprise—the very future of the series—was about characters and casting. The problem was that with only a treatment in hand, Abrams' team had to flesh out a sketchy cast of characters during an accelerated audition process with the start of pilot production looming. Also complicating matters was the

THE SURVIVORS CONFRONT EACH OTHER—AND THEMSELVES: **TOP:** MICHAEL SEEKS TO BOND WITH WALT. **RIGHT:** HURLEY LOOKS ON AS CHARLIE CARES FOR CLAIRE'S BABY. **LEFT:** SUN AND JIN CONTEND WITH A TROUBLED MARRIAGE.

fact that since the plane trip was imagined as an international flight, it would be an international casting call.

"A lot of our characters didn't exist, it wasn't all formulated and things had to come together very fast," noted executive producer Bryan Burk. "For 99 percent of the TV shows that get made, the writer has lived with the characters for months and months and gone through a process of getting notes and feedback. We just had this big, general idea and were putting things together as we went forward."

Without a script, Damon Lindelof began writing "sides," industry lingo for script pages for specific scenes. In this case, the audition sides were for imaginary scenes for characters still being developed. As

actors auditioned by day, Abrams and Lindelof wrote the pilot script by night.

Jorge Garcia, who won the part of Hurley, was one of those improbable success stories of Hollywood legend. Only a year and a half before, he had been working in the music department at a Borders bookstore in Westwood and getting a few acting gigs. In true serendipity, shortly before Garcia's audition, Bryan Burk recalled, they had seen Garcia's standout performance as a pot dealer on an episode of the HBO series, *Curb Your Enthusiasm*. "I heard that originally they thought of Hurley as a fifty–year–old redneck and then I showed up on TV and they went, 'Then again, maybe *that* guy!'" Garcia smiled. "So this [a role in *Lost*] happened, magically. When I came in to audition, I actually read Sawyer's sides, but with my more humorous flavor. I think, in many respects, that Hurley represents the audience. He's the everyman who asks the questions the audience is asking."

Dominic Monaghan auditioned for the part of Charlie, a has–been rock star and drug addict, and brought with him the renown of having recently played

ROSE (L. SCOTT CALDWELL) PROVIDES COMFORTING WORDS TO CHARLIE.

Meriadoc (Merry) Brandybuck, one of the intrepid hobbits in the acclaimed *The Lord of the Rings* trilogy. Monaghan recalls his audition wasn't a proper reading, that he walked into a room with Abrams, Lindelof, Burk and casting director April Webster and they all just started talking.

"No one else was reading for Charlie, it was just me," Monaghan explained. "I remember turning to J.J. and saying, 'It's just me?' And he went, 'Yup.' I found Charlie very sympathetic as a character because he pretends to be something he's not. He likes to think he's respected in the group and can be strong and make decisions, but one–on–one he turns to [individual survivors] and asks for help. I found that very charming and sweet. That was my initial 'in' with the character, that this guy was actually showing a side of himself that wasn't the real him. After my becoming most famous internationally for playing a character [Merry] who is undeniably good and sweet and friendly, I was keen to play someone who

seemed to have those qualities but was also a drug addict, had issues with his faith and problems with trust, his parents and women. I wanted to strip away those layers and find, at the core, this guy who's very hurt."

Maggie Grace, who turned twenty–one on the show, won the part of Shannon. When she auditioned, her character was presented as a twenty–year–old socialite who has a difficult relationship with her older brother, Boone. "And one can assume from the dialogue that she wasn't the easiest person to get along with, either!" Grace noted. "Shannon and Boone were some of the first characters J.J. and Damon came up with. There was always plenty of bad blood between them, even though the reasons for that deepened and evolved as the show progressed. Shannon has had a turbulent past, especially for someone so young. She's a master manipulator and has been destructive to herself and those she's closest to. She was a train wreck before the crash and after we're thrust into this insane situation, she has a long climb up that she's not terribly well equipped for. But I still think there's an innocence, a goodness, to Shannon. Every day on the island brings a choice to rise to the occasion or not."

Yunjin Kim had been a major star in Korea and in the Asian film world from her role as a deadly North

A LOT OF OUR CHARACTERS DIDN'T EXIST, IT WASN'T ALL FORMULATED AND THINGS HAD TO COME TOGETHER VERY FAST ... WE JUST HAD THIS BIG, GENERAL IDEA AND WERE PUTTING THINGS TOGETHER AS WE WENT FORWARD.

Korean assassin in the 1999 Korean production, *Shiri*. Her success in the Korean film industry meant she wouldn't have to audition for a role there again, she explained. But Kim, who had come to America when she was ten, had always dreamed of Hollywood success, and despite her career security and stature in Korea had entered into a "holding contract deal" with ABC, which meant she would be called in to audition for that network's projects. *Lost* was one of her first auditions.

"When I went to audition, my role was nonexistent," Kim explained. "J.J. had me read for Kate, but I don't think he ever thought of casting me in that part, those were just the only sides available. A day later, I got a call saying, 'You're on hold. They don't have a role for you, but J.J. will write you one.' Three days later, they were out looking for a character named Jin to play my husband and they got Daniel Dae Kim."

One of the most complex characters was Sayid, an Iraqi and former member of the Republican Guard. The role went to Naveen Andrews, a native Londoner of Indian heritage whose film roles have included *The English Patient* and *Kama Sutra: A Tale of Love*. "I couldn't believe primetime TV was to have such a main character! Usually, in Hollywood, such characters are at best peripheral or an extraneous element of any given story. One of the reasons I took this job was I couldn't believe they'd do a character like this! It was almost like, 'Where's the catch?'"

The original conception for Sayid was he would be the island's designated "techie" (for more on Sayid's evolution, see the Q & A with J.J. Abrams and Damon Lindelof). Andrews agreed that while Sayid's technological expertise made him vital to the group's survival, his character needed more than that to keep his interest. "He's a bit of a romantic and not unheroic," Andrews concluded. "In Iraq he was a torturer, but that's only part of a myriad of qualities. Like all human beings, Sayid is complex—and he's been allowed to be complex."

One of Andrews' creative requests was that Sayid be more of a romantic, which led to Sayid's budding love affair with Shannon. "In Hollywood you might see a white man with a black woman, but the other way around is not acceptable, for some reason," Andrews mused. "I said to Damon that the relationship shouldn't be what Middle America expects, so what you see is this Iraqi drawn towards someone who looks like Miss America. I thought that was exciting and unusual and I was sure there would be outrage—but there hasn't

been! From what I hear, people seem to like it. I think that just goes to show that Hollywood generally insults people's intelligence."

The character of Jack had been the first character Damon Lindelof had imagined on the deserted island and had been fated to die in the pilot episode. When

MANY OF THE SHOW'S FLASHBACK STORIES RETURN TO THE FATEFUL EVENTS LEADING UP TO OCEANIC FLIGHT #815. HERE, A DOCTOR (GEOFF HEISE) SHOWS JACK THE CORPSE OF HIS MISSING FATHER IN A SYDNEY MORGUE.

the decision was made to spare Jack, it changed the casting dynamic for the role. "Originally, we were going to hire a big movie star but we never actually made those calls," Burk recalled. "When we decided to keep Jack alive that changed who we were going to look for. You want Jack to be the guy you turn to for everything but you also want to see that he's fragile and fallible. We started meeting with actors and then Matthew Fox came in and he was perfect. There was no question— that was our guy."

Fox had also read for the part of Sawyer, along with Josh Holloway. "We always referred to Sawyer as our Harrison Ford/Han Solo character and Josh was that," Burk said. "When Holloway came in he was likeable and cocky and funny. We went, 'You could hate that guy but also want him as a best friend.'"

It was an unusually large cast, with fourteen series regulars. "We were blessed that all the casting came together in an absurdly short time," Burk concluded.

The only problem was the character of Kate, the beautiful girl with the secret past as a thief on the run.

Although *Lost* was an ensemble, Kate was to be the lead female role and a pivotal figure in the series. Burk estimated that casting director April Webster and casting associate Alyssa Weisberg looked at literally hundreds of actresses. But the start date for pilot production was getting closer and *Lost* still hadn't found its Kate. "We saw some incredible actresses, but they weren't what we were looking for in Kate," Burk noted. "To quote J.J., 'You'll know her when you see her.'"

To Burk this seemed the stuff of Hollywood legends, like Lana Turner being discovered while sipping a soda at Schwab's on Sunset. "I thought that was some kind of mystical Hollywood nonsense. The idea that our lead girl was going to walk in and we'd be like—*that's her*! Those things don't happen. But J.J. just kept saying, 'You're going to know.'"

Meanwhile, Webster had received two audition tapes from Canada. Both young women were flown down, one an unknown named Evangeline Lilly, who had only done a few commercials and had been an extra. Lilly went in to read for Abrams, Lindelof, Burk and April Webster while Alyssa ran the camera. As a first impression, Burk recalls Lilly as beautiful, but her face was obscured by her hair. But she began reading her sides and was doing well. Then, suddenly, Abrams stopped and asked Lilly to pull back her hair.

"Suddenly, we could see her face and it was surreal," Burk recalled. "I was—'It's her!' J.J. gave her some more direction and some adjustments from her previous reading and she was spot–on. Damon and I were writing each other notes. Damon's was: 'Home run!' I was like, 'I'm in love.' We just knew she was the girl. She was confident and fragile at the same time. We then brought her to the studio and the network and everyone loved her. It was a done deal."

"I love performing," Lilly explained. "I wanted to win them over in the audition, I wanted them to like me and want to work with me. I was trying to project all that which, as it turns out, are the characteristics of Kate! Kate herself is a performer, she's a con artist—she wins people over."

There was one major problem—being Canadian, Lilly needed a work visa and fast. The hard part was the American producers had to explain why someone with no professional resume was indispensable to their new show.

A week before shooting on the pilot was to begin, the work visa had still not arrived. The production had a little window of opportunity before the location work in Hawaii, with three or four days in Los Angeles scheduled for shooting interior plane scenes. Lilly was slated to begin work on Thursday of that week—*still* no work visa. The production pushed Lilly's start date to the following Monday. By then, it was looking as if Lilly might not get cleared and Burk, Thom Sherman and April Webster had begun meeting with other actresses in case they were forced to replace Lilly.

Meanwhile, Lilly had been spending two weeks in a strange city—it was her first time in Los Angeles—and she had to fill up the "empty space" waiting for the decision that would change her life. "It was a tense and exciting feeling, waiting to see if I would get the visa and knowing I could lose the most amazing opportunity of my life because of some red tape."

The news came on a Friday, Bryan Burk recalled—the visa had cleared and Lilly was going to get *Lost*. "It was that close," Burk said with a sigh. "If Evangeline's

JACK DROPS BY TO SEE SUN'S HERB GARDEN.
LILLY BECAME SKILLED AT TREE CLIMBING IN THE JUNGLES OF THE PHILIPPINES.
KATE AND JACK EXPLORE THE JUNGLE'S BOUNTY.

visa didn't clear I don't know what we would have done. No one else could play Kate."

"When I got the call saying I had the part it was insane," Lilly recalled. "I didn't expect to be doing anything like this."

Indeed, other than being a background extra, Lilly's only real on–camera "roles" had both been corpses—she had laid in a coffin for *Long Weekend* and in a pool of her character's own blood for *Kingdom Hospital*.

Lilly's career path had not been bound for Hollywood. She had moved to Vancouver where she was studying international relations at the University of British Columbia. There had been some gigs and work in the entertainment business. She spent nearly three years as an extra and enjoyed that because with all the downtime on a set she could sit in a corner and do the school work she would normally be doing at home, only get paid for it.

Despite dabbling in the business, Lilly was focused on getting her degree and interests other than acting. "I've always taken a sincere interest in helping people, in serving others. I had devoted about eight summers to work in kids' camps and at the university I started a human rights group."

One of her formative experiences was spending three weeks doing Mennonite missionary work in the Philippines, living in a grass hut in the jungle. "What struck me about that experience was the simplicity, it was the way we were meant to live. The sun would come up and the women would be up with it, pounding rice and you could hear that for miles in the jungle. A lot of the day was about finding food and taking care of the children. And then when the sun went down they went to bed.

"One of the things we did was to bring in medicines. A fifteen–year–old boy died of asthma in the middle of the night. Asthma! Something we wouldn't think about as life–threatening [in North America]. At the time, the Philippines was also suffering from a major drought. They were dependent on whatever the jungle could provide them. They had rice and whatever they could grow, they were digging up roots to make a stew.

"The big thing I had to struggle with was that as a guest of the tribe I never went hungry. We ate first and then they ate. I had protested [to the leaders of the missionary group] that it should be more equal. But I was told this was their custom—when you are their guest you are treated as a guest. To refuse that would offend them. It was still hard to stomach. While I was fed did *that* kid get enough to eat? I could only hope so. And then I knew that when I left I would be going home to a safe, rich place. That was my biggest struggle. But they were so happy—happiness doesn't come from having food on your plate."

Lilly is regularly asked if that experience in the jungles of the Philippines has helped her on the *Lost* island—"No," is the short answer, unless one counts the passion for tree climbing she developed when she was living in the jungle. "I don't draw on that, they're completely different experiences. One was a real experience, the other I'm on a set pretending to be someplace I'm not."

While some of Lilly's fellow *Lost* cast

members had struggled to make it in the business, some suffering years of disappointments, hers was literally an overnight success story. "I'm the opposite story of Josh [Holloway]—he hates that," she laughed.

The pilot had been Lilly's "baptism of fire." Other than a workshop camera test, some commercials and work as an extra, it was her first time before the camera—not counting the beautiful corpses she had played, of course. Her first scene was on the interior set in Los Angeles with the plane about to go down. Lilly credits being an experienced extra with making her feel at home and not over-whelmed on the set, even when she was in the unaccustomed featured position before the camera.

What carried Lilly through was that she identified with Kate's confidence and strength. In a dramatic episode in which Jack decides to take guns a U.S. marshal had brought on the plane and go after Ethan, the stranger who has kidnapped one of their own, Kate is right there—give me a gun, *I'm coming*!

Lilly, like Kate, is the girl who can compete with the guys, like the time she went one-on-one in a push-up contest with Matthew Fox.

Whether he let up on her or not, he barely beat her, forty–six to forty–two. "He won—by the skin of his teeth," Lilly laughed.

––––––––––

Although the cast was still close enough to California to fly back and forth during the season, the demands of the show required they all relocate to Hawaii. "They [the cast and crew] all love it out there," Bryan Burk noted. "They're all cut off and sequestered from everything that's going on [in L.A.]. I keep waiting for the 'island fever' to kick in, but it hasn't happened."

ALTHOUGH THE CAST WAS STILL CLOSE ENOUGH TO CALIFORNIA TO FLY BACK AND FORTH DURING THE SEASON, THE DEMANDS OF THE SHOW REQUIRED THEY ALL RELOCATE TO HAWAII.

"I'm from Ohio, so this place is surreal, it's fantastic," Maggie Grace noted of life on the island. "A lot of the cast members live close enough together that we can hang out on our downtime. We go bowling, kayaking, have barbecues at each other's back yards, order in food and have movie nights—given the male majority, more 'guy' films. It's pretty perfect. It's truly an extraordinary situation, working with J.J. and Damon, bonding with a cast about a billion miles from L.A. If you're going to be suddenly catapulted to this level of visibility overnight, I can't think of a better group to do it with!"

Being out on a real island and filming in real beaches and jungles enhanced the experience for all. All the production departments—from makeup to hair to costume—worked hard not to break the illusion of survivors stranded on an uncharted island. The approach even influenced fight scenes choreographed by stunt coordinator Michael Vendrell. "We've been developing a style of what *Lost* action is, which means realism," Vendrell said. "We have to make the fighting as rough–and–tumble as possible. But none of the characters, as far as we know, are skilled in any form of martial arts, so they can't look too professional. But on practically every episode there's a fight, so we've been slowly developing a fighting style for each guy. I talk to the actors about how their character would do it, so it's not Josh fighting but Sawyer, not Terry but Locke. That's what I try to do, let the actors create their own style. People believe Locke can throw a knife, so Terry has actually gotten pretty good at it—he can throw it thirty feet. That's the reality of it. We're like a reality show that's not a reality show."

As the season progressed, the actors began to get deeper under the skins of their characters. Through the show's flashback motif, the secrets of each character's past were revealed, but the actors were always kept in the dark about the potential evolution of their characters and the next twist and turn of the storyline.

"We're working for the CIA here, apparently," Josh Holloway grinned. "You get your script three days before you start shooting, while you're still shooting another episode or looping [dialogue tracks] for two episodes back. I've had to watch some past episodes to keep track of where I've been. Episodic television is such a whirlwind—once you've created the monster, it rolls!"

"I'm told very little," added Terry O'Quinn, a veteran actor who recently had a recurring role in *Alias*. "They might tell me when there's an upcoming Locke–centric episode, but they don't tell me what's in it. When we shot the pilot I didn't even know my character was wheelchair restricted, so I'm running over to help Jack. If I'd known, I probably would have been a little gimpy, rather than springing about like a young roebuck. But hey! It's quite alright. I don't blame them for playing it close to the vest. I would. This many people to try to keep things under your hat? In a series like this, that potentially could go on for years."

Some of the actors had suspicions about the directions their characters would take. In Dominic Monaghan's case, he always suspected Charlie would kick his heroin habit. "I knew ABC wasn't happy with me playing a drug addict for an entire season. But, I think, in the nature of television, you'll play one beat and it'll turn into something else to surprise and shock the audience.

"Charlie has done all the cliché rock–star bullshit that has damaged him and he's now learning that the righteous path is a bit more rewarding," Monaghan added. "Charlie is a big fan of girls. I think he likes Shannon initially, I think he has a crush on Kate. But Claire is someone who's small enough to fit under his arm, someone he can nurture and care for. I think that's what he sees in Claire, someone he can take care of. I think Charlie is naive enough to assume that anyone carrying a child is a good person and maybe the baby represents a different path, one of responsibility and maturity."

Malcolm David Kelley notes that at age twelve he's older than his character Walt, who's only ten. Kelley, who spent the first eleven months of his life in foster care until he was adopted by the Kelley family, brought not only a natural instinct for acting to the role but a resume with credits in movies, TV, commercials and music videos. "When I auditioned for Walt I played him as a little popular kid, but they made me play him like I have special powers and I'm an outsider. Walt can think of something and it happens, he just doesn't know how to use his powers yet.

JACK AND KATE WILL FIND CHARLIE ON THE TRAIL, LEFT HANGING ON A TREE BY ETHAN, AND SEEMINGLY DEAD. HERE DOM MONAGHAN GETS RIGGED FOR THE DRAMATIC SCENE BY ARCHIE AHUNA, SPECIAL EFFECTS CO–ORDINATOR. IN THE SCENE, KATE AND JACK CUT CHARLIE DOWN.

"When I'm acting it's like I have another personality in me and that brings out Walt. I can just get into my character. With all the beaches and caves and things when we're on set it *feels* like we're lost on an island. My acting skills are getting better except I'm still learning how to cry on the spot."

For Daniel Dae Kim, whose recent work included a recurring role in the TV show *24*, an intriguing aspect of the series was the international flavor of the cast and the fact that his character doesn't speak English. "If it's a flight from Sydney to Los Angeles there would be people who don't speak English. That it's reflected in this show is not only realistic but lends itself to a lot of dramatic situations."

"What I liked about *Lost* was it didn't look like what I had seen on network television the past few years, this homogenous and surface stuff," mused Harold Perrineau, a veteran of stage and TV whose movie work includes *The Edge*, and the second and third installments of *The Matrix* trilogy. "There have been shows where we're literally watching people go out on a date! I love being an actor, so I'm fascinated with new stuff. With this show, there was also this huge opportunity to have characters from different backgrounds, but their differences are not the topic. Who they are is the topic. I mean, whenever there's a show on TV with a black guy, it's usually about racism—he's either a crack head or 'streetwise.' Daniel [Kim] and I are friends and I have other friends who are Korean and it's never about me being black and them being Korean, it's about who we are. Because I live in New York and Los Angeles, this show is the way America looks to me. I don't think the show's creators had this idea, 'Let's change the face of TV,' because then it might have been screwed up. I think their intention was to do a character-driven piece and get the actors they thought could pull it off. I just saw this huge opportunity because all the different kinds of people on this show is the way America looks to me."

Naveen Andrews notes that a major difference between film work and television is the "relentless" nature of episodic TV. Happily, the show provided him a secure harbor far from Los Angeles and the "hype and bullshit machine" of the entertainment industry. He notes as major pluses for the *Lost* experience the

MATTHEW FOX WAITS FOR HIS CALL TO THE CAMERA DURING FILMING OF THE EPISODE, "ALL THE BEST COWBOYS HAVE DADDY ISSUES," WHICH FEATURES JACK'S FLASHBACK MEMORIES.

beauty of Hawaii and the island's mellow people, who welcomed the production but were not overly impressed by them. But, most of all, *Lost* was a chance to do some great work. "People seem to have responded to the character of Sayid. And if 'ordinary people' respond to a character who represents the so-called 'enemy,' it means they're trying to connect in a way that the government and the media don't necessarily allow them to do.

"I think it's rare to be involved in *any* project— whether film, television or theater—that has a moral force," Andrews concluded. "My character in particular, and the disparate nature of the people on the island, with everyone coming from all walks of life and different races, is a microcosm of the world situation we're all in. If we don't emphasize our similarities and stop emphasizing our differences, it's curtains for us, you know what I mean? In some small way our show is a real opportunity to emphasize to the audience the importance of pulling together."

As the season went on, Evangeline Lilly lost none of the appreciation for the chance to be Kate and develop her love of performance.

"One of the biggest things I've learned on this show is to be still on camera," Lilly noted. "In real life I'm active and animated. It was unnatural for me to hold back and just express emotions through my eyes. I remember the first time I went before a camera at a workshop, to do a screen test, I seemed so *big*! When I watched the *Lost* pilot, one of the people who stood out was Yunjin Kim— she's just stunning, breathtaking on camera. Her acting is so still, so minimal and precise and purposeful. I don't know her process, it's just seeing it."

As the season went on, Lilly was living the dream of Hollywood success. She had been named one of the "Breakout Stars of 2004" by *Entertainment Weekly*. There were interviews and magazine photo spreads with the cast, questions about stardom and fame, and image and career plans.

"I don't buy it at all," Lilly reflected of the adulation that comes with sudden fame. "I'm not starstruck, I've never wanted to be famous. It's not like this is the big chance I've been working towards for years—this all came out of nowhere. I have nothing to fear at this point. I always feel if this ends tomorrow, I had a great time. I had a golden opportunity and I embraced it and it changed my life."

THE BIG

SHOW

They call them "show runners" and in episodic television they do what the phrase implies, with a focus on "the creative functioning of the show," as *Lost* show runner and executive producer Carlton Cuse explained.

Lost necessitated two creative people to handle the day–to–day creative demands. Damon Lindelof was one half of the equation, but with J.J. Abrams busy with *Alias* and preparations for his directorial assignment on the third *Mission: Impossible* movie, Lindelof called on Carlton Cuse, a longtime friend who had given him a big break early in his career. Cuse, an experienced show runner, had created such television hits as the long–running *Nash Bridges*, the series on which Cuse first met Lindelof when he hired him as a writer. Cuse extricated himself from a development deal at another studio and by the seventh episode of the season was ensconced in the suite of *Lost* offices on Disney's Burbank lot.

SHOOTING IN HAWAII MEANS SOMETIMES DEALING WITH NASTY WEATHER, BUT HERE B–CAMERA OPERATOR RICK TIEDEMANN (AT THE CAMERA) AND SECOND ASSISTANT DIRECTOR KRIS KRENGEL PERSEVERE.

"I'm experienced at overseeing the managerial aspects of producing a television series, which is a huge operation," Cuse explained. "Running a show involves the creative vision you have to put forth each week and also the managerial aspects of running this gigantic company, which is about 250 people working on this show."

As with most shows, there were layers of companies involved. The show was created under the umbrella of Bad Robot, J.J. Abrams' production company, while

BASICALLY, YOU MAKE A TELE-VISION SHOW THREE TIMES: WHEN YOU WRITE IT, WHEN YOU SHOOT IT AND WHEN YOU EDIT IT.

Touchstone Television provided funding and owned the series, which ABC broadcast. Burbank was the show's creative headquarters, where the overall mythology was designed and the scripts for each episode prepared under the guidance of Abrams, Lindelof, Cuse and a team of writers.

The production of the scripts were then realized in Oahu, Hawaii, with the outdoor locations, including the main beach set at the fabled north shore. Heading production duties there was executive producer Jack Bender and producer Jean Higgins. "Jack is a tremendously talented, artistic guy who is our liaison in charge of creatively realizing the scripts we send him, he works with the directors and oversees the actual look and style of the show," Cuse explained. "Jean oversees the financial side, basically making sure Disney's money is well spent, but that also requires a creative mindset in figuring out how to give the show the best look at the best value."

Once an episode was shot, the film would be sent back to Burbank for postproduction work ranging from editing and visual effects to scoring the music. "When the show comes back here that's Bryan Burk's purview, he applies his creative vision in helping shape the show in post-production and he and I work very closely on the cuts [final edits] of the show," Cuse added. "Basically, you make a television show three times: When you write it, when you shoot it and when you edit it."

When Cuse joined the production, Abrams and Lindelof steeped him in the

LEFT TO RIGHT: IN A SCENE FROM THE "WHITE RABBIT" EPISODE, LOCKE GIVES JACK A HAND DURING A CLIFFHANGING SITUATION. IN ONE OF THE SHOW'S TRADEMARK FLASHBACK SCENES, EMILIE DE RAVIN'S CLAIRE SITS DOWN FOR A FATEFUL PSYCHIC READING AS DAN LIPE AND JOHN MUMPER RECORD THE SOUND.

A HONOLULU HARBOR WAS TRANSFORMED BY KEVIN BLANK'S VISUAL EFFECTS DEPARTMENT INTO THIS WATERFRONT VIEW OF SYDNEY FOR A SCENE FROM THE "OUTLAWS" EPISODE. THE DIGITAL MATTE PAINTING AND COMPOSITE WORK BY ERIC CHAUVIN OF BLACKPOOL STUDIOS (AN EFFECTS HOUSE BASED IN WASHINGTON STATE) INCLUDED BLENDING TWO SEPARATE PHOTOS OF THE SYDNEY OPERA HOUSE AND SYDNEY SKYLINE INTO AN IDEALIZED VISION OF THE CITY.

"ultimate mythology beats of the show," as Cuse called it. Although Abrams and the creative insiders have stated there is a master plan and definite story arc, the vagaries of a serial drama keep the creative dynamic fluid. Abrams, talking about *Alias* (for the book *Alias: Declassified*), once likened the start of a season to driving through a fog towards a distant mountain with landmarks to aim for along the way, the fog clearing the deeper one went on the journey.

Cuse also used the journey metaphor to describe *Lost*, imagining a road trip from Los Angeles to New York where the beginning and end are clearly established, but the journey itself—the roads and detours and stops along the way—unfold spontaneously, sometimes serendipitously. "The mythology elements on *Lost* are sort of landmarks along this road trip, but the actual journey is a daily process of discovery," Cuse elaborated. "A show is a very organic entity and you don't just force your will upon it. A lot of what happens is a two-way street. We get feedback watching an actor's performance and the qualities they bring to a character, there's the dynamics we discover when two actors are paired and we see how they interact."

The medium of television itself creates its own challenges. Commercials alone can lop off fifteen minutes or more of an hour of episodic television and, of course, the stories themselves have to be structured to account for those mandatory breaks. The television creator also has the challenge of holding the attention of channel-surfing viewers who have the potential to get lost among hundreds of channels. TV's commercial nature, the domesticity of the "tube"—these are some of the reasons the medium has traditionally been looked down upon by the movie side of the entertainment industry. But many in the business feel television is finally getting some respect.

"Episodic television has changed, thanks to cable," Jack Bender mused. "There's no more, 'It's good enough for television.' Even [big theatrical] movies end up on the small screen, eventually. But, basically, it's the quality—episodic television has to look like a feature film. The big difference is all good episodic television has to deliver that quality in eight days. I think good episodic television is, by far, the hardest [medium] to maintain quality week–by–week, to not slip into a pattern of, 'That's good enough.'"

Another big difference between movie and television, Bender noted, is in modern movie–making the director's vision is foremost, with the production crew "cast" to the director's personality. But in a weekly television series, a number of directors can be assigned to different episodes throughout a season. "On television, you cast a crew who can live together long–term. You're creating a family because, truly, we end up seeing each other more than we see our own families. There's no slacking off because you've got a cold or don't feel like it—that yawning mouth needs to constantly be fed."

As with the cast, *Lost* required the production crew to relocate, at least temporarily, to Hawaii. Producer

Higgins, for one, notes that during the first season about the only times she managed to get back to her home in Los Angeles was two weeks between the pilot and the start of the series and over the Christmas break.

Director of photography (DP) Michael Bonvillain, a veteran of such shows as *Alias*, noted that during the first season Pat Churchill was a welcome addition as unit production manager. Up to then, Jack Bender and Jean Higgins had been running everything themselves. "This show is so enormous, it's like a feature," Bonvillain explained. "Even breaking down the scripts is an incredible puzzle, but Jack Bender and the other producers do that. But it's just a hard show to do. It's a circus, with all the equipment trucks and crew and dealing with logistics and weather and shooting in places where there's mud and steep slopes and flash–flood danger. We've got it down to a science, although it seemed the show actually got harder to shoot because the scripts

CHARLIE RUNS FROM THE FRENCH WOMAN'S RIFLE FIRE.

kept getting more ambitious and we were trying not to repeat ourselves."

Bonvillain added that one of the best things that he and fellow series DP Larry Fong (who shot the seminal pilot) did was to hire a great crew. "Our crew is all A–list feature guys," Bonvillain explained. "Paul Edwards, our

A–camera operator, has done a ton of features. Jim Grce, the gaffer, is a topflight guy who has done a lot of the Roland Emmerich movies, like *Independence Day* and *Godzilla*, and he runs his crew really well and takes care of his equipment. Chuck Smallwood, the key grip, is another topflight guy. Tony Nagy, our first assistant A–camera, turned down *Pirates of the Caribbean 2* and *3* to work on this show and runs a great department. Basically, all these guys protect me so I don't have to think too much about the elements, because when you shoot on the beach on the north shore, especially in wintertime, there can be so much salt spray blowing off the water that when it's backlit it looks like fog. I mean, I *do* think about the elements when it's raining and I'm standing in ankle–deep mud, but I know that because of those guys the camera's being protected and the lenses cleaned, the lights are working. I wouldn't say I'm superfluous, because I get to work really closely with the directors and they've gotten a lot of good directors for this show. But Paul Edwards can set up a shot that's so good and well designed and cuts so well that I'm like an editor, I get a variety of options. It's not just about dollies and sets. The crew and the producers—they're all filmmakers."

In addition to camera and lighting and sound, production departments in Hawaii included the art department headed by production designer Stephen

A CLASSIC VISUAL–EFFECTS "JEOPARDY" EFFECT FOR THE "NUMBERS" EPISODE. THE LIVE ACTION FILMED ACTOR JORGE GARCIA CROSSING A CREAKING ROPE BRIDGE, WITH GREENSCREEN BACKING TO BE REPLACED IN POST-PRODUCTION WITH THE ILLUSION OF A DIZZYING HEIGHT.

THE FINAL SHOT BY BLACKPOOL STUDIOS' ERIC CHAUVIN. THE NEUTRAL GREENSCREEN WAS REPLACED WITH A DIGITAL MATTE PAINTING THAT COMBINED A PHOTO OF A LOCATION IN IDAHO WITH PHOTOSHOP SOFTWARE TOUCHES, WHICH INCLUDED ADDED COLOR, GREENERY AND WATER EFFECTS.

Storer, makeup by Steve LaPorte and assistant makeup artist Mark Sanchez, the hair department headed by Susan Schuler with assistant hairstylist James Sartain, the costume department run by Billy Ray McKenna, special effects coordinated by Archie Ahuna, and stunt work coordinated by Michael Vendrell. There were the on–set departments, from set decorator Rick Romer to

"plates" (the live–action photography that could be composited with computer–graphics imagery).

Kris Krengel, second assistant director on *Lost*, had returned to the business after a four–year break during which she moved to Costa Rica. She was lucky, she noted, to get the *Lost* job upon her return, which put her in Hawaii and not the frantic L.A. scene she had

MICHAEL BONVILLAIN, ONE OF THE *LOST* DIRECTORS OF PHOTOGRAPHY. VETERAN MAKEUP ARTIST MARK SANCHEZ TENDS TO DOMINIC MONAGHAN. SPORTING A *LOST* T–SHIRT, FIRST ASSISTANT A–CAMERA TONY NAGY ADJUSTS CAMERA SETUP ON THE BEACH SET.

departed. Her job was to help the first assistant director and handle such vital logistics as the preparation of "call sheets," the one–sheet distributed throughout the production that was the bible detailing all the particulars of a day's shoot. Krengel always tried to find ways of making things fun, a necessity given the typical twelve–hour workdays, so *Lost* call sheets would be embellished with a "Do You Know" item or a priceless quote of the day.

"I had to get back to this," Krengel smiled. "There's nothing like the adrenalin and joy you feel when you're on a great set. It's like you're surrounded by this great family and everyone knows everything about you, about your personal life, about your work life. You miss that when the season's over and it takes a couple days to kind of recover. There's no other business like it!"

on–set dressers Michael Gilday and John Lee. To secure all the locations, from wilderness locales to Honolulu, was the responsibility of location manager Jim Triplett. And while visual effects supervisor Kevin Blank was based in Burbank, his island connection was visual effects co–supervisor Ivan Hayden, who handled such hands–on work as setting up greenscreens and shooting

"In theory, we're making low–budget films," Paul Edwards observed. "It's a big hit show with a great ensemble cast, quality writing and a great premise, which allows a great deal of license in what they [the creators] do with the show. But you don't have time to do every shot you want. It's the nature of the beast. You have to move fast, you have to get your day's work."

Each day's shooting schedule mandated specific scenes and a quota of script pages to be shot. "This show, in many respects, is like a feature in that with every shot and setup [the cast and crew] is giving it the max," said Michael Moore, a new sound mixer who joined the production before the Christmas break. "The difference is the last feature I worked on [*Exorcist: The Beginning*] we averaged [less than] a page each day; on *Lost* we average seven and a half pages a day."

There was an efficient, logical order to filming, explained Tucker Gates, one of the series directors. The usual process was to open with the wide "master" shot of a scene, then move in for close–ups and reverse angles, giving the editors back in Burbank all the "coverage" they could hope for. "A lot of the concerns are time oriented, so you'll maybe shoot in a certain direction because you're lit in that direction," Gates added. "To create an episode is usually about a three–week process. The director will have maybe five days of prep and three days after that [to get ready]. Then, we shoot for about nine days. I'll have four days to edit."

JAMES GOLDMAN, SECOND ASSISTANT B–CAMERA, MARKS A TAKE FOR THE GRAVE SCENE FROM THE EPISODE, "WHATEVER THE CASE MAY BE." CAMERA **BOOM SETUP FOR "CONFIDENCE MAN."** BOONE **EMBRACES SHANNON IN "HEARTS AND MINDS."**

LIVE–ACTION EXPLOSION OF THE WING ON THE MOKULEIA BEACH SET. ACTORS JORGE GARCIA AND MATTHEW FOX ARE VISIBLE IN THE FOREGROUND. NOT VISIBLE IS EMILIE DE RAVIN'S PREGNANT CHARACTER, WHO IS AGAIN BEING SHIELDED FROM HARM BY FOX.

THE FINAL SHOT, ENHANCED WITH ADDITIONAL PYROTECHNIC ELEMENTS COMPOSITED BY STEVE FONG.

One of the important (and usually unsung) jobs on a production is that of key grip. Chuck Smallwood, key grip on *Lost*, worked closely with the gaffer and first assistant camera. "My job basically combines art and technology," Smallwood explained. "The DP and the director talk about what they want for a scene and we discuss how to provide the camera move they want—whether we should go with a dolly, which can be big articulated arms to boom on something or tiny dollies to move on tracks, or use cranes or mount a camera to a moving vehicle. The grip basically puts the camera where it needs to be. We provide equipment and manpower, but it's all a collaboration. The art of it is understanding the equations of how to do things safely in the briefest time period."

On the lighting side, Smallwood worked with gaffer Jim Grce, who was in charge of running the lights to get the look the director of photography wants. "We process the lighting, put light where it needs to be," Smallwood explained. "Like when we're out in the natural light and filming women we'll put up silks, which are on twelve–by–twelve–foot frames that modify the light so the contrast isn't so harsh [on their faces]. On a set there are many ways to isolate movie lights, to add light, redirect it, modify it, to shine it in an intentional way to create a mood, to create a space of light and dark."

Smallwood also works with the art department when a set needs a translight or backdrop, he works with the visual effects department and helps them put up greenscreen used in effects shots, and he works with physical effects to make sure cameras are mounted and stabilized properly.

Smallwood feels *Lost* is the greatest experience of his career. "Here in Hawaii it's such a beautiful environment. I've learned so much about filming on remote beaches and wilderness. It is a unique job description to be standing on a beach and see whales and turtles, to see spectacular rainbows and sunsets. It's the most fantastic thing to be driving down some dirt road before dawn, it's pitch black, and know that somewhere at the end of the road you're going to come to the set where you're going to be working."

Once filming in Oahu is completed, the film goes back to Burbank for postproduction. Visual effects work for the series might include digital matte–painting extensions to enlarge the cave set in Honolulu (one of the only stage sets in the entire show), creating computer generated (CG) environments and creatures (including those fearsome polar bears), removing telltale wires used in stunt scenes, and digitally enhancing special–effects explosions where needed. Other than possibly those charging polar bears, *Lost* visual effects are usually what are called "invisible effects," meaning the shots don't necessarily betray the fact that they might be digitally processed or enhanced. For example, for the "Outlaws" episode, a Sawyer flashback to Sydney harbor was shot in a Honolulu harbor against a green-screen that Blank replaced with a background featuring the Sydney Opera house. (Blank proudly points out that such invisible effects were recognized by the Visual Effects Society, which awarded *Lost* the award as Best Supporting Visual Effects in a Broadcast Program at a banquet and award ceremony held in Los Angeles on February 16, 2005.)

Ultimately, Blank noted, J.J. Abrams' vision for *Lost* was that as much as possible be done "practically," meaning live and "on camera." A science fiction television show, for example, might have a $100,000 budget per episode, with story points dependant on visual effects to create spaceships, alien creatures and fantastical environments—the visual effects budget per episode for *Lost* was only $15,000 to $20,000, using an average of ten shots, Blank estimated.

Blank recalled that his department came to the rescue for the "Walkabout" episode, in which a pack of boars enter the main fuselage wreckage to feed on the moldering corpses. The original plan had been to run real boars through the scene, so a boar "wrangler" had been hired and live boars brought to the set. Then things went wrong, when the boars refused to cooperate.

"To get boars to run through, the wrangler runs ahead with food and they follow," Blank explained. "The story I heard was apparently some of the extras had been feeding the boars all day, so when it came time to shoot the scene the boars weren't hungry—they didn't move, they didn't do anything! So, you basically had a production company held hostage. So, they asked me to help. I had to take shots that were not intended for visual effects but we managed to produce eight shots with CG boars. I had to look at every frame of footage, check the eye lines of the actors, basically see where CG boars would logically fit in."

Other times, Blank has been an advocate for visual effects. J.J. Abrams wanted to stay away from computer graphics for the polar bear that charges Sawyer in the pilot, he just wanted a few terrifying glimpses. But Blank kept pushing to do it CG. As Blank recalls, a metal device was moved through the tall grass at the location to effect the sensation of a giant creature lumbering through, while a "stuffed bear" hung on a wire was flown through the scene. "J.J. wanted to see grass breaking and he asked if we could put in some CG grass breaking. I wanted to take charge of the polar bear, so for

JACK AND LOCKE CONVERSE WHILE THE CREW RECORDS IT ALL. CREW MEMBERS, LEFT TO RIGHT: PAUL EDWARDS, TONY NAGY AND CASEY ALICINO, WITH DAN LIPE ON BOOM MIKE IN THE BACKGROUND.

THE CAMERA CREW INVADES THE FRENCH WOMAN'S LAIR.

shots with flashes of fur of the bear running through the jungle, that's *me*, wearing furry polar–bear chaps.

"But I got the shot and said, 'I'm just going to make a [CG] bear!' The bear on wires swinging to camera was used on two frames, so there's no time to perceive this hundred–pound stuffed bear. But we live in the world of DVD and TIVO and people do freeze–frame. So we replaced that with a CG bear and J.J. liked it—if you freeze–frame that shot, you'll see a CG bear, not a silly thing on wires. That was the blueprint when it came time to do a polar bear for the series."

One of the final stages in the creative process is music, with the *Lost* score created by Michael Giacchino, a rising composer in Hollywood who writes the scores for *Alias* and created the music for *The Incredibles*. Before the *Lost* pilot was even shot, Giacchino and J.J. Abrams had long conversations about "the soul and voice, the emotional center of the

show," which would be reflected in the music, Giacchino recalled. One early concern Giacchino expressed to Abrams was that they had to avoid the cliché music associated with an island, the lull of woodwinds and flutes. (Abrams himself created the opening theme, a "synth patch" on a synthesizer, Giacchino noted.)

"Essentially, all the characters are lost souls, they're nervous and frightened and in a place where they don't know what's ten feet into the woods," Giacchino explained. "They don't know where they are, what the island is. So we wanted the music to have a dual personality—sad and longing, and then completely uncomfortable, nervous and unsure."

Giacchino describes the *Lost* sound as exotic percussions and a signature echoing note on the low register of a harp string. To evoke the imagery of the downed airplane itself, the orchestra even utilized metal objects as Instruments, from pieces of chain-link fence

to metal cooking bowls. Giacchino's scores would also be written so string instruments like violin and cello and bass would be bowed in a non–traditional way to purposely produce a discordant sound.

Giacchino credits his orchestra, a veteran group he regularly works with, with being able to bring his musical vision to life. "In this business there's no time for

THEY DON'T KNOW WHERE THEY ARE, WHAT THE ISLAND IS. SO WE WANTED THE MUSIC TO HAVE A DUAL PERSONALITY—SAD AND LONGING, AND THEN COMPLETELY UNCOMFORTABLE, NERVOUS AND UNSURE.

rehearsals, so studio musicians have to be ready to go. The greatest thing about working in L.A. is you throw down sheet music and these musicians can read it. And using the same people over and over we have developed a kind of shorthand for dealing with all the

weird sounds on this show. For example, when I was a kid I had a dog named Muffin who would make these weird, grunting sounds and we have a percussionist who has this piano board with just the strings that he hits with a mallet—we call that sound a 'Grunt Muffin.' I'll just write 'Grunt Muffin' on the sheet music."

Giacchino also specifically asked J.J. Abrams *not* to share secrets of the series mythology with him—in fact, Giacchino doesn't even read the scripts. Just like the actors and crew, he wanted to be surprised week–to–week, he didn't want his scores to betray or foreshadow advance insights. Giacchino would wait to view the final edited episode, write the music within two days and record with his live orchestra on the third day. *Lost* music also comes sparingly—Giacchino estimated that while *Alias* might have twenty–seven minutes of music, *Lost* will only have eleven or seventeen minutes. "*Alias* is a fantasy world, it's a ride. *Lost* is about the people and the music is more related to the perspective of the characters, so I want to be with the characters, to stay in the present. In *Alias* I'll get scripts and look ahead. *Lost* is more in the moment, so I've tried to keep myself in the moment."

Like a painter limited to a few colors on his palette, Giacchino was also conscious of not making wild musical mood swings when stories shifted from the island to flashbacks. The music, he noted, had to keep within "the realm of the show."

While there's no dramatic musical motif for characters—like the distinctive "Darth Vader" music in *Star Wars*, for example—subtle themes signal the spirit of each character: Sawyer's is a moody, low harp note, Sun and Jin get more romantic tones, Locke's sound is "almost ticking," conveying his restless mind, while music for Jack emphasizes a repeating theme that evokes the memories and anguish over his father that keeps running through his head, over and over.

Ultimately, *Lost* music echoes the brooding heart of lost souls, it's the eerie sound coming out of the island itself, like a night wind stirring, that whispers of mystery and secrets. "I wanted the music to be as alien as the monster in the jungle," Giacchino noted.

THE   LOST

MYTHOLOGY

Throughout most of the first *Lost* season, hanging over the production like the proverbial sword of Damocles, was a promise from the show's creators that a main character would die before season's end. Naveen Andrews was not alone in wondering if his character would be the one. "The reality was if this was really about survival, then some people were not going to make it, brutal as that may sound."

Maggie Grace noted that audiences had already been primed to accept, if only for a few moments, that Charlie had been killed (hung by Ethan but resuscitated by Jack) and that the island's mysterious monster had killed Shannon (Boone's drug–induced hallucination). "I knew someone would have to really die for the audience to keep buying into the high–stakes moments that are so intrinsic to our show. I don't think any of us thought it would happen so soon. It's been tough, we're a really close–knit group."

In the 17th episode of the regular season, a dream of Locke's leads him and Boone to a plane that once crashed deep in the jungle, a plane Locke is convinced will provide answers to the island's secrets. Boone

THE REALITY WAS IF THIS WAS REALLY ABOUT SURVIVAL, THEN SOME PEOPLE WERE NOT GOING TO MAKE IT, BRUTAL AS THAT MAY SOUND.

climbs up into the plane, which tips over and crashes to the ground, mortally wounding him. In episode 18, despite Jack's surgical skills, Boone succumbs.

But while *Lost* fans will miss Boone, they need shed no tears for Somerhalder himself. The twenty–six–year–old actor, who previously had the lead role on the TV series *Young Americans*, has been in such films as *Changing Hearts*, playing opposite Faye Dunaway, and *In Enemy Hands* with William H. Macy. By April 6—the date the Boone death episode aired—Somerhalder was preparing to head to South Africa to shoot a movie and his summer travel plans included four weeks in London, "drinking tea and engrossing myself in Shakespeare and seeing great theater."

The actor was philosophical about Boone's death, "At any point, anyone in this cast, with the possible exception of Foxy [Matthew Fox], could have been killed for the sake of shock value or story point. The beauty of this show, and the dynamic that J.J. and Damon created, is that every character is always on the precipice of dying."

But while reflecting on his *Lost* season, Somerhalder admitted it was still a jolt to be told that Boone would be the first major character to die.

Q: When J.J. Abrams and Damon Lindelof telephoned you about the decision to kill Boone, what was that conversation like and what was your reaction?

Somerhalder: It hurt, it hurt for sure. It was right after the Golden Globes and I was in California, just hanging

WHEN I GOT THAT CALL I WAS FLYING THROUGH THE SANTA YNEZ WINE COUNTRY IN A CONVERTIBLE WITH A BEAUTIFUL GIRL. I SAID TO J.J. AND DAMON, "GUYS, THIS IS NOT A CONVERSATION I THINK I SHOULD BE HAVING RIGHT NOW. LET'S TALK ON MONDAY."

out and about to go back to Hawaii to look for a house to buy. When I got that call I was flying through the Santa Ynez wine country in a convertible with a beautiful girl. I said to J.J. and Damon, "Guys, this is not a conversation I think I should be having right now. Let's talk on Monday." I just needed to get off the phone and sit, process it and then go, "Okay. Cool." But it definitely stung for a second and it was more about not being in Hawaii and around the Josh Holloways and Matthew Foxes and Maggie Graces of the world.

Q: Did they try to break the news gently?

Somerhalder: There is no gentle way to break something like that and I don't want anything sugar coated for me, anyway. They just said, "Look, we'll be working with you time and again, but we've decided to kill Boone."

By the way, from a writer's standpoint it made absolute sense. You build up a character, make the character sympathetic to the audience and then kill him! That's shock, that's intensity, that's all the good things about storytelling—it just happened to be my character.

On this show art clearly imitates life and then life starts imitating art. You have a bunch of actors living on an island which is wildly conducive to the context in which we're shooting. It's a strange dichotomy of living, going off–set into the jungle by yourself or horseback riding on the beach, when two hours before you were in this fight–or–flight scene running through the jungle, thinking you're going to die! There's something beautiful in all of it.

Q: When you got back to the creators, what was that conversation like?

Somerhalder: I had a great conversation with Damon. I also don't envy those guys for doing this. We all have a bond that began when we started shooting this project over a year ago, and they don't like having to make those phone calls. I just have a feeling of gratitude to J.J. and Damon because living in Hawaii has given me such an incredible sense of calm and well–being.

Q: What was that like, living and working in Hawaii?

Somerhalder: I've been hiking on beautiful cliffs and peaks, scuba diving and swimming in waterfalls and in the ocean. That's an everyday thing, and there are so many memorable experiences they all sort of blend into one.

One of my favorite places [on Oahu] is an ancient burial ground on a plateau above the ocean where you can sit and look out over the world. It's a lava rock formation that people created probably 1,500 years ago and in front of you is the ocean and you're so high up the world kind of rounds. There's a little offering area where people leave fruit and gifts for the spirits. It's so magical.

I always said, in regard to this show and being on

this island, that it was too good, something bad had to happen. But then I realized it's the way things should be and to just appreciate it because it will go away.

Q: What has it been like working with Terry O'Quinn? The whole story line of Locke and Boone discovering the hatch was so important to the series.

Somerhalder: I think it was a blessing that Locke sort of took Boone under his wing, because it's just a great notion to wake up each morning and go, "I'm going to spend a week in the jungle with Terry O'Quinn." Terry O'Quinn is such a calm, ridiculously talented man who's got such a great way about him. He made this experience even better.

Actually, I didn't really know anything about Boone until the "Hearts and Minds" episode [the Boone and Shannon story]. Up until then my character really hadn't done too much and there wasn't a lot to hold on to. When you actually have a place to go, then you can start rolling.

Q: That episode featured Boone and Shannon, his stepsister, having sex. Did that plot twist surprise you?

Somerhalder: I thought it was genius. Here you have these two bickering, spoiled rich brats that no one has sympathy for and you start to understand where they're coming from. When we were shooting that episode, I saw Carlton [Cuse, who wrote the episode] on the set and I just ran up to him and gave him a huge hug and thanked him and Javier [Grillo–Marxuach] for creating a great script and for this great dynamic.

Q: I know the show's creators haven't told you the ultimate significance of the hatch, but what do you think the hatch is all about?

Somerhalder: There's something obviously in there. But it's not going to be the final answer, it's going to be ten more questions. The hatch encompasses mystery,

Locke's obsession with it is the reason for Boone dying, it's going to be a reason why the island is split—leaders will be born. I don't know how far they [the creators and writers] will go with it. I hope they go so far that it's ridiculous.

Q: How would you sum up your *Lost* experience?

Somerhalder: I spent a year surrounded by some of the most incredible people I've ever met and developed relationships that will stand the test of time. I'm grateful I had this experience that was given to me through the visions of J.J. Abrams and Damon Lindelof and Bryan Burk, the studio and network and everyone. I will be coming back to this island and crashing on all their couches as much as I possibly can.

> THE HATCH ENCOMPASSES MYSTERY, LOCKE'S OBSESSION WITH IT IS THE REASON FOR BOONE DYING, IT'S GOING TO BE A REASON WHY THE ISLAND IS SPLIT—LEADERS WILL BE BORN.

Q: And going to sit on that plateau above the ocean, I imagine.

Somerhalder: Absolutely. I want to add that we [the *Lost* production] have such respect for this island. It just commands respect and you easily and willingly give it because it nourishes you. There is a spiritual presence here that's beyond belief. It's something to be appreciated and embraced.

THE LOST

MYTHOLOGY

The *Lost* Writer's Room is where the series' grand design and mythological beats are broken down into episodes, where the destiny of each character turns on freewheeling creative discussions. What would it be like to be a fly on the wall when the writers put their collective heads together?

Take this moment in time: February 15, 2005, the *Lost* Writer's Room, Burbank, California, around the noon hour. On a far wall is the board on which anyone can take a marker and write out an idea for an episode. One side of the board is a column of notes headed "Extant Mysteries" that includes: "Who is Ethan? Who/

THE SURVIVORS TURN TO JACK IN EVERY EMERGENCY. HERE CHARLIE (WITH "FATE" WRITTEN ON HIS FINGER BANDAGES) ALERTS JACK TO SWIMMERS IN TROUBLE.

what are the Others? What is the hatch? What is the black rock?"

Today, the writers are trying to crack the 20th episode of the season, in which Michael is mysteriously poisoned. Sitting counterclockwise around a long table

are Edward Kitsis, Adam Horowitz, Jennifer Johnson, Leonard Dick, Javier Grillo–Marxuach, David Fury, Paul Dini and Monica Macer. Propped up on an adjacent sofa is writer's assistant Matt Ragghianti, typing the record of the freeform creative exchange on his laptop computer.

The story discussion is picking up on Michael's desperation to get off the island. His first raft has been burned, he and Jin have built a new one, and there's a narrow window of opportunity to launch before bad weather will force them to wait for months for their next chance. The raft has room for four people and it seems settled that Michael and Walt will take two seats, along with Jin, who helped make the raft and is an expert fisherman, with Sawyer taking the final spot (before Michael's first raft was burned, Sawyer had bartered for a seat).

The day's discussion is wondering whether Kate will do *anything* to get a seat on the raft. For Kate, even being stranded on an island has taken on a semblance of settling in and that scares her. Escape is all she knows when she's cornered, she's still the fugitive on the run. The creative ideas contemplate whether Kate, to ensure she gets on the raft, poisons Michael to take his place. Then more pondering—what if Sun still loves Jin too much to let him go and she uses her plant knowledge to create a poison that'll make Jin

minus the trappings of a drawing–room mystery. There's talk of Sawyer going after Kate with a gun—too repetitive, David Fury feels, there's been enough episodes with drawn guns. Jennifer Johnson proposes that Kate

CLOCKWISE: JACK IN A RARE SOLITARY MOMENT. LOCKE BROODS, EVER–PRESENT KNIFE AT THE READY. JACK RESCUES BOONE AFTER BOTH FAIL TO SAVE A SWIMMER WHO'S SWEPT OUT TO SEA.

WHAT IF SUN STILL LOVES JIN TOO MUCH TO LET HIM GO AND SHE USES HER PLANT KNOWLEDGE TO CREATE A POISON THAT'LL MAKE JIN TOO SICK TO MAKE THE TRIP?

has masterminded the poisoning of Michael but Sawyer "outs" her. There's the idea of Kate's toy plane being in the mix—it's her heart, Johnson adds.

An idea is floated that Walt seek retribution for his father, that he's finally detached from Locke and bonded with Michael. (The notion of Walt seeking "retribution" for his father being poisoned would fall by the wayside. But there would be a dramatic season–ending moment between

too sick to make the trip? Perhaps Kate put her up to it … maybe Michael drinks the potion by mistake …

Show runner Carlton Cuse comes in for a while and suggests they "play it" like an Agatha Christie story,

Walt and Locke.) Dini wonders if there's a way to have Walt confront Kate with Locke's knife. The plot thread could provide the "last hurrah for Walt's psychic powers," Grillo–Marxuach muses.

Someone wonders if Rousseau, the mysterious French woman, could be used as a *deus ex machina*: "'Hi! Is this Act Three? I was told to report for an action scene!'" A wave of laughter goes around the room.

David Fury gets up and paces. He stops and picks up a slinky toy and begins shifting it from palm to palm as he notes that Jack doesn't trust Kate.

"Kate will sacrifice trust with Jack to get on the raft," Johnson adds.

Grillo–Marxuach wonders about Jack and Sawyer teaming up to get the truth from Kate. It's an intriguing idea, having Jack and Sawyer, the two men in Kate's life on the island and bitter rivals, being in the same emotional place.

He also wonders if Sawyer could just take Kate "out of the game" to protect her from the suicidal risk of the raft voyage. Someone wonders if it's too soon after the

TOP AND RIGHT: AS THE ONLY DOCTOR, JACK TENDS TO ALL, FROM SAWYER TO A U.S. MARSHAL (FREDRIC LANE). MIDDLE: SHANNON BEGS SAWYER, THE ISLAND PACKRAT, FOR A SPRAY TO KEEP OFF SAND FLEAS.

injury and death of Boone to have the poisoning angle, another "sick" episode.

"No one needs to know about the poisoning," someone offers.

"Is *Sawyer* the right guy to be poisoned?" Leonard Dick rhetorically asks.

It's suggested that Michael get poisoned and Kate simply steals the raft.

"Michael is the heart and soul of the raft,' someone says.

The raft may be the object of desire for those wanting to get off the island, but it's far from a safe passage. It will be a risky voyage—the raft represents either salvation or suicide.

A FRUSTRATED MICHAEL STARES INTO SPACE AS HIS SON GETS LOST IN A STRANGE COMIC BOOK FOUND IN THE WRECKAGE. MIDDLE: AFTER A COUPLE OF WEEKS ON THE ISLAND, THE BEACH CAMP MUST RELOCATE FURTHER UP THE COAST AS HIGH TIDES BEGIN SWIFTLY ERODING THEIR ORIGINAL CRASH–SITE CAMP. LEFT: IN AN UGLY CONFRONTATION, BOONE HAS MICHAEL UNDER THE KNIFE.

There's not only a freeform energy to cracking a story in the Writer's Room, the conversation crackles with shorthand lingo that cuts to the chase: "I have a wild pitch!" "emotional beats," the "heat up," "action pop" and "Where's the heat?" Matt Ragghianti recalls that Damon Lindelof once remarked that the extras were all potential victims for the island monster, and that they resembled "meat–filled socks." This was later shortened to just "socks."

Ultimately, a creative communion and consensus emerges as a story is cracked. Sometimes ideas hit the Room like a bolt of lightning and it becomes electric. Ragghianti, speaking for the group, recalls the "palatable energy" in the Writer's Room when the idea was introduced that Locke be revealed to be in a wheelchair.

It's a mercurial process that can produce happy accidents, such as the unexpected comic balance and affinity between Hurley and Jin, a seemingly unlikely pairing. There was the dramatic story arc of Boone becoming Locke's acolyte and partner in his mission to open the mysterious hatch, a relationship that unexpectedly took the characters—and the Writer's Room—

explained, for the creative directions he and Lindelof propose. "That this show is on the air is a small miracle and I do think the studio and network have been great in understanding that our show is different, that our characters are really complex. They are willing to embrace the wild, mythological notions that hook the audience into the show, but they also provide a measure of balance."

That creative feedback started with the early, emphatic notes not to kill Jack. The network had also suggested that the secret of the "Others" who might exist on the island not be revealed too quickly, so the murder of the enigmatic Ethan left that question still shrouded in mystery.

Cuse also recalled the pivotal story in which Boone was mortally injured had initially been proposed to have Locke and Boone investigate a twin-engine plane that had just crashed in the jungle canopy. "The network felt this was too extreme a move, too early in the series to introduce an outside element onto the island," Cuse recalled. "We took their notes and then came up with the idea that Locke sees this plane crash in a dream that is so vivid that when he wakes up he follows the signs in his dream and locates this plane that crashed at some past point in time. It ended up being a much better approach."

down the dark path to Boone's death, which became the catalyst for another arc of stories encompassing the emotional aftermath.

"It's an unusual occurrence—a smart show where the story is the star," actress Maggie Grace observed. "J.J. is famous for giving A treatment to B-genre concepts with mass appeal. It's escapist—everyone's dreamt of this sort of situation. The creators walk a line between entertaining and exploring some bigger questions. It's also interesting to me to watch a society being built from the ground up, to watch characters struggle with themselves. The audience gets to know the characters as they get to know each other. We each have a choice to deceive, to reinvent."

The creation of *Lost* mythology doesn't happen in a vacuum—the network and studio gets advance scripts and provide the "litmus test," Carlton Cuse

IN THE WRITER'S ROOM, THE CONVERSATION CRACKLES WITH SHORTHAND LINGO THAT CUTS TO THE CHASE: "I HAVE A WILD PITCH!" "EMOTIONAL BEATS," THE "HEAT UP," "ACTION POP" AND "WHERE'S THE HEAT?"

An outside element would be a "large seismic event in the series," Cuse agreed. A prime example of an "outside element" was on the old *Gilligan's Island* show, which practically every week featured some new visitor

ONE OF THE HAPPIER TURNS IN THE SERIES MYTHOLOGY IS WHEN GOOD-NATURED HURLEY BUILDS A GOLF COURSE. TOP: CAMERA TRACK AT THE GOLF-COURSE SET AT KUALOA RANCH ON OAHU. BOTTOM: HERE MICHAEL WATCHES JACK LINE UP A SHOT.

to the castaways' supposedly uncharted desert isle. It was easy to see why *Gilligan's Island* leaned on that narrative crutch—it's hard to plot a lost island story without an outside element, with just the daily challenge of finding food, shelter and security to inspire dramatic situations. In general, most dramas provide clear protagonists and antagonists—a police show, at its hardboiled essence, pits cops against robbers. But *Lost* has no overt antagonist.

"In any given episode, when you're doing a present-day island story, what is the force of opposition?" Cuse mused. "Some of our shows are man versus nature—Jack and Charlie get caught in a cave-in. Ethan was

to know more about the characters and the flashbacks go back to the seminal events in their lives.

"J.J. and Damon have created a mythology to this island that exists and ultimately, over time, this mythology will be peeled back and revealed," Cuse concluded. "I think the first season has been about the survivors coming to the conclusion they may be on the island

LEFT: YESSICA HOLLOWAY, JOSH'S WIFE, AND CHRISTIAN TAYLOR, ONE OF THE SHOW'S WRITERS, JOIN MEMBERS OF THE CAST FOR A GROUP SHOT ON THE GOLF-COURSE SET. RIGHT: HURLEY AT THE FIRST ISLAND OPEN.

an example of an external antagonist. There is also a contradiction in that some [fans] would say Locke is a bad guy while others would say he's their favorite character—if they were on the island he'd be the guy they'd follow! We love that contradiction, but it does make it hard to tell stories."

Cuse credits the flashbacks with not only providing storytelling opportunities, but in having the show work at all. "If the show was just about a bunch of people stranded on an island and trying to get off, even if it were a mysterious island, I don't think the show would have the broad appeal it has. The flashback stories are the emotional core of the series and give a much broader audience access. There's a genre audience that enjoys the mythology, but the broader audience wants

for a while and becoming aware of their environment. There's a growing sense that maybe all of these people are possibly here for a reason, that the island is putting tests in the path of these characters that mirrors things that have happened in their past.

"The mission of this first season was the discovery and opening of the hatch, which is an important part of that mythology. It will lead to the next step of understanding what is going on."

J.J. ABRAMS AND DAMON LINDELOF

At one point, Abrams generously noted he wanted to set the record straight about the collaborative nature of *Lost*. "At a certain point it became apparent that Damon, with the help of Carlton Cuse, who's a genius, was not just running the show but as much or more the creative vision as I was. [Damon] and I together shoulder the responsibility of where the stories go forward. But the truth is I got a lot more credit for the show, incorrectly, just because people are more familiar with the work I did on *Alias* than what Damon did on *Crossing Jordan*. I always feel a

FAR LEFT: *LOST* CO–CREATORS DAMON LINDELOF (LEFT) AND J.J. ABRAMS. MIDDLE: DAMON LINDELOF. BELOW: ABRAMS DIRECTS MONAGHAN AND LILLY.

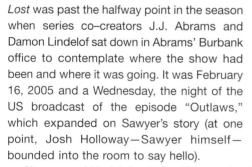

Lost was past the halfway point in the season when series co–creators J.J. Abrams and Damon Lindelof sat down in Abrams' Burbank office to contemplate where the show had been and where it was going. It was February 16, 2005 and a Wednesday, the night of the US broadcast of the episode "Outlaws," which expanded on Sawyer's story (at one point, Josh Holloway—Sawyer himself— bounded into the room to say hello).

Abrams and Lindelof noted, with some trepidation, that the network had not yet renewed the show for a second season. But it seemed the proverbial Sure Thing: That morning's *Los Angeles Times* had published the national rankings for network prime–time shows for the week of February 7–13 and *Lost* was number six, with an estimated 19.48 million viewers.

little guilty when I hear, 'Wow, I love J.J.'s show!' I'm happy to be a part of it, but I'm certainly not entirely responsible for it."

The nearly ninety–minute interview session (which has been edited for continuity) touched on the nature of collaboration, the art of storytelling, musings on the coolest movies ever, the series mythology and the creative journey that lies ahead.

Q: J.J. and Damon, your creative collaboration has been credited for the success of *Lost*. Could you describe your working relationship?

Lindelof: J.J. and I had separately been asked the question: "How do you make a TV show about plane–crash survivors stranded on a deserted island work?" We were complete strangers coming in, although I was a huge fan of J.J.'s for all his work in television and the way he tells stories. I'd actually been trying to get in a meeting with him and I had wanted to write on *Alias*, but the timing never worked out. Finally, the stars aligned and this was our opportunity to finally meet. I approached it as a fan of J.J.'s. It wasn't until after about five weeks of working together that, in my head, we became partners. I think J.J. approached it as a partnership from the word "Go" because that's his normal approach. It's not, "You're working for me."

I think the key to why our collaboration has been successful is we sort of speak the same language in all the movies and books and literature we love, so we immediately developed a quick and facile shorthand. We both also realized the key to cracking the show was it had to be about not only the people who crashed on the island but the island itself. We didn't know how we would do that, but very quickly our approach was that we would do it in a mysterious way. We would start, in a disoriented way, with a guy who wakes up in the middle of a jungle, and as the series went on we'd peel back the [hidden] layers of the people and the island.

Abrams: With Damon it was instantaneous, this feeling that I knew him. Working together has been effortless where it should be effortless and an effort in the way it should be an effort. As any writer who enjoys collaboration will tell you, finding that other person is an incredible gift.

… One of the reasons it was so easy to invest completely with working with Damon was he came into the room for our first meeting with such a vital sense of what the pilot story would be—he pitched it shot–by–shot.

There are so many layers to what needs to get figured out when you're trying to construct a story, so many points of entry into figuring out how a story works, and Damon just goes right to the heart of what makes a story work or not. So, you get to talk about the essence of a story real quickly. One of the most fun aspects of my job is I love riffing when someone pitches an idea, that feeling of hearing an idea that makes you go—Oh! One idea causes another idea. Everything was a choice at the beginning, from what it would be like when the plane went down to who the fugitive would be to ideas

> ONE OF THE REASONS IT WAS SO EASY TO INVEST COMPLETELY WITH WORKING WITH DAMON WAS HE CAME INTO THE ROOM FOR OUR FIRST MEETING WITH SUCH A VITAL SENSE OF WHAT THE PILOT STORY WOULD BE— HE PITCHED IT SHOT-BY-SHOT.

about when we would reveal certain elements, like the monster in the jungle. Then there was the time Damon pitched the idea that Locke was in a wheelchair before the crash, which is one of the favorite ideas I've heard in my life.

Q: What was your reaction when Damon pitched the idea that Locke was in a wheelchair?

Abrams: Damon had pitched me on instant message on the computer and my reaction back was, "Oh"—send—"My"—send—"God!"—send. I just started to *see* that. It was exactly like when he pitched the idea of opening with this guy in a suit who wakes up in the jungle—I wanted desperately to be there to direct that moment, because you just get it. Damon and I both think visually, but it's not so much what the idea exactly looks like as the emotional component. To me, the epitome of the process is an idea will be pitched to me and at the beginning it's irrelevant what it means as long as there's that feeling of, "That's really cool" or, "Oh, my God!" It's an emotional component that gets me excited, it's usually the scene I see in my head. Then the question becomes, how do you reveal it? The idea then usually comes down to what is translatable in film.

Q: Damon, where did you start in trying to crack the challenge of Lost?

Lindelof: We both had those same building blocks—a plane has crashed on an island. Well, that might be a cool movie or a miniseries, but where's the show? Episodic television needs to be a sort of franchise, so what would the franchise be for Lost? As I said, it had to be cool and mysterious and about what you don't know, as opposed to what you do know. I approached it from the point of view that if you invest the audience

THE THING THAT WAS REALLY COOL WAS IT WAS HUGE, BUT EVERY ASPECT WAS CRAZY. COULD WE, IN NO TIME, FIND THE LOCATIONS, WRITE THE SCRIPT, CAST THE ACTORS, FIGURE OUT THE VISUAL EFFECTS—WAS THAT EVEN POSSIBLE? BUT THE CHALLENGE OF PULLING IT OFF WAS EXHILARATING.

in the stories of the characters and who they might be—make them as mysterious as the island—you have a lot more fodder for television. J.J. had instantly gravitated

towards this idea and almost from the word "Go" he had this idea of a hatch on the island. The hatch became symbolic not only because of who might have put it there and what you could find if you opened it, but of all the things on the island. I also remember J.J. very clearly saying that whatever we wanted to do in Lost we had to build all that stuff into the pilot, we had to stock this world with all the elements and hints and clues. So if we were going to do non–linear storytelling, like the flashbacks, we had to have flashbacks in the pilot. We couldn't decide to do stuff we hadn't set up from the beginning or the audience would smell a rat.

Q: One of the opening scenes in the pilot is a sneaker hanging from a tree. Is it supposed to be the shoe that Locke is missing?

Abrams: It's just meant to be the sort of morbid thing you see when something horrible has happened.

Lindelof: Some things are intentional in terms of clues for the show, other things are more subjective. If someone thinks it's Locke's shoe, who's to say it's not, because he is missing a shoe.

Q: Where did the idea of the flashbacks come from?

Abrams: To me, it came when Damon said we should start on a guy who's in the jungle having been on a plane crash. That was, "Oh, my God," because it had who, where, why, what—every important question was right there. So, clearly, you would want to see what it was like to have been on that flight. I think flashbacks were implicit, it came with the territory of starting with the guy in the jungle.

Lindelof: What was cool about those flashbacks in the pilot [of the plane cracking up] was J.J. directed them in such a terrifying way that ABC was able to sell the show. I think America and the world has a macabre, bizarre fascination with plane crashes and that sort of imagery, so the tail section ripping off and the plane going down was something people really wanted to see.

But the way we designed the flashbacks to the plane was they would be about character. We showed the different stages of the plane crash through the different perspectives of Jack, Charlie and Kate. We felt that in the [aftermath] of the crash it was hard to get a sense of who the characters are, so we needed to see them at rest before this intense thing happens. So on the plane we see Jack take that drink and he flirts with the flight attendant, we realize Charlie's a drug addict, and when we see Kate at the end of the two hours we see the handcuffs on her and we realize, "Oh, my God—she's the fugitive!" The premise of the show is that the mystery of who these people are is as interesting as the island itself.

Q: Did you try to avoid the clichés of the old disaster movies?

Abrams: I love those movies!

Lindelof: Me, too. *The Towering Inferno* is like the greatest movie, ever.

Abrams: I grew up on movies like *Earthquake, The Poseidon Adventure*, the *Airport* movies. I mean, please! Damon and I share a love of certain pop genres and when *Lost* got on the cover of *Starlog* magazine that was *it* for us—there is nothing cooler … *Lost* felt like our version [of the classic disaster movies]. But it was not an homage, not a conscious thing.

Q: You like to say, "Take a B–genre and do it A."

Abrams: That's like my favorite approach … The approach was not to consciously avoid any clichés or stylistically borrow from some other genre, but to take a storyline that might easily fit into the classic 1970s disaster movies and then tell it in a way that felt committed and real and scary and unique.

Q: J.J., what was it like to direct the pilot?

Abrams: The thing that was really cool was it was huge, but every aspect was crazy. Could we, in no time, find the locations, write the script, cast the actors, figure out the visual effects—was that even possible? But the challenge of pulling it off was exhilarating.

It was a two–hour pilot taking place on a canvas that was vast compared to what we had done in the past. When I directed the pilot of *Alias*, the wide shots were limited because we were essentially always in Burbank. So I wanted desperately to make this thing look big. But there were so many logistical things to figure out. There were no interiors in the pilot except for the first days of the airplane interior shot here [Los Angeles], the rest was shot in Hawaii. You could count as an interior the actual cockpit we used in Hawaii, but that couldn't have been less practical or comfortable because we were in the middle of real rainstorms in the middle of the jungle. It was three days in there and the first time I went up into the cockpit it was claustrophobic, there was all this mud and this putrid smell that made you feel like you were inhaling spoors from Venus or something. There were challenges like that.

But the biggest thing was there are fourteen series regulars and when you're doing a pilot you're trying to find the voice of every character and you're working with actors and pairings of actors and they themselves are desperately trying to find out what they sound like. Thank God, Damon was there. We would have these sidebar conversations with the actors telling them what we were thinking about their characters. With Josh Holloway, for example, we had a number of ideas about Sawyer while we were scrambling to make the pilot. So when we did his scene where he's reading his letter we told Josh, "We're trying to figure out what the letter is, but for the purpose of this scene you're reading your own suicide letter that you had written." So, that was what he was playing when we shot it. Now, it ended up being a different thing.

Q: Sawyer's letter is symbolic of his parents being killed, right?

Abrams: Yes, in the show. But the point is, at the end of the day, the biggest challenge [in the pilot] was finding a way within scenes so you could quickly understand and feel a connection with these characters. It was a lot of information for an audience to take in and it's a testament to the actors and their absolute commitment to finding the truth in what they were doing, to bringing to life their moments, that allowed audiences not to be confused.

Lindelof: There's a real collaborative process to this show. The thing about the pilot that was so exciting was J.J. kind of assembled his Dream Team of production people, but it wouldn't be anybody else's Dream Team. He had to sell the network on Larry Fong, who had basically done commercials and music videos and had never been the DP on anything else, and he shot that pilot so beautifully, some of the most amazing television I've ever seen photographed. Larry was able to develop a look for the show and then Jack Bender was able to come in for the series and carry that on and bring a whole look to that, with Jean Higgins producing the show on a weekly basis. One criticism we got from the pilot was, "You guys will never be able to keep this up, it won't look this good." I feel it still does, which is a testament to all the people involved.

Q: The character of Boone dies, which fulfilled the promise that you would kill someone off in the first season. Did that promise come back to haunt you?

Abrams: It was a very tough decision because we really love all the actors. One of the down sides to doing a show is inevitably there's going to be a change in some form and you never want to say goodbye to someone you love working with. So we had been discussing the most effective and shocking way to do it [kill off a main character]. It was never in the long–term plan to kill Boone, but Damon, Carlton and the other writers came up with this storyline involving Locke and Boone. Also, given the jeopardy these characters are supposed to be in on the island, to go through a season without a main character dying felt like a cheat. In fact, if we did our job effectively the audience won't like it, either. But this is the cost of living on this island, what they have to contend with. So, even though people might miss Boone, they know enough people so it would be, "Thank

God" that Claire is still there or Jack or Sawyer or whomever you enjoy watching.

Lindelof: We had sort of used up our fake deaths — we have the psych–out death of Charlie where he's been hung and Jack resuscitates him and a psych–out death with Shannon where the monster seems to have killed her on Boone's vision quest. You lose the audience's faith if you just fake the death of a character.

We didn't know who we were going to kill until we came back from the Christmas break, sometime in January. Literally, the day we decided it was going to be Boone, we called Ian. I think the audience will find it very surprising that we're killing off Boone in episode 18, not in the season finale. We also didn't make this promise to kill off a character to boost ratings. Killing off Boone, we felt, would really change things up! Early in the series, Boone emerged as this guy who wanted to do good, but he was always going to be the lifeguard and not the doctor. But Boone was also a character who sort of bounced off a lot of other different characters. We felt it would be really tragic if Boone died in how it would affect Locke, Shannon and Sayid, by proxy of his relationship with Shannon. We realized Boone's death would force dramatic confrontations and relationship evolutions on the show in a way no other character would … And we can always use the flashback device to see Boone again.

Q: Or have Boone reappear, like Jack's dad?

Lindelof: Yeah — who's to say?

Q: There's the motif of the eye–opening, which usually begins each episode. Where did that idea come from?

Abrams: That was one of the first things Damon pitched — eye opens, we then see this guy in the jungle.

Lindelof: It was this visual concept to signal to the audience that the show is always about the people, that we're experiencing this island with them.

I think one of the things that makes this show accessible to people all over the country and, now, in foreign

countries, is the characters on the show are as confused about things as we [the audience] are! Also, there's a lot the characters aren't telling about themselves, but the flashbacks are letting the audience in on the joke. For example, Kate knows that Jack's dad died in Australia, but she doesn't know that his coffin was on the plane and that Jack's been seeing him on the island. In the same way, nobody knows exactly what the island is and the audience experiences their exploration and discovery of the island through the characters.

Q: Is it even an island?

Lindelof: Is it even an island, indeed! … One of the jokes, when the studio was asking us to shoot an alternate ending for the pilot, was [the survivors] would be trying to send this transmission and two guys in overalls come walking out of the jungle and say, "You're not on an island, you're in Florida!" "Oh!" And that would have been the end of the show! [laughs]

Q: The character of Sayid, as a former member of Iraq's Republican Guard, seems to be the one character who sort of hooks into current events.

Abrams: It was the idea of a character who is our enemy in theory, but seeing the living, breathing person.

Lindelof: There were two separate evolutions to that character. The first part was we wanted to have someone on the island who's the techie, like the *Gilligan's Island* show had the Professor. We wanted to put our own spin on that idea and our first impulse was to make the techie a woman. But then we had this discussion about how, in the 1960s, Gene Roddenberry used *Star Trek* as a sci–fi analogy of the times, so the Klingons were supposed to be the Russians. Then, in the late eighties, *The Next Generation* did this cool innovation where they put a Klingon in Starfleet, so now the enemy was serving on the bridge of the *Enterprise*. So we sort of cross–pollinated that with the idea of a techie and since we were doing this in September of 2004, we wondered: "What if the techie were an ex–member of the Republican Guard?" The poetry of it is that the people on the island are still living

in October of 2004 and their perspective is not our perspective. We felt it would be cool [to have an Iraqi character] because obviously we wanted to have as many different sorts of nationalities and ages and everything on the island.

Abrams: Also, [the Sayid character] helped us represent that what we really wanted the show to be about was the person you would never in your life have met suddenly becomes the person you need to survive, the stranger who becomes your brother–in–arms. I just couldn't wait to direct the scene where Sayid reveals to Hurley he was in the Republican Guard. It was a great moment because Hurley had been bonding with this guy and when he hears he was in the Persian Gulf War it doesn't even occur to him [that the man didn't fight on the American side]. The Sayid character basically says to him, "I was your enemy." It was the kind of moment when the framework that people base their lives on suddenly shifts. It felt like that was a great moment to drive that home, that the people on the island were not just going to be concerned with what they're going to eat and drink and where they're going to sleep, but what their society was going to be. That was the epitome of that aspect of the show, that you're forced to interact with someone you never in a million years would have met given what your life was like before the crash.

Q: When you think about being "*lost,*" the word itself has deep emotional connotations and connections.

Lindelof: We've said that our show is about lost people on a lost island. When all is said and done, when you peel back season one, you'll know why every character was in Australia and that these are all sort of lives interrupted. I think audiences have taken this concept to mean that they're all in Purgatory, that these people are literally dead and resolving their past lives. But what is death, really—what's the difference, isn't it the same thing? They're all on an island and if they get off the island that's the end of the show. So, for all intents and purposes they are dead.

Q: Since the creative process involves dreaming things up as you go along, were there any surprises in the first season?

Lindelof: Actually, we're a little defensive about, "Making it up as you go along." We get accused of that and it signals there's an arbitrary nature to the creative decision–making process. I don't want anyone to feel we're stumbling around in the dark, that it's been a case of, "Gee, what are we going to do this week?"

We did decide a lot of things early on in terms of what we did know and didn't know. There is a design to everything, but we can jettison things that aren't working in favor of things that are. I think that's what makes it good, that we can sort of change our minds about things, like deciding not to kill Jack. The "making it up" part is just our acceptance that this is a collaborative process, that the show is about writers and actors and directors and all these voices. There's a jazz–like quality to *Lost*: I'm really good at the sax, J.J. is really good on the piano, Matthew Fox is on the drums and we're all sort of listening to each other and maybe there's a five–second period where things go off–rhythm a bit because Foxy is changing things up. That's the sense in which we're making things up. It's all about trusting each other.

Q: Can you give any hints of what might be in store for the second season?

Abrams: There are a number of stories for characters we wanted to tell this season that we didn't get to. With Hurley, for example, one of the stories we were expecting to get into but didn't was why he had been in a mental institution and why his name is Hurley. There's the mystery of exactly what happened with Kate and why she's on the run. By the end of the first season they'll have been there approximately forty days, but they've explored very, very little of the island. So, there's the idea of this vast landscape they'll begin to explore and the opening of the hatch is one of the clues and mysteries of the island.

Early on, one of the things Damon said, which was a moment of clarity for me, was there shouldn't be one answer to the island. The questions people have now are —why can Locke walk, what's up with the real or imagined powers Walt seems to have, what is Kate up to, what is the monster in the jungle, why are there polar bears—some of these questions will be answered sooner than others. What makes me feel safe with the show and the story I would love to ultimately tell isn't in my head as scenes, it isn't in my head as locations.

WHEN ALL IS SAID AND DONE, WHEN YOU PEEL BACK SEASON ONE, YOU'LL KNOW WHY EVERY CHARACTER WAS IN AUSTRALIA AND THAT THESE ARE ALL SORT OF LIVES INTERRUPTED.

It's the *feeling* I have for a righteous explanation for a good number of things on the island, that we can get to that place where things will be explained that satisfies me in a grand way. Will it answer every question? No! But it shouldn't, because it's not all about one thing. And how we end up telling it, exactly, is part of the collaboration Damon was describing.

We've discussed the journey of getting there as if it were a great big cinderbox of a Stephen King novel and the first forty days is just the first couple chapters of this story. And the end is spectacular. But to get there you have to earn it through the body of the book, which is just what we're getting into on this show.

DREAMING IT UP

II.   CHARACTERS

Based on our meeting, here's what we have so far for the new and improved cast o' castaways (plus a few lame ideas I've tossed in just for talking points). While the island itself should always pose an exigent threat, there probably needs to be ongoing conflict within the group itself.

Therefore, I've broken them down into two groups (although which "side" they're on shouldn't manifest itself until we're well into the series) –

THE GOOD GUYS

JACK (THE ALPHA MALE)

He's our guy. The lead. The first thing we see in the show. The one who wakes up on the beach and brings us to the CRASH SITE. Our guide for the first two acts. He's cool. Intelligent. Handsome. Self-deprecating. A natural born leader. And his name is "Jack" so he can't possibly die.

Except for the part where he does.

KATE (OUR HERO)

Remember that chick from "V?" The one who starts off as the shy, unassuming and vulnerable doctor but eventually becomes the leader of the fucking resistance and gets away with saying things like – "Get away from me YOU STINKING LIZARD!" as she empties the clip of her Uzi?

Well, Kate's kinda like her – minus the medical training (whatever she did in her pre-crash life is up for discussion, but she shouldn't be defined by her career).

She is our star– the character we primarily view this new world through. Despite the protests of some of the survivors, she is the de facto LEADER of the group. She is the one they all trust – she is mega-smart, cool under pressure and highly motivated.

QUESTION: Is it too Bristowesque to make Kate *the one who was flying with her husband (now missing and presumed dead) – her primary motivation is not just exploring the island but in finding* him*? This way, when the guy shows up at the end of the first season (or beyond) and she's already fallen for one of our other castaways, we get a helluva lot more bang for our buck?*

It was in a January 12, 2004 e–mail that Damon Lindelof touched base with J.J. Abrams and company about incorporating all their brainstorming for what would become *Lost*. The result of Lindelof's "Midnight Document," as he called it—the 1/12/04 outline titled, "What We Know So Far"—included crafting Jack as a heroic figure and killing him at the end of act 2 of the pilot, thus emphasizing the island's mortal dangers, Lindelof adding *"anyone's expendable."* A grisly end was imagined, with Jack joining Kate and Charlie to explore the plane's cockpit when the thing–in–the–jungle attacks Jack and leaves his broken body high in a tree—*without his head*! (The scene would remain, only the creature's victim is the pilot, who at least got to keep his head.)

The show's creative evolution—a tantalizing alternate *Lost* universe—can be traced through the production's e–mails, outlines, treatments and early pilot scripts.

Familiar final characters would evolve and mutate:

- Kate, imagined as the central hero figure, particularly after Jack's death, was to be a happily married woman flying with her husband. During the crash

COINS. Quarters, nickels, dimes... SCATTERED. She moves to   *
the coins -- Charlie behind her.   *

                         CHARLIE
              ... what's that about?   *

Kate senses it before she sees it. Slowly tilts her head up
as we follow her gaze skyward --

And she GASPS.

We are looking up the trunk of AN ENORMOUS TREE. Gnarled and
battle-scarred with centuries of living, the thing's gotta be
SIXTY feet tall...

And thirty feet up, something is WEDGED in the branches. At
first, it doesn't seem to make sense -- maybe it's a pair of
pants someone hung up there to dry...

But that's not what it is.

It's JACK.

The position of his limbs horrible, unnatural.   *

He's dead.

                    END OF ACT TWO

they would be separated and her missing husband's fate remain a mystery.

- Charlie was envisioned as an anti–hero but in a January 13 follow–up outline, Lindelof proposed combining the idea of a drug addict character with Charlie. "This guy is still Han Solo ... but what if Han had to kick heroin before he fired up the Falcon and ditched Mos Eisley? Instead of molding an entirely new character to be our 'druggie,' maybe it's worth considering grafting the addiction onto our rogue." Sawyer would ultimately fulfill the role of island "rogue."

- Locke was a wealthy young CEO slated to join Jack in oblivion. Lindelof summed up the original Locke, in the 1/13 outline: "Entitled, cocky, arrogant ... he's Thurston Howell with BALLS. 'I make $3.4 million dollars a year, my friend—why don't you go gather some fucking firewood?'"

- Kate, Charlie and a core group of fifteen other survivors would return to camp and discover the other survivors had *vanished*.

THE LOST DIARY

EPISODE SUMMARIES

If an airliner crashed on a deserted island a few survivors would scrounge for paper and pens to record personal reflections, just as Claire does in her diary. Some might become historians of life on the island. It's a human imperative, this urge to chronicle and document life, particularly in times of crisis and challenge. If such an island scribe had a god–like omniscience, the *Lost* characters' flashbacks would also seep into such a journal, making for a record of the secrets of all these strangers that Fate has thrown together. Such a chronicle by an unidentified observer might read like this …

PILOT EPISODE
PART I

TELEPLAY BY
J.J. ABRAMS
AND DAMON
LINDELOF

STORY BY
JEFFREY LIEBER
AND
J.J. ABRAMS
AND DAMON
LINDELOF

DIRECTOR OF
PHOTOGRAPHY
LARRY FONG

DIRECTED BY
J.J. ABRAMS

It's a traveler's worst nightmare and we're living it— our plane from Sydney to Los Angeles has crashed on an island in the middle of nowhere. By some miracle dozens of us have survived. But it's been chaos on the beach. Smoking metal and wreckage is everywhere, bloodied bodies, people screaming. The most horrible sight was when one of the engines, still spinning, sucked in a poor bystander and exploded.

A heroic presence on the beach was Jack, a surgeon back in the States who seemed to be everywhere, coming to the rescue, tending the injured. It was only when things settled down that he saw to a bleeding cut on his back. He asked a young lady named Kate to sew him up with a regular sewing needle and thread. Gutsy guy—and girl! Jack talked to Kate about fear and how, as a surgeon, there were times he had to let fear in—but only for a second. With a patient on the operating table and their life in your hands, you had to be strong, for them.

By nightfall a signal fire was going and the entire beach lit up with campfires, the flames casting weird shadows against all the twisted metal. Less than fifty of us are alive, and certain individuals are beginning to emerge among our group. One of the natural leaders is Sayid, who seems to have a military background. A young guy named Charlie used to be in a band called Drive Shaft. A big fellow named Hurley checked in with Claire, a very pregnant young Aussie, to see if there was any "baby stuff" to worry about. Two young people, a brother and sister named Boone and Shannon, have been bickering, but I saw Shannon earlier this morning and she was screaming. Jin, a man from Korea, seems terribly distressed and has told his wife, Sun, to stay with him at all times. They don't seem to speak any English.

There is also an older fellow named Locke who actually seems happy about things. When a sudden rain sent everyone scrambling for shelter, Locke

TOP AND RIGHT: **JACK SHEPHARD SURVEYS THE WRECKAGE OF OCEANIC FLIGHT #815.** BELOW: **A MANACLED KATE BREATHES FROM THE OXYGEN MASK BEFORE THE PLANE BREAKS UP.**

stayed out in the downpour, reveling in it like it was a heavenly baptism.

As the initial shock wears off, some are trying to piece together what happened. Jack recalls we were at 40,000 feet when the plane hit turbulence. All he remembers is telling an older woman named Rose that turbulence is normal and he'd keep her company until her husband got back from the restroom. Then the plane shook, oxygen masks dropped—all Jack remembers is waking up, lying in the jungle and seeing a dog run past (the dog's name is Vincent and belongs to a ten–year–old boy named Walter, who has survived with his father, Michael).

Jack reasons that if the cockpit fell into the jungle, there might be a radio, and we could call for help. But then the strangest, most unsettling thing happened—a roar from the jungle and crashing sounds,

as if some gigantic creature were lumbering around. Something unnatural.

Jack, Kate and Charlie found the cockpit and the pilot, who was miraculously alive. The pilot explained

that six hours into the flight the radio had gone out and they had turned back to land in Fiji. The plane was a thousand miles off course when we hit the fatal turbulence, so no rescue planes or ships could possibly know where to look for us. There was more bad news—the transceiver wasn't working.

Suddenly, the pilot was yanked through the cockpit window by that thing from the jungle! Jack grabbed the transceiver and everyone scrambled out of the cockpit. They found the bloody corpse of the pilot, high in the branch of a tree.

"Guys, how does something like that happen?" Charlie asked.

PILOT EPISODE
PART II

TELEPLAY BY J.J. ABRAMS AND DAMON LINDELOF	STORY BY JEFFREY LIEBER AND J.J. ABRAMS AND DAMON LINDELOF	DIRECTOR OF PHOTOGRAPHY LARRY FONG
		DIRECTED BY J.J. ABRAMS

It's the day after the crash and many are still coming to grips with harsh reality. Some ignore reality altogether—Shannon is sunbathing on the beach, still certain rescue is imminent. But, as Jack and Kate and Charlie learned from the doomed pilot, our plane went off course and we're stranded far from the normal air and seafaring traffic lanes.

The thin veneer of civilization is already chipping off. A tall, lanky Southerner named Sawyer picked a fight with Sayid, convinced Sayid blew up the plane in a terrorist act. Kate shouted at them to stop and Jack pulled them apart. Sawyer seems contemptuous of "the doc" and sarcastically muttered, "You're the hero." Jack keeps tending the injured, including a delirious man with a jagged piece of shrapnel in his stomach, whose condition seems of interest to Kate.

Sayid checked the transceiver from the cockpit and noted the batteries were still good. It was possible to broadcast "blind," but that would waste the battery. He proposed getting a signal from high ground. When Hurley heard that Sayid fought in the Persian Gulf War he assumed Sayid was all–American—he was taken aback when Sayid said he was a veteran of Iraq's Republican Guard.

Sayid was joined in the hike to find high ground by Boone and Shannon, Charlie and Kate. Sawyer also caught up with the party: "I'm a complex guy, sweetheart," he told Kate, who seems to see right through him.

The group was in an open field when a creature suddenly rushed directly at them. Sawyer stood his ground and pulled out a gun and killed the creature. It was not the "thing," but just as weird—a polar bear! The strangeness of an Arctic creature in a temperate zone was forgotten as the matter of the gun came up. Sawyer claimed he got it off the ankle holster of a U.S. marshal who'd been on the flight. Kate grabbed the gun, gave the clip to Sayid and the now–empty gun to Sawyer.

The marshal is actually the wounded man, whose shrapnel Jack finally removed. But he has lost a lot of blood and has been unconscious. When he awoke, he grabbed Jack and demanded, "Where is *she*?" Kate was his prisoner!

Kate's last words to the marshal before the crash were: "I have one favor to ask." Then, in the turbulence, a piece of luggage flew out of an overhead compartment and smacked the marshal unconscious. Kate took his key and unlocked her handcuffs, which are among the pieces of wreckage.

It's clear there's treasure to be had in the wreckage, particularly personal possessions and luggage. Jack has already asked Hurley to search for antibiotics. Walt found a superhero comic book written in Spanish. Walt has struck up an unlikely friendship with Locke, who showed the boy how to play backgammon. Walt told Locke he had been living in Australia with his foster dad and his mom, who had died a couple weeks ago. Michael, the real father he never knew, had been taking him back to live with him in America.

Meanwhile, the party out in the high ground had been working with the transceiver and realized they couldn't send out a distress signal—another transmission was blocking it, a voice in French. Shannon, who has a rough knowledge of the language, translated the looping message: "Please help me ... I'm

BELOW: **SAYID, THE "TECHIE" AMONG THE SURVIVORS, WORKS WITH KATE ON ANTENNAS WITH WHICH TO BROADCAST A DISTRESS SIGNAL.**

alone on the island … The others, they're dead. It killed them, it killed them all … "

Sayid realized the shocking truth—this transmission was sixteen years old!

A mysterious thing lurking in the jungle, a rampaging polar bear, a radio transmission from the past—Charlie spoke for all when he blurted out:

"Guys, where *are* we?"

TABULA RASA
EPISODE 101

WRITTEN BY
DAMON
LINDELOF

DIRECTOR OF
PHOTOGRAPHY
LARRY FONG

DIRECTED BY
JACK BENDER

Today Jack saw the mug shot of Kate that the lawman was carrying. "Dangerous, she's dangerous," the marshal kept repeating.

As the days stretch on, it's becoming clear a rescue party might not be coming soon. Sayid's group returned to the beach but Sayid had told them not to tell anyone about the mysterious transmission, particularly the cryptic comment about whatever "killed them all." It would rob people of hope and hope is too precious to lose.

Indeed, everyone seemed to be echoing Charlie's question, "Where are we?" Hurley, who has been helping Jack with the marshal, wondered if the unseen thing in the jungle was a dinosaur. Jack had to remind Hurley that dinosaurs are extinct.

Sayid asked for electronic equipment so he could post another signal. He also argued that we had to begin organizing. The water supply, for example, is the bottled water pulled from the wreckage and that supply is quickly running out.

Meanwhile, Locke has given young Walt a glimpse of his secret, telling him "a miracle" happened to him—this island has given them all a miracle, he declares. Michael, out in the jungle looking for Vincent, Wally's lost dog, accidentally walked in on Sun, the young Korean woman, who was washing herself—an awkward moment, made more so by Michael's embarrassed mumbles of apology in a language he knew she could not understand.

Kate tried to play it cool when she asked Jack how the injured man was doing, not knowing that Jack and Hurley knew her secret. But there's a growing bond between them. Kate confided in Jack about the mysterious sixteen-year-old distress signal.

Kate's memory has drifted back to Australia and the time she was sleeping in a sheep pen when an old rancher rousted her. She passed herself off as "Annie" and he gave her breakfast and kept her on to help him run his ranch. But, damned luck, the day she tried to walk away, she accepted his offer to drive her to the train station, not knowing he would turn her over to the marshal for the $23,000 reward.

There was another confrontation between Jack and Sawyer when the doctor entered the fuselage, a grim task given the dead bodies still in there. The doc was looking for medicine while Sawyer had scrounged up some booze, smokes and a couple of *Playboy* magazines, which about summed things up, Sawyer noted. Sawyer and Jack instinctively bristle in each other's presence—they're from opposite sides of the tracks and both know it. Sawyer resents the doctor, who seems to be playing by civilization's rules and doesn't realize this is survival of the fittest—"I'm in the wild," Sawyer declared as he left the wreckage.

Kate finally entered the tent where the mortally wounded marshal was sleeping. She bent over him

LEFT: BOONE AND HURLEY WATCH AS CLAIRE LEADS THE MEMORIAL SERVICE TO HONOR THOSE WHO DIED IN THE CRASH OF OCEANIC FLIGHT 815. RIGHT: SAYID AND KATE PREPARE RADIO EQUIPMENT.

and he suddenly awoke and began choking her. Jack walked into the tent in time to separate them, but the wounded man began going into convulsions, bleeding internally.

Jack's valiant efforts to save the marshal caused grumbling and discontent as the man's agonizing howls made it a sleepless night for everyone on the beach. Sawyer finally sat down by Kate and noted there was still one bullet left in the gun. Inside the tent, between his death throes, the dying lawman warned Jack about Kate and asked to talk to her alone. "She got to you, too, huh?" the marshal said, to Jack's surprise.

Kate went into the tent and the marshal asked what was the favor she was going to ask him before

the plane went down. She just wanted the rancher to get all the reward money—he had a hell of a mortgage. The marshal had something else to ask: "Are you going to do it, or what?"

Sawyer would "do it," but botched it. He aimed for the dying man's chest and perforated a lung, wasting the last bullet. His efforts had just prolonged the inevitable.

Jack angrily ordered Sawyer out of the tent. The death cries soon stopped. Somehow, Jack ended it.

Thankfully, a lighter note the next day. Locke had made a whistle and Vincent answered his call. Locke had the pleasure of telling Michael he'd brought Walt's dog back and he could give it to his son.

Jack was sitting alone at the beach and Kate

joined him. She wanted to tell him why she was arrested, but Jack didn't want to know. "It doesn't matter, Kate, who we were, what we did before this, before the crash," Jack declared. "Three days ago we all died. We should all be able to start over."

WALKABOUT
EPISODE 102

WRITTEN BY
DAVID FURY

DIRECTOR OF
PHOTOGRAPHY
LARRY FONG

DIRECTED BY
JACK BENDER

The fourth day on the island and a huge scare on the beach as horrible sounds came from the main section of fuselage wreckage. Everyone feared the thing from the jungle had descended, but it was wild boars come to feed on the twenty or so dead bodies inside. The decaying corpses were a critical problem, baking under the hot sun for days, so despite Sayid's protests that we honor the dead with a proper burial, Jack successfully argued the fuselage be set on fire that night to burn the bodies.

Sayid turned to his other project, the radio. He concluded there must be a significant power source on the island for the radio transmission he had earlier picked up to be playing continually for sixteen years. With an antenna, the transceiver could be used to triangulate a distress signal.

Meanwhile, Locke put an exclamation point on the problem of the dwindling food supply when he tossed a knife and stuck it into an empty airplane seat next to Sawyer and declared: "We hunt." The boars represent hundreds of pounds of meat on the hoof, but their tusks and surly disposition make hunting them a challenge. Locke is prepared, with a case full of deadly looking knives he'd checked on to the plane and which he's recovered from the wreckage. As Hurley muttered, "Who *is* this guy?"

Kate volunteered to go along. Michael also joined the hunt and in sign language asked Sun to watch his boy as he headed into the jungle. Meanwhile, Charlie and Hurley tried spearfishing with some success (although Charlie had done so at Shannon's request, so she could pass off the fish to Boone as if she had caught it).

On the beach, Claire approached Jack about whether he should lead a memorial service that night. "No, it's not my thing," Jack said. Jack is still the one everyone turns to but he seems uncomfortable with the responsibility. Nevertheless, he checked on Rose, the older woman who sits silently on the beach awaiting the return of her missing husband. To Jack's trained eyes she seemed to be suffering post–traumatic shock. He kept a silent vigil with her until Rose simply said, "His fingers swell." The high altitude during a flight caused her husband's fingers to swell, which is why she was wearing his wedding ring on a chain around her neck. Jack knows her husband was in the rear lavatory when the tail section broke off and is probably dead. He asked Rose if she wanted to honor her husband, Bernard, at the memorial service Claire was organizing. Rose declined—she's convinced Bernard is still alive, somewhere. She also told Jack she was "letting him off the hook" on his promise to stay with her until her husband returned.

Rose's faith is probably a natural defense mechanism in the face of her loss. But Jack is beginning to doubt his own physical senses—he keeps seeing a phantom of a man dressed in a suit.

Meanwhile, Locke was expertly leading the hunting party until a charging boar sideswiped Michael. Kate felt they should return to camp. Locke replied, strangely: "Don't tell me what I can't do!" And then the gigantic thing in the jungle attacked and Kate hurried off with a wounded Michael. But Locke, left behind, saw it—and it was beautiful.

Back at camp, Kate told Jack, "Locke's gone. That thing was moving in his direction. There wasn't time." It was a shocker, then, when Locke appeared, tired and bloody—with a dead boar in hand.

That night the fuselage was set on fire and the memorial service was held. Boone held a torch so Claire could read the names of the dead or missing and try to personalize the lost strangers with whom we feel somehow connected.

Locke kept watching the funeral fire and saw something in the wreckage, a link to his old life. No one knows the fearless knife–thrower and hunter, the guy who seems hardwired with survival skills, was a lonely, desk–bound office worker who had come to Australia to be part of an organized walkabout, the traditional aboriginal rite of passage in the wilds. When Locke arrived he was rejected for a simple reason—he was in a wheelchair.

That had been the "miracle," the day of the crash, when Locke found himself flat on his back in the sand—his shoeless foot twitching, his legs working again. Locke saw his abandoned wheelchair burning

in the funeral pyre and despite the somber, silent mood, he smiled.

KATE AND CHARLIE CAUGHT IN AN EXPECTANT MOMENT.

WHITE RABBIT
EPISODE 103

WRITTEN BY
CHRISTIAN
TAYLOR

DIRECTOR OF
PHOTOGRAPHY
MICHAEL
BONVILLAIN

DIRECTED BY
KEVIN HOOKS

The sixth day on the island and our number has dwindled by one, to forty–six survivors. A woman named Joanna had gone swimming and the tide swept her out to sea. Boone had tried to rescue her but was going under when Jack first swam out and pulled him back to shore, and then made a valiant attempt to swim back out for Joanna. But it was too late. Jack seemed to take her death personally.

But life and survival goes on. We were down to our last eighteen bottles of water when more bad news hit—someone had stolen the cache of water.

Claire, because of her pregnancy, was suffering from lack of water. Charlie—he with the tattoo that reads, "Living is easy with eyes closed"— has tried to comfort her. Claire feels people aren't looking her square in the eye, she feels she's a "time bomb of responsibility" and people are dreading the moment she goes off. "You don't scare me," Charlie told her.

And everyone keeps looking to Jack for answers to everything. But who can explain to Jack why he keeps seeing a phantom he recognizes as his dead father, whose body he had been bearing home from Australia when the plane went down?

This island seems to stir our deepest fears and secrets. Jack remembers as a boy his dad's harsh words to him—"You don't have what it takes." His dad, a successful chief of surgery, could coldly go about his business because he realized he couldn't always be a hero, he couldn't save everyone.

Jack and his dad were estranged, hadn't talked in two months, when his mother told him, "Your father's gone." He had been drinking too much, had lost his old friends, he was alone—"Why do you think that is, Jack?" his mother asked, prodding the open, psychic wound that shamed Jack into going to Australia.

Jack finally gave chase to the phantom and almost fell off a cliff. He was hanging on for life when a hand reached down to help him up—it was Locke. Jack, his guard finally down, confessed he couldn't possibly be a leader for the survivors, that he "doesn't have what it takes." How could he lead, he revealed, when he was chasing a ghost, his own white rabbit?

"I'm not a big believer in magic, but this place is different, special," Locke told him. "The others don't want to talk about it because it scares them. But we all know it, we all feel it. Is your white rabbit a hallucination? Probably. But what if everything that happened here happened for a reason … I have looked into the eyes of this island and what I saw was beautiful."

Locke tells Jack he has to finish whatever it was he started and do it alone. A leader, he adds, can't lead until he knows where he's going. So Jack, alone, with a torch to light his way through the night, followed the jungle sounds that led him to a cave with

TOP: **LOCKE LISTENS AS JACK REVEALS HIS PURSUIT OF HIS OWN PERSONAL "WHITE RABBIT."** LEFT: **THE "GHOST" OF DR. SHEPHARD, JACK'S FATHER (JOHN TERRY), WHICH JACK KEEPS SEEING IN THE DISTANCE.**

scattered pieces of the plane, luggage—and an empty coffin. But the cave also had springs and pools of clean, sweet, flowing water.

That night, back at the beach, it was discovered that Boone had taken the water bottles in a well–meaning but misguided attempt to safeguard the dwindling supply. And then Jack emerged with news of the cave and the unlimited supply of fresh water. "It's been six days," Jack announced, "we're all waiting for someone to come. What if they don't? We have to stop waiting, we need to start figuring things out. A woman died this morning just going for a swim … Every man for himself is not going to work! It's time to start organizing. We need to figure out how we're going to survive here. Now, I found fresh water up in the valley. I'll take a group in at first light. If you don't want to come then find another way to contribute. Last week, most of us were strangers—but we're all here now … But if we can't live together we're going to die alone."

Afterwards, Jack sat alone at a campfire and Kate joined him, bringing a glass of water. She asked where he had gone when he disappeared into the jungle.

"I just had to take care of a few things. My father died in Sydney … "

TOP: JIN PRESENTS SUN WITH A WEDDING RING. BOTTOM: JIN GIVES SUN A DOG TO KEEP HER COMPANY FOR THOSE LONG NIGHTS WHEN HE'S AWAY DOING HER FATHER'S BUSINESS. BUT SUN DOESN'T WANT DOGS OR DIAMONDS, ALL SHE WANTS IS TO MAKE A HAPPY LIFE WITH JIN.

HOUSE OF THE RISING SUN
EPISODE 104

WRITTEN BY	DIRECTOR OF	DIRECTED BY
JAVIER GRILLO-MARXUACH	PHOTOGRAPHY LARRY FONG	MICHAEL ZINBERG

It was a beautiful, sunny day but violence disrupted it when Jin suddenly tackled Michael in the surf. Sayid and Sawyer pulled them apart and they used the dead marshal's handcuffs to lock Jin to a piece of fuselage. Sayid announced that Jin would stay handcuffed until they knew what happened.

Meanwhile, Jack, Locke, Kate and Charlie had gone into the valley to explore the cave. After being chased by some angry bees, they took shelter in the cave and Kate found two skeletons with withered clothes hanging from their bones. "Our very own Adam and Eve," Locke said. Jack saw no evidence

SUN IS READY TO DITCH HER HUSBAND AT SYDNEY AIRPORT— UNTIL JIN OFFERS HER AN ORCHID, THE DELICATE FLOWER THAT FIRST WON HER HEART.

Shaft, he even had both their albums! Music to Charlie's ears. Charlie then confessed the eight days stranded had been eight long days without the guitar he'd brought with him on the trip to Australia. Locke is also on to Charlie—does Charlie want his guitar or his drugs?

Locke demanded that Charlie give him the drugs. "This island just might give you what you're looking for, but you have to give the island something," Locke told him.

Charlie handed over his stash. "Look up, Charlie," Locke smiled.

And there, literally overhead, stuck in a tree branch, was Charlie's undamaged guitar.

Meanwhile, the situation at the beach was humiliating for the young Korean couple. Sun remembered an elegant night, a garden party lit by mellow lantern light and a waiter serving champagne—Jin. That night they'd talked about marriage, and Jin vowed to talk to her father, a wealthy and powerful businessman. As a token of his undying affection, Jin gave Sun a beautiful orchid.

Now, on this lost island, Sun had to watch her proud husband chained like a dog. She remembered the day he finally gave her a diamond ring—he had convinced her father he was worthy to take his daughter's hand and had gone to work for her father. But then came the long hours alone, the quiet evenings at home she'd planned that were interrupted by the phone calls that took Jin away. The worst night was when Jin came home, splattered with blood, and it seemed obvious what he did for her father. She had finally planned to escape and had secretly learned English. While with her husband at the airport in Sydney to catch a flight to Los Angeles, she planned to slip away to a waiting car that would spirit her away. But at the last moment she couldn't leave him—maybe it was the orchid he held up to her in the airport that drew her back.

of trauma and observed that, given the condition of the clothes, they probably had lain there for fifty years. Then it became clear that "Adam and Eve" probably lived here. The cave was a source of fresh water, the jungle canopy provided shade from the sun, the cave itself shelter against predators. It was crystal clear to Jack. Instead of bringing the water to the people, they should bring the people to the water—we should live in the caves.

Charlie tried to slip away for a little privacy to indulge in his dwindling stash of heroin. The only problem was Locke began following him and just when he really wanted Locke to bugger off, Locke said he recognized him as the bass player for Drive

Sun finally approached Michael alone and spoke to him in English. He was shocked, but agreed to keep her secret. But she had to explain that the watch Michael was wearing, a watch he'd picked up from the wreckage, belonged to her father. That was why Jin attacked—it was a question of honor. Michael returned the watch to Jin, venting a little anger. "Time doesn't matter on a damn island," Michael shouted as he brought an ax down and cracked the chain, freeing Jin.

But there is a larger development now, with Jack pushing for everyone to relocate to the caves. Sayid is an advocate for the beach and even lobbied Michael, apologizing for earlier doubting his innocence and asking for his support in keeping a beach camp to watch for a passing plane or boat and tend the signal fires. Sawyer decided to stay put at his beachfront tent. Kate is another who decided on the beach. "I don't want to be Eve," she told Jack. "I can't dig in."

By night, new people were arriving at the caves. Soon campfires were blazing and Charlie began playing his guitar. Sun and Jin had come and were settling in and Locke was there too. Jack sat by himself thinking, I believe, of Kate.

THE MOTH
EPISODE 105

WRITTEN BY
JENNIFER
JOHNSON AND
PAUL DINI

DIRECTOR OF
PHOTOGRAPHY
MICHAEL
BONVILLAIN

DIRECTED BY
JACK BENDER

Morning of a new day, our little colony now divided into two camps. But with water at the caves and fish off the beach, there will be exchanges back and forth.

For Charlie it was an agonizing new day without

drugs. Drugs were his way of coping when he was briefly caught in the rock–and–roll spotlight, and had become a comfort in facing the disappointment of being *out* of the spotlight. He remembered his

ABOVE: **JACK COMFORTS CHARLIE AS HE KICKS HIS HEROIN HABIT.**
OPPOSITE: **CHARLIE IS PULLED DEEP INTO THE ROCK-STAR LIFE BY HIS AMBITIOUS BROTHER IAN (NEIL HOPKINS).**

struggles trying to be a good Catholic, kneeling in the confessional to ask forgiveness for his latest bit of rock–star debauchery and the unflappable priest telling him that life was a series of choices. And Charlie chose the rock–star life with his older brother Ian. Charlie remembered how he made his brother vow that if things got too crazy, they'd walk away. But Ian stole the spotlight, broke their vow and treated Charlie more like a baby brother than a rock god.

Charlie finally confronted Locke and asked for his stash back. Locke made a deal: Charlie could ask for his drugs three times—this was the first—and if he still wanted the drugs the third time, Locke would hand over the stash.

Meanwhile, Sayid erected an antenna on the beach and was working out a complicated method of triangulating a signal. In addition to the beach antenna, another antenna would have to be positioned two kilometers into the valley and a third on higher ground. All three would have to be switched on simultaneously, with bottle rockets fired as signal flares. Boone offered to man the beach antenna, Kate the post in the valley and Sayid would take the high ground. They only needed fresh

batteries. A laptop seemed an ideal source, which involved wrangling with Sawyer, as usual.

"It must be exhausting always living like a

parasite," Kate told Sawyer. " … All you had to do was say 'Please,'" he told her. It's hard to tell whether Sawyer enjoys attention, likes to make people grovel or if Kate simply shamed him into it. Maybe, like he said, he's a complicated guy.

But as Sayid's team prepared to send out their signal, a cave–in trapped Jack at the caves. Hurley told Charlie to run to the beach to tell Kate, but she was gone by the time Charlie brought the bad news. Boone rushed off to help, leaving the job of shooting the signal flare to Shannon. Sawyer promised he would head into the valley to tell Kate about Jack.

Sawyer reached Kate and Sayid before they split up and seemed genuinely hurt when Kate blurted, "What the hell are *you* doing here?" Maybe that's why he didn't tell her about Jack. He did help climb a tree to attach Kate's antenna while Sayid headed for high ground. Sawyer let it slip about the cave–in and Kate dropped everything to run for the cave.

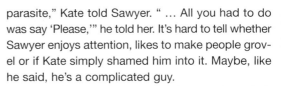

At the cave, Michael took charge of the dig—eight years working construction taught him a lot about load bearing, how to keep a rock wall from further collapsing. When a narrow opening was made, Charlie insisted on being the one to crawl through. Jack was alive in a little chamber but his shoulder was dislocated and he asked Charlie to pop it back in. It was brutal, but Charlie did it.

In the cramped space that reminded Charlie of the confessional booth, Jack talked to him about his obvious drug addiction. But then Charlie saw a moth. Taking a flashlight, he followed and the moth led to an opening to the surface.

When Jack and Charlie walked back around to the cave, it was the happiest scene since the crash. Kate rushed into Jack's arms and when Hurley heard Charlie had found a way out, shouted, "Dude, you rock!" Charlie just grinned, he was so happy. It was a beautiful thing to see.

For Charlie, the moth in the cave was a reminder

of earlier in the day when, soon after the cave–in, Charlie came upon Locke, who was skinning a boar. Charlie had asked, the second time, for his drugs. Locke just pointed with his knife at a cocoon where a moth was struggling to emerge. He could use his knife to widen the opening and help the moth be free, he explained, but it would be too weak to survive—struggle was nature's way of strengthening a creature.

That night, after rescuing Jack, Charlie saw Locke alone and asked for his drugs. The third and final time. Locke handed it over. And Charlie dropped it in a fire. "I'm proud of you, Charlie," Locke said. And, honestly, a moth flew by at that very moment.

With Jack rescued, talk turned to whether Sayid managed to get a signal. Shannon had switched on the beach antenna at the agreed–upon time and shot off her flare. Although Kate had left her post to Sawyer, the second signal had been fired. Sayid had turned on his antenna and was acquiring a signal when someone came from behind and knocked him unconscious.

CONFIDENCE MAN
EPISODE 106

WRITTEN BY	DIRECTOR OF	DIRECTED BY
DAMON	PHOTOGRAPHY	TUCKER
LINDELOF	LARRY FONG	GATES

Another day, more violence. Boone discovered Sawyer's hidden stash in the jungle and Sawyer beat him up for messing with his things. Boone, however, was looking for Shannon's asthma inhalers. It seems Shannon was too self–conscious to let people know she has an asthmatic condition. Boone was convinced Sawyer had them because he's been on the

beach reading a novel that had been in Shannon's bag, along with her inhalers. Sawyer said the book had been among the debris on the beach.

Kate went to see Sawyer and ask for the inhalers. Sawyer calls her "Freckles" and agrees to hand them over—for a kiss. Kate told him she wasn't buying his act—she'd seen him reading and rereading a carefully folded letter. Somewhere beneath that hard–boiled exterior was a real human being …

"Shut up," Sawyer said—and handed her the letter. It was a strange, anonymous note from someone describing how "Sawyer" had sex with his mother and stole his dad's money and how his dad killed her and then himself.

Kate walked away, there was no kiss.

Meanwhile, Sayid returned with the troubling account of being attacked by some unknown assailant. Locke suggested someone could have used a cigarette to make a time–delay fuse on the second flare and gotten to Sayid's position (an obvious reference to Sawyer). Locke handed Sayid a knife—"In case there's a next time."

The Shannon situation then took an ugly turn. She was having trouble breathing and Sayid told Jack that during five years in the Republican Guard he was trained in torture—ten minutes with Sawyer

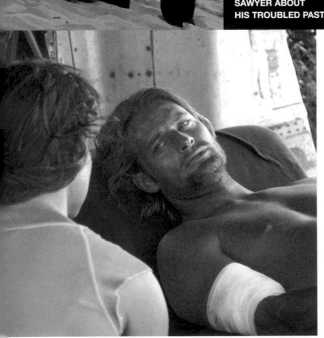

He just asked to see Kate alone.

"Baby, I'm tied to a tree in a jungle of mystery," Sawyer declared when Kate appeared, alone. "I just got tortured by a damn spinal surgeon and a genuine Iraqi … You really going to let that girl suffocate because you can't bring yourself to give me one little kiss? Hell, it's only first base. Lucky for you, I ain't greedy."

Kate gave him the kiss and Sawyer said, "I don't have it … never did."

A furious Kate punched him, stomped off. Sayid and Jack rushed back as Sawyer was loosening his bonds and in the scuffle Sayid's knife cut an artery in Sawyer's arm. With blood spurting, Jack had to tend to him or he'd die.

Under the stress, Sawyer remembered how he'd bedded a woman whose wealthy husband put up the front money for a bogus oil deal. But when he visited their home he saw their little boy and suddenly he called off the deal.

Sawyer had blacked out and when he came to, Kate was there. She had his neatly folded letter and she noted the envelope was postmarked from Knoxville, Tennessee, in 1976, America's Bicentennial year. "You wrote this letter," Kate declared. Sawyer told her to get the hell out. He later burned the letter.

Something about this island … it makes you confront your past. It can also renew you. Sun, constantly lectured by Jin to keep buttoned up and modest, has started to rebel and is wearing more comfortable clothing. Sun has also revealed a green thumb and made a salve from eucalyptus that helped Shannon breathe, even without her inhalers.

At the end of the day, Kate saw Sayid on the beach—he was leaving the camp because he'd broken a personal vow to never again engage in torture. But he was leaving on more than a self-imposed exile. "Someone has to walk the shore and map the island, to see what else there is," Sayid said to Kate. "I can't think of a better person to do it than the only one I trust. I hope we meet again."

Sayid kissed Kate's hand and headed off, following the coastline.

and he'd get the medicine. Sawyer was asleep in his tent when Jack and Sayid dragged him out and tied him to a tree. Sayid was right. The threat of losing an eye had Sawyer pleading he'd had enough.

SOLITARY
EPISODE 107

WRITTEN
DAVID FURY

DIRECTOR OF
PHOTOGRAPHY
LARRY FONG

DIRECTED BY
GREG YAITANES

Sayid had not ventured far when he discovered a cable stretching from the ocean across the beach and deep into the jungle. His soldier's instincts were still strong—down a jungle path he discovered a trip wire. But when he stepped over, it was into another trap—a rope hooked his leg and swung him into the air, leaving him dangling until someone cut him down and he fell, unconscious.

Sayid woke up manacled to a bed of springs, heard someone muttering "Where is Alex?" He realized he was wired to an electric panel as his captor sent electric shocks through him. He shouted he was one of the survivors of a plane crash, that he had found the wire, that they heard sixteen–year–old transmissions, a Mayday from a French woman …

"Sixteen years," said a woman, stepping out of the shadows. "Has it really been that long?"

It was the French woman! Sayid saw a jacket stenciled with her last name: "Rousseau." She seemed paranoid, a little crazy—she talked about "Others" in control. She had been going through Sayid's backpack and found a photo of a woman—what was her name? "Nadia," Sayid said.

Sayid's capture and strange interrogation was a complete contrast to the mood back at the settlement. Hurley found some golf equipment among the mass of luggage, secretly built a two–hole golf course in a beautiful valley nearby, and then invited everyone to the first Island Open.

Michael thought it a colossal waste of time. "Dude, listen, our lives suck," Hurley replied. "Everyone's nerves have been stretched to the max. We're lost on an island running from boars, monsters, freaking polar bears … we need some kind of relief … some way to have fun … or else

we're just going to go crazy waiting for the next bad thing to happen."

Hurley's logic was impeccable. Jack and Michael begin golfing. Word spread and a crowd began heading to the valley to take their swings. Kate came

SAYID GETS KARMIC PAYBACK FOR HIS PAST AS A SOLDIER AND TORTURER IN IRAQ WHEN HE IS TRAPPED AND TORTURED BY THE MYSTERIOUS FRENCH WOMAN (PLAYED BY MIRA FURLAN), WHOSE TRUST HE FINALLY WINS.

just to see superserious Jack actually having fun. Sawyer teased her—there's a new one, *a doctor playing golf*—but even Sawyer showed up and when Jack was lining up a big shot he grinned and bet two tubes of sunscreen and a flashlight that Jack would choke. Kate took that action.

Back at the French woman's lair, Sayid gained her trust by repairing an old music box. But before he fixed it, he asked for her first name. "Danielle," she said. And Danielle Rousseau told of how she had been part of a science team on a boat three days out of Tahiti when a storm left them shipwrecked here. They built temporary shelter … but *it* killed the rest of the team. She talked of the Black Rock and "the Others" that she had heard, whispering in the jungle.

Suddenly, they had heard a growl. The French

woman sprang to her feet, grabbed a rifle and clambered up a ladder of what was a survival lair built below the jungle floor. Sayid worked his chains loose and freed himself. He grabbed a rifle and some maps and documents, but accidentally left behind the photo of Nadia.

Somehow, with his own incarceration and imprisonment, Sayid's vivid memories of Nadia and Iraq had come back as if it were happening all over again, how Nadia had been captured and accused of being part of the resistance and how Sayid was assigned to get the truth from her. But they had known each

instead Sayid helped her escape. When his superior suddenly appeared, Sayid shot him dead and then shot himself in the leg to make it appear Nadia had used a gun in her escape. Before she left, Nadia took the photograph of herself and scribbled a message on the back.

The inscription had intrigued the French woman, she had wanted it translated. She got her chance when she and Sayid encountered each other on the jungle path. Sayid had the drop on her, but Rousseau coolly noted that even Robert didn't know the pin on that gun was missing when she shot *him*. But he was sick …

"I'm not sick," Sayid said.

"I can't let you go," Rousseau said. "To have someone to talk to, to touch."

Sayid told her the inscription Nadia wrote: *"You'll find me in the next life, if not in this one."*

Rousseau lowered her rifle as Sayid explained it had been seven years since he parted from Nadia and he had held on to the hope she was still alive.

Sayid asked her to come back with him to the camp, but Rousseau refused. Before they parted, Sayid had to ask: "Who is Alex?"

Alex was her child, Rousseau answered.

Sayid headed back to our beach camp. But it was now night. And he heard … the whispers.

RAISED BY ANOTHER
EPISODE 108

WRITTEN BY
LYNNE LITT

DIRECTOR OF
PHOTOGRAPHY
MICHAEL
BONVILLAIN

DIRECTED BY
MARITA
GRABIAK

other since they were kids—he couldn't torture her. He kept her alive, but after a month his superiors ordered him to take her out and shoot her. But

The other night, everyone's slumber in the caves was broken by Claire's screams. She awoke, bloodied— she had made fists so tight her fingernails had gouged her palms. Her vivid dream had been of her following a baby's cries into the jungle and finding Locke at a table, playing solitaire. "It was your responsibility, but you gave him away, Claire," said Locke, who had a bad eye. "Everyone pays the price."

The nightmares would return and Claire again woke up screaming, with another vivid account of someone coming at her with a knife and trying to hurt her baby. Charlie believes her but Jack feels Claire is simply stressed.

Claire's pregnancy has been rough from the start, when she was abandoned by the boyfriend who had gotten her pregnant. Then there was a visit to a psychic who broke out of his trance to stop their reading—he had seen something terrible in Claire's future. Claire convinced the psychic to do another reading and he made it absolutely clear she had to raise her child herself. When she was at a meeting to put her unborn baby up for adoption and several pens handed to her to write her signature on the document all failed to work, she took that as a sign and walked out. She had been on the doomed Oceanic flight because the psychic claimed he had found a couple in Los Angeles who were the only ones who could adopt her child.

The chance that Claire could have been attacked did cause concern about who exactly is among us. Hurley began conducting a census to determine who was living in the caves, who was settled at the beach. (Locke gave a characteristically enigmatic response when Hurley asked his reason for traveling and Locke replied: "I was looking for something." When Hurley asked if he found it, Locke stated, "No, it found me.")

Kate also told Jack she was concerned about Sayid. Jack was down at the beach in what has emerged as a barter system between our two settlements, with water brought from the cave in exchange for fish caught on the beach. Jack also shared the cave news of Claire having awoken screaming the last two nights, fearing she was being attacked. He thinks it's textbook anxiety—other than her self-induced bloody palms, there are no marks on her body. But with the baby due in a few weeks another anxiety attack could trigger an early labor.

At the caves, Jack tried to get Claire to take some mild sedatives that wouldn't hurt her baby but would make her relax. Claire was indignant—"You don't believe me!"—and announced she was returning to the beach. Charlie rushed after her, which was good because she suddenly went into contractions on the trail. Ethan Rom, a survivor who'd given his name to Hurley's census and had gone on some hunting expeditions with Locke, was also on the trail and rushed off to get Jack. The contractions stopped and Claire began talking to Charlie about the psychic and it dawned on her—

CLOCKWISE: **CHARLIE ON THE TRAIL WITH CLAIRE AS SHE FEELS CONTRACTIONS. LOCKE MAKES A STRANGE APPEARANCE IN ONE OF CLAIRE'S TROUBLED DREAMS. THE ADVICE OF PSYCHIC RICHARD MALKIN (NICK JAMESON) WILL SEND CLAIRE ON HER DOOMED FLIGHT. CLAIRE'S BOYFRIEND THOMAS (KEIR O'DONNELL) CAN'T COPE WITH IMPENDING FATHERHOOD AND ABANDONS HER.**

ALL THE BEST COWBOYS HAVE DADDY ISSUES
EPISODE 109

WRITTEN BY
JAVIER GRILLO-
MARXUACH

DIRECTOR OF
PHOTOGRAPHY
MICHAEL
BONVILLAIN

DIRECTED BY
STEPHEN
WILLIAMS

Ethan kidnapped Claire and Charlie. A rescue party comprised of Locke, Jack, Kate and Boone plunged into the jungle in pursuit.

Locke was taking it personally—he had hunted with Ethan. Jack also felt responsible and angry with himself for not believing Claire's fears for her safety. The trail was still hot when some of the finger bandages upon which Charlie had written "LATE" were discovered—but then the trail diverged. Kate announced that one might be a dummy trail—it turns out Kate is an expert tracker! So the teams broke up, Locke and Boone heading down the trail that Charlie seemed to be marking, Jack and Kate following the footprints.

As if to ease the tension, Boone asked Locke what he did back in the "real world." "I was a regional collection supervisor for a box company," Locke replied. "We made boxes." Boone thought Locke was joking. Boone himself ran a subdivision of a wedding business his mother owned.

Jack and Kate were also asking each other personal questions. Kate recalled joining her dad for hours of hiking and tracking deer.

Jack didn't talk about it, but rushing down the trail, he kept remembering how his father's eclipse as a surgeon and a man was bound up on an operating table where Jack unsuccessfully tried to resuscitate a dying woman. His father, in the room

there was no couple in Los Angeles, the psychic knew what was going to happen with Flight 815!

Meanwhile, Sayid had returned. He talked of meeting the mysterious French woman. "We are not alone," he announced.

The census was matched to the flight manifest, which was in Sawyer's possession. One of us was *not* on the manifest—Ethan, who had returned without Jack to confront Claire and Charlie on the trail.

with him, kept telling Jack it was over, to "call it." It had been his father's patient and the only reason Jack had taken over was a nurse told him his father's hands were shaking. Jack knew the awful truth about his father's drinking—and now his dad had made a fatal mistake. His dad wanted him to sign a document asserting they did everything possible to save the patient, if Jack didn't sign the document his father would be stripped of his license. It was almost pitiful, his father's weak smile, his praise that Jack was becoming the most successful young surgeon in the city. Jack signed the document.

While the rescue attempt was going on, an ugly incident happened at the caves, where Sayid, wounded from the French woman's trap in the jungle, was alone and resting. Sawyer had come upon him and it seemed there would be bloody payback. Sayid expressed regret for the torture, and after a few menacing moments Sawyer left Sayid unharmed—Sawyer *is* a complicated guy.

Meanwhile, back on the rescue mission, Locke wanted Boone to head back to camp. Boone refused. Locke suddenly told Boone it was going to rain in about a minute, and it did.

During the rain, Jack and Kate discovered they had taken the right trail—they encountered Ethan. Ethan fought fiercely and knocked Jack unconscious. Before Jack blacked out, Ethan declared that if they kept following he would kill his prisoners.

Kate awakened Jack and while they pushed on, Jack remembered a meeting with hospital brass about the dead patient. When Jack learned the deceased woman had been pregnant, he revealed that his father's drinking had made him "incapacitated." It was the correct moral decision, but pushed his father into the downward spiral that would drop him into a morgue in Sydney.

Jack and Kate came upon the horrible sight of Charlie hanging from a tree. They cut him down. Charlie seemed dead. For Jack, so much was lost on that operating table where he had exhorted a dying patient to come back and that memory

TOP: IN THE FLASHBACK THAT JACK CAN'T SHAKE, HIS FATHER (JOHN TERRY) IMPLORES HIM TO COVER UP A HORRIFIC CASE OF MEDICAL MALPRACTICE. RIGHT: SAYID RECOVERING FROM WOUNDS SUFFERED DURING HIS ENCOUNTER WITH THE FRENCH WOMAN.

seemed to keep him pushing on Charlie's heart, trying to revive him, repeating, "Come on, breathe, Charlie." It seemed desperate, futile …

But then, Charlie gasped, came back to life! Another miracle on the island.

But, back at the cave, harsh reality settled in. Claire was still missing and Charlie in shock. "Claire, that's all they wanted," Charlie finally said.

Out in the jungle, Boone was convinced they were lost. Locke, undaunted, wanted to keep going. He tossed Boone the flashlight—which dropped and hit something metallic.

WHATEVER THE CASE MAY BE
EPISODE 110

WRITTEN BY
DAMON
LINDELOF AND
JENNIFER
JOHNSON

DIRECTOR OF
PHOTOGRAPHY
LARRY FONG

DIRECTED BY
JACK BENDER

Claire is missing and Charlie in shock, but life goes on. So many of the nearby fruit trees had already

KATE, AN ACCOMPLICE OF BANK ROBBERS, FIRST POSES AS A HOSTAGE, THEN DEMANDS THE SAFE-DEPOSIT BOX THAT HOLDS A KEY TO HER PAST.

been picked clean that Kate ventured deeper into the jungle to pick more fruit. Sawyer appeared on the trail, saying he was keeping a protective eye on her. Together they discovered a waterfall and pool but when they took a swim to the bottom, they made a grisly discovery—corpses from the flight, still

belted into their seats. There was something else, a silver Halliburton case. Kate asked Sawyer to bring it up—she clearly wanted it—but when Sawyer declared he wanted it, she didn't fight him. "Something you want to tell me about this little suitcase, Freckles?" Sawyer asked, suspicious.

Meanwhile, a major disaster as the tide suddenly began eroding the beach. It was clear the settlement would be washed away, so an emergency move was made up the coast where there was still plenty of beach. Rose helped Charlie keep his mind off Claire, getting him to help her move a piece of fuselage to the new camp.

Jack had come to the beach to observe the situation. Sayid told him the group still didn't want to move to the cave. Claire's kidnapping made the jungle seem more dangerous than ever. Jack asked about the French woman's maps and papers Sayid had brought back—perhaps they might reveal the island's secrets.

Meanwhile, Boone and Locke had made it back to camp, but kept returning to the jungle, making Shannon suspicious. Boone, as usual, keeps telling her she's "useless" and Shannon seems resigned to this image. She was actually sunbathing on the beach when Sayid asked her to help him translate the mysterious French notes in the papers he took from Rousseau's lair. But Shannon, self-conscious and easily flustered, only made out snatches of what seems to be nonsense verse: "The sea of silver sparkles that change … blue infinity." Maybe, Shannon declared, these are the ravings of a madwoman.

Meanwhile, all Kate could think about was the silver case. Sawyer prides himself on being able to pick any lock but this one was impossible—Michael told him that only "impact velocity" would open a Halliburton. Sawyer had gone into the jungle to drop it from a tree when Kate appeared and grabbed the case. Sawyer caught her and offered a deal—tell him what was inside and he would *give* her the case. Kate just walked off.

Back at the cave Kate asked Jack for help getting the case back from Sawyer, explaining it had been checked by the marshal and held four nine–millimeter guns and plenty of ammo. The idea of Sawyer in possession of the island's only arsenal got Jack's attention. Kate further explained the marshal kept the key to the case in a wallet he kept in his back pocket. Jack had buried him, so all they had to do was dig up the corpse and get the wallet. Jack, suspecting there was something else in the case, agreed to help—provided they open the case together. They dug up the moldering corpse and Kate pulled out the wallet, which was crawling with maggots. She dropped it and palmed the key, but Jack forced open her clenched fist.

Maybe it was his anger at Kate's betrayal, but Jack confronted Sawyer and declared if he didn't hand over the case he would withhold the antibiotics needed to heal Sawyer's knife wound. Back at the cave, Jack and Kate opened the case together. Guns and ammo were inside, just as Kate said. But Jack knew there had to be something more. There was a folder marked, "Personal Effects." And within that was a small envelope and inside was a small toy–airplane model.

It was a plane model Kate had obtained while robbing a bank in New Mexico as "Maggie," a professional photographer who had gone into the bank to talk to an executive about a loan application. In the setup, masked bank robbers barged in and used her as a fake hostage to get the executive to unlock the money cage. When it looked like her cohorts were going to start killing, she grabbed a gun, wounded them all, and demanded the executive open up a safe–deposit box to get what she was really after, the little model airplane.

"It belonged to the man I loved," Kate told Jack.

Jack wanted the *truth*.

"It belonged to the man I *killed*," Kate cried.

HEARTS AND MINDS
EPISODE 111

WRITTEN BY
CARLTON CUSE
AND JAVIER
GRILLO–
MARXUACH

DIRECTOR OF
PHOTOGRAPHY
MICHAEL
BONVILLAIN

DIRECTED BY
ROD HOLCOMB

Kate discovered that Sun's been tending a garden for fruits and herbs. Kate, drawn to the garden, had been talking to fill the silence and realized Sun

understood her! Sun asked Kate to keep her secret— even her husband didn't know she spoke English.

Locke's priority is figuring out how to open the mysterious sealed hatch he and Boone discovered on the jungle floor. This is where they have secretly gone every day, instead of hunting. But Boone is losing his nerve. Every night they return empty–handed only arouses suspicion. Boone was also upset by the growing attraction between Shannon and Sayid and had confronted Sayid about it. But Locke doesn't care whether they bring back a boar, or what others think—it's all about the hatch.

Boone wanted to reveal the secret of the hatch. "They're not ready," Locke argued. But Boone had to at least tell Shannon. For all their bickering,

LEFT TO RIGHT: SHANNON STRUGGLES FROM HER BONDS WITH ASSISTANCE FROM BOONE. SHANNON AND BOONE CHASED BY THE THING IN THE JUNGLE. BOONE FINDS SHANNON, SEEMINGLY THE VICTIM OF THE ISLAND'S MYSTERIOUS MONSTER.

theirs may be the most complicated relationship on the island.

Shannon is Boone's stepsister and she had a little routine, traipsing off to some exotic port with a new guy, causing Boone to come after her and write a check to make the problem lover go away. And that was the setup that had brought Boone to Sydney. He thought he was rescuing his wayward sister but discovered Shannon and her new lover, Brian, were

going to take the $50,000 check and start a new life together. Later, Boone found Shannon standing at his hotel–room door. Brian had taken the money and run. Shannon knew Boone would try to rescue her because he had always been in love with her. It was so obvious. That was crazy, Boone said. Shannon moved in closer, embracing him, nuzzling him. "Stop," Boone whispered. She didn't stop.

Locke finally asked Boone if he had thought through the ramifications of revealing the existence of the hatch to Shannon. "Yes," Boone said. Locke then knocked out Boone with the butt of his knife.

Boone woke up, tied to a tree. Locke was calmly mixing a bowl of paste, then dabbed the paste on the wound where he hit Boone. Locke declared that the camp was four miles due west and tossed a knife into the ground near Boone. When Boone summoned up "the proper motivation" he'd reach the knife and cut himself loose. And then Locke left him.

It attracted some notice when Locke returned, alone, to sit by himself on the beach, calmly staring out at the ocean. "Any ships?" Jack asked, sitting down for a rare one–on–one with Locke. He asked about Boone and Locke just shrugged—no Boone! Jack asked about the lack of boar meat, Locke noted the boars seemed to be migrating out of the valley.

Later, while Jack was ministering some pills to Charlie to ease the pain of his heroin withdrawal, the subject of Locke came up. "Trust him?" said Charlie. "No offense mate, but if there was one person on this island I would put my absolute faith in to save us all, it would be John Locke."

Meanwhile, back in the jungle, Boone heard Shannon scream for help. He wriggled out of his bonds, reached the knife, cut himself loose. He found Shannon—Locke had tied her to a tree! Then, suddenly, they heard the island's unseen monster moving after them. Boone managed to tell his stepsister about the hatch before the thing scooped her up and away. Boone soon found her bloody, battered dead body.

That night, Boone made it back to camp and rushed at Locke with a knife. "You killed her!" he shouted. Locke, almost effortlessly, got Boone under control. Locke simply asked why Boone had no blood on him. The salve Locke had applied to Boone had been an hallucinogen. "I gave you an experience that I believe was vital to your survival on this island," Locke revealed. " … It was only as real as you made it."

Locke asked what it was like to see this vision of his stepsister's death. Boone finally admitted, "I felt relieved."

"Yes," Locke nodded. "Time to let go."

Boone then saw Shannon talking to Sayid in the campfire light. He turned back to face Locke.

"Follow me," Locke said. Boone followed Locke back into the nocturnal jungle.

SPECIAL
EPISODE 112

WRITTEN BY
DAVID FURY

DIRECTOR OF
PHOTOGRAPHY
LARRY FONG

DIRECTED BY
GREG YAITANES

Ten–year–old Walt has become attracted to Locke, looking up to him as a father figure. Perhaps that is what set off Michael today, when he went looking for his son and found him in the jungle with Boone and Locke. If Michael had walked in a few moments earlier he would have seen Locke teaching Walt how to throw a knife and he would have seen Walt throw a perfect strike. Instead, Locke told Michael his boy should be allowed to realize his potential on the island while Michael angrily told Locke to stay away from his son.

Michael had never known his son. Once, so much hope had been alive when he and his pregnant lover, Susan, talked about their future, when he promised to help her make it through law school, when Michael named their unborn baby after his

RIGHT: MICHAEL AND SUSAN (TAMARA TAYLOR), STAR–CROSSED LOVERS. BELOW: MICHAEL PLAYS WITH THE INFANT SON FROM WHOM HE WILL SOON BE SEPARATED.

own father. But when Walt was a one–year–old, with the couple still unmarried and Michael an unemployed construction worker, Susan left with their baby for a job opportunity in Amsterdam. Later came the long–distance phone call and Susan announced she was seeing Brian Porter, the man who had hired

brought Michael to Sydney, to take Walt home.

"Who are you?" was the boy's first question when he met Michael.

Now, on the island, Michael felt his chance at finally being a father for his son was slipping away. That night, Sun noticed he seemed upset and asked what was wrong and Michael talked about Walt. "He can't grow up here," he declared.

Meanwhile, Sayid felt the French woman's papers could be coordinates for some location on the island. But Michael wasn't interested in learning about the island, playing golf, planning water filtration systems, building "a sweet little home here." They had to get *off* the island. How about a raft? They had airplane seats that could float, plenty of timber to build with. He was determined: "My son and I are leaving."

But Walt remained distant. If not looking for Mr. Locke, his nose was buried in that strange, superhero comic book with its images of polar bears and space aliens.

Michael saw him reading the comic and tried to reach out. He suggested that together they would collect the pieces of airplane wreckage that would help them build a raft.

The raft became the talk of the island, but another little drama was also playing out—Sawyer had Claire's diary. When Kate and Charlie came asking for it, Sawyer mercilessly teased Charlie, pretending to read a passage. Charlie hit him, Sawyer hit back. But Sawyer finally handed the diary to Kate, assuring her he hadn't read it.

Meanwhile, the raft–building project was having troubles getting started. At one point, Walt saw Locke and walked after him. Locke told Walt they shouldn't be together. But in more bad timing Michael appeared and angrily confronted Locke. Michael was beyond listening and then Walt hit him where it hurt: "You're not my father." Michael tossed the superhero comic into the fire and Walt saw the polar bear drawing engulfed by the flames. Jack, Boone, Shannon and others witnessed the ugly scene.

her. It got worse when, after vowing to come to Amsterdam and get Walt, Michael hung up the phone, stepped out into the street and was hit by a car. He was convalescing when Susan visited him unannounced and explained she and Brian were getting married and moving to Italy, and Brian wanted to adopt Walt.

Years later, when Susan suddenly died of a blood disorder, a grief–stricken Brian had appeared at Michael's house to break the bad news and ask Michael to take Walt back. Michael was angry—he hadn't been the boy's father in nine years! Brian admitted he was not up to being a father, but there was more: "There's something about him," Brian said. "Sometimes, when he's around, things happen. He's different, somehow." And that was what

The spat had its predictable consequence as a rebellious Walt took Vincent and disappeared into the jungle. Michael confronted Locke, who finally got to explain not only that he had not seen the missing boy, but that he had earlier told Walt not to visit him in respect of his father's wishes. Michael realized Walt had headed off by himself. "Let's go find your boy," Locke said.

They discovered Walt, calling out "Dad!" in terror, trapped in a thicket of trees by one of the polar bears. Locke and Michael climbed an overhead branch and Michael dropped down into the thicket to tie a rope of vines around Walt, which allowed Locke to lift the boy to safety. Michael was now cornered, but Locke dropped down a knife and Michael made a quick stab at the ferocious beast, causing the animal to roar in pain and ramble off. After this ordeal, father and son seem emotionally united. Locke and Michael also looked at each other with respect.

That night, by their campfire, Michael gave his son something he'd retrieved from the wreckage, a box Walt's nanny had given him that was full of the cards Michael had sent him over the past eight years, each illustrated with his delightful cartoons. Walt's mother had never shown them to her boy but, Michael noted, she hadn't thrown them away, either. Michael was sure his mother meant for Walt to have them some day.

This night there was another major development. Charlie had been reading Claire's diary—he was happy to find himself described as "so adorable and sweet … Charlie makes me feel safe"—but there was also a strange passage. Charlie brought the diary to Jack and Sayid and explained Claire had been recording her dreams and one described a "black rock." Wasn't that what the French woman had mentioned? And could it possibly be the triangle–shaped object that appeared when they pieced her maps together?

At that moment, deep in the jungle, Locke and Boone were up to their usual nocturnal wanderings when they heard something coming through the thick brush towards them. They froze, waiting in the moonlight, Locke intently staring as he pulled his sheathed knife out and held it at the ready.

A figure broke through the brush and stood in front of them.

It was Claire.

HOMECOMING
EPISODE 113

WRITTEN BY
DAMON
LINDELOF

DIRECTOR OF
PHOTOGRAPHY
MICHAEL
BONVILLAIN

DIRECTED BY
KEVIN HOOKS

A lot has happened since Claire stumbled out of the jungle and fainted in Locke's arms. He and Boone brought her back to the cave and her first reaction on gaining consciousness was fear. Claire not only doesn't remember anything about her kidnapping but the entire month we've been stranded! All she remembers is being on a plane bound from Sydney

LEFT TO RIGHT **LOCKE AND ETHAN ENGAGE IN LIFE–OR–DEATH COMBAT. CLAIRE IS THE BAIT AS KATE, ARMED AND READY, WAITS FOR ETHAN TO FALL INTO THE TRAP.**

be brought back to this very spot, or he would kill one of us every day.

Jack and Locke talked on the beach and Jack proposed moving everyone to the caves for protection. Locke thought that a bad idea and proposed they "circle the wagons"—tell a select few and post guards around the perimeters of the camps. Later, Kate approached Jack and pointed to the key to the silver case with the guns he'd hidden somewhere. But Jack was adamant against firearms. So, traps were set and guards posted.

But when morning came, Scott Jackson, from California, was found dead on the beach, his neck broken. Now we were in a real crisis. Jack huddled with Locke, asking if he could track Ethan. Locke shook his head, "We're on Ethan's turf." Jack then took Locke to where he had hidden the silver case, unlocked it, and handed Locke one of the guns. A dramatic plan was concocted—they would use Claire as bait, leaving her in the clearing as Ethan had demanded. If Ethan bit, they'd spring out of hiding and subdue him, only using the guns as a last resort.

Jack would take one of the guns and after arming Locke, the tracker supreme, it made sense to give the third gun to Sayid, the former soldier. When Charlie heard of the plan he was upset—use Claire as bait?! But Claire was willing. Charlie offered to go along and asked for the final gun. "Charlie's right," Locke agreed. "Four guns, there should be four men."

It speaks to the gravity of the threat that Jack gave the fourth gun to Sawyer. Although Sawyer had botched the mercy killing of the marshal, he had shot down a charging polar bear and clearly knew guns. Kate wanted to come along and Sawyer noted that with a hundred rounds there was ample ammo for a fifth gun—the one that had belonged to the marshal. Sawyer's logic was impeccable: "Five guns

for Los Angeles. But there's no evidence Claire was injured in any way and her baby seems fine.

She has no memory of Charlie, either, and he has been trying to rebuild the trust they had. The chance of losing Claire reminded him of the time he traded on his dwindling Drive Shaft fame to gain the trust of Lucy, a young woman with a wealthy father. He'd been put up to it by Tommy, a smack dealer who saw a chance to get his boy nestled comfortably in the grand old house so Charlie could swipe a valuable heirloom and pawn it. It was a sloppy plan, and Charlie botched it. Charlie had tried to make things up to Lucy, told her he really wanted to take care of her. Lucy dismissed him with the cutting comment, "You'll *never* take care of anyone!"

While Charlie was on a walk with Jin, they were attacked and Jin knocked unconscious. It was Ethan. He literally lifted Charlie up, demanding Claire are better than four." But as Sayid reminded everyone before setting out, "We want him alive."

It was dusk and raining when Claire walked into the clearing and Ethan appeared. Jack tackled him, dropping his gun in the process. The surprised Ethan unleashed a savage attack, but this time Jack held his own and kept pounding Ethan into submission. By then, everyone had scrambled out of hiding with guns drawn. But, suddenly, gunfire rang out—Charlie had followed, picked up Jack's gun and shot Ethan four times at point–blank range.

"Why did you do it, Charlie?" Jack asked back at the cave. They had missed a golden chance to find out Ethan's secrets. But Charlie didn't believe Ethan would have told them anything. Besides, he "deserved to die." No way would he allow "that animal" to threaten Claire again.

Ethan's death removed, at least for the moment, the pall of fear. Claire had even come up to Charlie to tell him that she remembered something—peanut butter. Charlie smiled. It seemed a lifetime ago, but he had once sat on the beach and shared a jar of imaginary peanut butter with her, to Claire's delight.

"I want to trust you," Claire told Charlie before they said good night.

OUTLAWS
EPISODE 114

WRITTEN BY	DIRECTOR OF	DIRECTED BY
DREW	PHOTOGRAPHY	JACK BENDER
GODDARD	JOHN BARTLEY	

What's in a name? For Sawyer it's the lifetime of hurt that began with the sound of his father pounding on the front door, his mother hiding him under the bed—and then the shouts, the gun shot, the body falling. He saw his father's boots appear in

his doorway, heard the final shot of his father killing himself. Frank Sawyer—that was the name of the con man whose schemes had made a little boy an orphan. Sawyer—the name the boy took when, years later, he got as lost as his dead dad.

The nightmares of his past have been haunting Sawyer. They seem to have come with a massive boar that invaded his tent the other night and dragged the tent into the jungle. It was when he gave chase that Sawyer heard the *whispers*.

But just as crazy was when Sawyer became convinced the boar was personally tormenting him. So he went out with a gun to kill it. Jack was upset at Sawyer for being the last person who had not turned in his firearm after the bloody Ethan business. Kate promised she would go and get the gun.

Meanwhile, there is the realization that what happened with Ethan hasn't ended so neatly. Charlie and Hurley buried him yesterday. Hurley was concerned about Charlie, who seemed to be suffering from post–traumatic shock. After all, he had fired four bullets into a defenseless man's chest. At Hurley's urging, Sayid talked to Charlie and told him that the consequences of taking a life—even in the line of duty—would be with him for the rest of his life. "You're not alone," Sayid said, "so don't try to be."

Meanwhile, Sawyer did find his tent but heard the whispers again—and the boar nearly rammed him. Kate met up with him and found it hard to believe a boar was personally harassing him. But she made a deal to help him track it.

The boar situation seemed to be rooting up Sawyer's worst memories. He remembered getting the compact .357 with hollow point loads to kill the man whose con had triggered his parents' death. The man was in Sydney and that info came courtesy of Hibbs, an old con artist. They weren't on the best of terms—in fact, Sawyer had said he would kill Hibbs the next time they met. But Hibbs had said the magic words: "How about the known where-abouts of the man who runs your life?"

It had been easy—in retrospect, too easy—Hibbs pointing him straight to Sydney harbor and the "Sweet Shrimp" truck where Frank Sawyer whipped up shrimp in mild or hot sauce. It was a rainy night when Sawyer gunned down the man who, with his dying breath mentioned "Hibbs" and how he was going to pay him back. Hibbs had gotten Sawyer to do his dirty work, to kill a man over a gambling debt. "It'll come back around," he said before he became a dead man.

It was the next morning on the boar hunt when Sawyer awoke to realize the boar had ripped through their camp, tearing up only *his* stuff—the boar had even pissed on his shirt! Locke then appeared, explaining he had picked up their trail, and told him about a sister who had died and how his foster mother wouldn't forgive herself. One day a dog suddenly appeared and stayed at their home, sleeping in his sister's old room and keeping his mother company until she passed away and the dog disappeared. His mother always believed the dog was her daughter incarnated, come back to say the accident wasn't her fault.

Whether Locke's story had any meaning for Sawyer, he did meet up with the boar. It was a face–off, the boar staring at him, Sawyer with his gun cocked and aimed. But he lowered his gun and looked at Kate. "It's just a boar," Sawyer said. "Let's get back to camp."

Sawyer turned his gun over to Jack, but not without first aiming the weapon and saying "stick 'em up." Jack had replied, "That's why the Red Sox will never win the Series." It was an old expression his dad always used, his comment on fate, Jack explained.

In that moment, Sawyer remembered how he

had been in a Sydney dive, drinking to blot out his troubled past. The place was deserted except for an older man who told him the air conditioning was useless and Australia was as close to hell as you'd get without being burned. "That's why the Red Sox will never win the Series," said the man, who was once a head of surgery and had talked about a son who was about Sawyer's age. "He's not like me, he does what's in his heart. He's a good man, maybe a great one." Right now his son thought he hated him, but he didn't hate him. "But what I feel is gratitude and pride because of what he did to me — what he did *for* me." The man could step over to a payphone and make a call and he could fix *everything*.

"Why don't you?" Sawyer asked.

"Because I am weak … "

That was what Sawyer remembered when he asked Jack if his daddy had been a doctor, too. Jack had said yes — why did Sawyer want to know about his father?

"No reason," Sawyer said, and he walked away.

... IN TRANSLATION
EPISODE 115

WRITTEN BY	DIRECTOR OF	DIRECTED BY
JAVIER GRILLO-MARXUACH AND LEONARD DICK	PHOTOGRAPHY MICHAEL BONVILLAIN	TUCKER GATES

The big event on the island was Michael's raft. He had built it using bamboo for a deck, pieces of fuselage to form a cabin and some hoarded building material provided by Sawyer, who "bought" a ticket for the big launch. But the other night all hell broke loose — someone burned the raft. The prime suspect — Jin.

That morning Sun had been on the beach in her

bikini and Jin had tried to drape a towel over her and was a bit rough about it. Michael had run over to intervene — and got slapped by Sun. She later told Michael she did it for his own protection, he didn't know what her husband was capable of.

Jin is haunted by memories of bad choices and moral compromises. To win permission to marry Sun he had gone to work for her father, Mr. Paik. But his father–in–law was demanding. Even on their wedding day, before the big reception, Jin had told his beautiful bride he had to delay their honeymoon until after management training for his new job. Because of his ambition, Jin had also told everyone — even Sun — that his father was dead, too ashamed for them to know that his father was a humble fisherman.

Now, Jin even suspected that there was something going on between Sun and Michael. He had gone off to cool down and the irony was that he had seen the raft burning and singed his arms trying to put out the fire. Sawyer had gone to find Jin and roughly brought him to the beach. With Jin not able to speak English and his accusers unable to speak Korean, the burn marks seemed damning evidence. When Michael saw Jin on the beach he could not

Sun's secret, but it was a shock to everybody to realize she could speak English—most shocking to Jin. Locke then appeared and broke things up by chastising us for fighting amongst ourselves. He pointed out to the jungle from whence Ethan had come. "We're not the only people on this island and we all know it," he declared.

For Jin, the shame of his wife having kept such a secret from him caused him to move out of the caves. A lot of his shame is his own self–loathing. He remembers Mr. Paik promoting him as a special assistant and how that led to his giving a message to Mr. Han, a secretary for environmental safety. And then came the night when a cell phone interrupted another special evening Sun had planned and he was called to face the wrath of Mr. Paik, who declared that Mr. Han had closed one of his factories. To prevent the man's death by one of Paik's assassins, Jin beat the man in his home—Sun saw the blood on his hands that night.

Jin did reconcile with his father and had asked for his forgiveness. For the moment he cannot reconcile with Sun.

Locke had a gut feeling about who burned the raft. When he sat down to play backgammon with Walt, the boy, in confidence, confessed. "I don't want to move anymore," Walt said. "I been moving places my whole life. I like it here."

"I like it here, too," Locke said.

Earlier, Locke had told Shannon, "Everyone gets a new life on this island." Shannon herself has begun hoping for a fresh start, without worrying about her brother, without using a man. Maybe she'll get that new life with Sayid—a romance is kindling between them.

Sun was back on the beach the other day, walking to the surf in her bikini. She had the towel around her, the one Jin had tried to wrap around her. She let it fall away in the wind.

be restrained. Even Jack backed off—this was between Michael and Jin, *mano a mano*. Michael would knock Jin down and he would get up, defiant, not striking back. Suddenly, Sun cried out in English, "Leave him alone!" Michael and Kate knew

On another part of the beach, Michael has begun rebuilding his raft. He was astonished to look up and see Jin join him, carrying building supplies. "Boat," Jin said in English.

NUMBERS
EPISODE 116

WRITTEN BY DAVID FURY AND BRENT FLETCHER	DIRECTOR OF PHOTOGRAPHY JOHN BARTLEY	DIRECTED BY DANIEL ATTIAS

On an island of secrets, each survivor has their own secrets. But who, in their wildest dreams, could have imagined jovial Hurley being worth $156 million? The full import of this secret life came to a head the other day when Michael, whose raft–building project is going full speed, asked Jack about being able to send a distress signal from sea. Hurley and Jack approached Sayid about finding the French woman and asking her for batteries to power such a signal. Sayid thought it a bad idea, noting that Danielle Rousseau had ominously christened the area where Sayid had originally discovered her "Dark Territory."

It was during this exchange, while Sayid brandished some of the documents he'd taken from Rousseau's lair, that Hurley happened to get a close look at one of the papers, one with columns repeating a sequence of numbers: 4 8 15 16 23 42. They were the exact numbers Hurley used back home in Los Angeles to win the "Mega Lotto." Initially, the money seemed cursed, the bad luck beginning at the big Lotto victory press conference, during which his beloved grandpa Tito keeled over, dead. Later, when Hurley took his mother to the surprise dream house he'd bought her, in the space of a minute she broke her ankle getting out of the car, a mysterious fire

began burning the vacant house, and Los Angeles police suddenly descended upon him with drawn guns and put him in handcuffs.

At a subsequent meeting with his accountant, it dawned on Hugo "Hurley" Reyes that it wasn't the lottery monies but the *numbers* that were cursed. Even stranger, Hurley realized that he stood unscathed even as the cursed numbers seemed to widen their circle of influence. As his accountant told him, his stocks were all up, including orange futures that were skyrocketing after a tropical storm wrecked Florida. And between his settlement with the LAPD for false arrest and an insurance payout for a fire that cost eight lives at a factory in which he had an interest that meant a "windfall of cash", Hugo had almost doubled his net worth in a few months.

And now, on the island, Hurley had come face–to–face with the numbers that had become the bane of his existence. He had to find the French woman—perhaps she knew the meaning of the numbers. Hurley headed down the beach to the point where Sayid had found a cable that stretched from the surf into the jungle area where he had encountered the French woman. But Hurley's abrupt departure concerned

knowing he was protected by his curse, easily leapt out of the path of the pendulum–swinging log. His luck continued to inexplicably hold when they came to a fragile–looking rope bridge and he easily crossed over, although Charlie barely made it before the bridge came crashing down.

Thus separated, Jack and Sayid stumbled upon the French woman's lair—or what was left of it when Jack tripped a wire and a booby–trap explosion blew it up. It was clear to Sayid that Rousseau knew he or others would come looking for her, so she had moved on. Sayid found a fragment of the photo of Nadia he had left behind in the ruined lair, but nothing else, certainly no batteries.

Meanwhile, Hurley was closer to his rendezvous with the French woman, picking up the thread of his earlier efforts to find a meaning behind the cursed numbers. Hurley had been a patient at a mental institution and had gotten the numbers from Lenny, a fellow patient. Hurley had gone to the hospital to see Lenny, whose mind was still lost, his attention drifting, his "conversation" a stream of meaningless babble—until Hurley mentioned he had used the numbers to win the lottery. Lenny was suddenly lucid: "You shouldn't have done that—you've opened the box! … It doesn't stop!" Before Leonard was dragged away, he managed to shout out that he had gotten the numbers from Sam Toomey, a man in Australia. It was a scrap of information that led Hurley to a lonely house in the outback where he met the widow of the man, who had been dead four years. The woman shared a strange story about her husband and the numbers.

Sixteen years ago, her husband and Leonard had been stationed together at a listening post in the Pacific, monitoring long–wave transmissions. A

FAR LEFT: HURLEY HOLDS THE WINNING LOTTERY TICKET. MIDDLE: HURLEY FOLLOWS THE CABLE INTO THE JUNGLE—AND INTO THE RIFLE SIGHTS OF THE FRENCH WOMAN (ABOVE). LEFT: LOCKE PRESENTS CLAIRE WITH A BABY CRIB.

Charlie. Realizing that Hurley was going alone into the Dark Territory, Charlie, Jack and Sayid headed out to find him.

They caught up with Hurley in time to realize their friend had just stepped on a pressure trigger and if he moved it would release a spiked log. Hurley, boring job, listening to hours of crackling static—until the night they clearly heard a voice repeating the numbers. Sam had used them at a fair in Calgary to guess the beans in a jar and the numbers had been correct to the last bean. They won a lot of cash but on the way home a pickup truck hit them head–on. She had lost a leg in the accident but Sam barely suffered a scratch.

Hurley's search for meaning had been interrupted by the plane crash on the flight home, but now, with the numbers on a scrap of paper in his fist, he had picked up the thread—even as he found himself surprised by Rousseau and staring down the barrel of her rifle. "You must be the French chick," Hurley said. And he held out the numbers and fearlessly asked—*What do they mean?*"

The French woman lowered her rifle. She revealed that when her research ship was at sea they had picked up transmissions of a voice repeating those numbers and had changed course to investigate and were subsequently shipwrecked. But the transmission source was somewhere on the island and they found a radio tower—up by the Black Rock. After her team had been lost to "the sickness," Rousseau changed the transmission to the distress signal Sayid had picked up weeks before. "I suppose you're right—they are cursed," Rousseau concluded of the numbers. Hurley, grateful that someone finally believed him, gave the surprised, lonely woman a warm bear hug.

It was a total surprise to Charlie, Sayid and Jack when Hurley suddenly reappeared and handed them a battery. "She says, 'Hey,'" Hurley shrugged.

That night, Claire was with Locke, who had asked her for help on a little carpentry project. Claire was grateful to feel useful. It was also her birthday, she admitted. Locke noted it was auspicious that her birthday and her child's birthday were going to be so close together. And then he turned over what they had been working on—a baby cradle. "Happy birthday, Claire," Locke smiled.

Elsewhere that night, Hurley and Charlie shared a campfire and Charlie revealed the secret of his heroin addiction. When it was Hurley's turn to reveal something, he got no further than saying back home he was worth $156 million dollars. "Fine, don't tell me!" Charlie said, before indignantly striding off. "I bare my soul! And all I get is bloody jokes."

But the mystery of the numbers will not go away—they may be the key to the mysteries of this strange island. Inscribed on the hatch Locke and Boone discovered are those accursed numbers: 4 8 15 16 23 42.

DEUS EX MACHINA
EPISODE 117

WRITTEN BY	DIRECTOR OF	DIRECTED BY
CARLTON CUSE	PHOTOGRAPHY	ROBERT
AND DAMON	MICHAEL	MANDELL
LINDELOF	BONVILLAIN	

For two weeks Locke and Boone have been trying to break open the hatch, without success. Locke, normally serene and confident, appears to be suffering a crisis of confidence—the island spirit, with which he always seemed in communion, seems to have deserted him. Still, he tells Boone "the island will tell us what to do." But Boone is awakening from Locke's spell and finally questioning Locke's fervent certainty that their destiny is wrapped up in opening the hatch. To Boone, they've hit a dead end; to Locke, their faith is being tested.

Locke, who asked the island for a sign, got it in a dream so vivid that he awakened Boone at dawn. In his dream, Locke saw a plane crash in the jungle and he was convinced Boone and he would find the dream plane. Locke led the way into the jungle. Soon they discovered a sign that they were on the path to the plane—the skeletal remains of a priest in the low branches of a tree. There was a thick wad of Nigerian money, a rosary—and a gun. They moved on, but Locke's legs began to give way. Locke finally revealed to Boone that for the past four years he

For the past few days, John Locke has been remembering the strange time before he lost the use of his legs. He was working in a department store when a mysterious woman entered his life, a woman named Emily Locke, who claimed to be the mother he never knew. She told him he was "special … part of a design."

Hooked on discovering the secrets of his lineage,

CHILDREN OF DESTINY: BOONE, EAGER ACOLYTE TO THE MYSTIC HUNTER LOCKE. TOGETHER THE TWO BLAZE A TRAIL INTO THE ISLAND'S FOREBODING JUNGLE—AND ITS HIDDEN SECRETS.

was paralyzed and relegated to a wheelchair. The island had made him whole and now the island seemed to be taking back its gift.

John secured the services of a private investigator who led him to his long–lost father, a wealthy man named Anthony Cooper. Cooper himself didn't have a family and he seemed eager to embrace his new-found son. The two began sharing hunting trips, and on one of their hunting dates, John got the time mixed up and got to Cooper's house an hour early and saw him hooked up to a dialysis machine. Bad kidney, Cooper explained, and the prognosis wasn't good, given his age and distant place on the donor waiting–list. For John it would be an act of filial love when he finally told his dad he would give him one of his kidneys.

Back in the present, John still had hope in the spirit of the island, despite completely losing the use of his legs. They had found his dream plane, high up in a tree. With Locke immobile, it was up to Boone to climb up to the plane. Inside was a map of Nigeria, along with small statues of the Virgin Mary, each filled with bags of heroin. But there was also a radio and Boone was in the midst of sending out a "Mayday" when the plane began shifting and fell, crashing to the jungle floor.

Suddenly, the strength began returning to Locke's legs and he pulled a bloodied Boone from the wreckage and staggered back to camp with Boone on his back. A feeling of crisis and despair gripped Locke, a feeling like the day he woke up in the hospital bed after the kidney operation and found his father gone. He had been betrayed by Anthony Cooper, who got a new lease of life at his expense and then cruelly shut John out of his life.

Meanwhile, back at camp, Sawyer had been suffering daily headaches. He finally let Jack conduct a diagnosis, fearing he might have a brain tumor. Jack's verdict: Sawyer was farsighted and had been doing so much reading lately that he was getting headaches. All he needed was reading glasses. Despite the bad blood between the two men, there was relief and grins all around.

That night Locke appeared at the cave with a bleeding Boone, crying out to Jack for help. Locke, after explaining that Boone had fallen off a cliff, disappeared. Jack is determined to save Boone's life, but it doesn't look good.

If anyone had followed Locke they would have seen him at his secret spot, huddled over the hatch, crying out to the island: *"I've done everything you've wanted me to do!"*

And then suddenly a light shone behind the glass of the hatch.

DO NO HARM
EPISODE 118

WRITTEN BY
JANET TAMARO

DIRECTOR OF
PHOTOGRAPHY
JOHN BARTLEY

DIRECTED BY
STEPHEN
WILLIAMS

By morning, a medical tent had been set up in the caves. Boone's lung had collapsed and he was gasping for breath, but with a piercing blow to

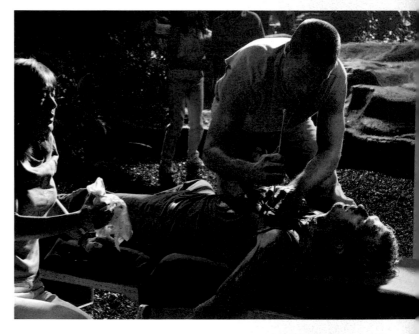

Boone's chest, Jack opened a breathing passage. He ordered Kate to run to the beach camp and get all the alcohol she could gather from Sawyer. "Boone, you are *not* going to die," Jack declared to his patient. But the young man had lost a lot of blood and his right leg was fractured.

Meanwhile, Kate was heading back from the beach with Sawyer's alcohol when she heard something in the brush. It was Claire, staggering and gripping her swollen abdomen in pain—she was about to have her baby! Kate cried, "Help!" and Jin, working alone on the raft, ran into the jungle and found them. "We need *Jack*," Kate explained and Jin was off to the caves.

FAR LEFT: JACK PREPARES TO OPEN A BREATHING PASSAGE FOR BOONE—THE HARD WAY. TOP: WITH JACK OCCUPIED, KATE MUST HELP CLAIRE DELIVER HER BABY. BOTTOM: JACK AND MICHAEL GET SET TO SEVER BOONE'S LEG.

Jin arrived at the medical tent in time to see Jack giving his own blood to Boone in a makeshift blood transfusion. Jin blurted out Claire's plight in Korean and Sun translated. But Jack wasn't about to leave—Kate had to deliver the baby. He told Charlie to go back with Jin to help.

By nighttime, Claire's water had broken and Kate faced the daunting reality of having to deliver the baby. Claire was scared, Kate was scared, Charlie and Jin nervously kept watch. But in that crisis moment, Kate resolved they would all get through this challenge together.

Meanwhile, back at the cave, Jack continued working on Boone by torchlight. Boone became lucid again and mentioned a plane. Jack was confused—Locke said Boone had fallen off a cliff. "The hatch," Boone whispered. "John said not to tell about the hatch." But Jack had other things to worry about. "It's not working," Sun declared after the blood transfusion. Not only that, it was clear Boone hadn't broken his leg in a fall—some mighty force had *crushed* it.

The task seemed impossible, but Jack had promised Boone he would save his life. Jack's thoughts went back to his marriage with Sarah, a former patient who had suffered a terrible car crash. Jack had saved her and even on the eve of his wedding was wondering if he was marrying her simply because he had saved her life. Jack even confessed his fears to his dad, who told him, "Commitment is what makes you tick, Jack. The problem is you're just not good at letting go."

And "letting go" was what Sun was finally imploring Jack to do with Boone. Jack was planning to amputate Boone's mangled leg by slamming down the blade–end of the cargo hold like a guillotine.

"You can't save him, Jack," Sun declared.

"Don't tell me what I can't do," Jack said, echoing the exact words Locke once blurted out to Kate when they first went into the jungle to hunt boar.

Sun looked at Jack with accusing eyes before turning away. It was Boone who finally stopped it, coming back to consciousness and saying, "Wait!"

"This is our best chance," Jack told him.

"I know you made a promise, I'm letting you off the hook," Boone said, repeating words Rose had once said to Jack. "Let me go, Jack."

By the following morning, our island community

was changed forever. One life had expired, a new life had arrived—a beaming Claire had a healthy infant son in her arms. Kate had successfully delivered the baby and Jin and Charlie had been there to embrace each other in the joy of that moment, a joy shared with everyone on the beach who crowded around the young mother and son.

Locke was still nowhere to be found. Shannon, who also had been missing during the crisis, had been off on a romantic idyll with Sayid, during which she had revealed the big secret that Boone was her stepbrother and in love with her, although she didn't share those feelings. The two of them were strolling up the beach to where the crowd had gathered around Claire when Jack saw them and walked over to break the sad news of Boone's death.

Later, when Kate saw Jack on the beach, she asked if he wanted to talk about Boone dying. "He was *murdered*," Jack declared. As of this writing, he has gone off into the jungle to find John Locke.

THE GREATER GOOD
EPISODE 119

WRITTEN BY
LEONARD DICK

DIRECTOR OF
PHOTOGRAPHY
MICHAEL
BONVILLAIN

DIRECTED BY
DAVID
GROSSMAN

Kate found Jack while he was in the jungle looking for Locke and convinced him to return to camp. Jack, fatigued from lack of sleep and the blood transfusion, was furious at Locke's lie about Boone's "fall" and felt it had affected his diagnosis and treatment, resulting in Boone's death.

At the beach everyone was assembled as Boone's body was lowered into the fresh grave Hurley had dug. Shannon was too upset to say any final words so Sayid did the honors. He was concluding his

remarks when a familiar voice said: "It was my fault." Locke had reappeared. He began explaining about the Beechcraft airplane stuck in the jungle canopy,

how his leg was hurt and Boone had to climb up to the plane. Suddenly, Jack tackled him, shouting that Locke had lied. It was scary to see our de facto leader lose control, particularly when he has the key to the gun case around his neck. Kate had to give Jack some juice mixed with sleeping pills in order to get him to rest.

A distraught Locke did approach Shannon to explain and apologize. But something about Jack's fury fortified her resolve and she went to Sayid and declared that Locke had *killed* her brother and she wanted him to do something about it.

Sayid, trained interrogator, asked our inscrutable survivalist to take him to the plane to salvage its radio for the transmitter he was building for Michael's raft. They found the plane, as Locke promised, but Sayid was not satisfied. If Locke had a leg injury, how could he have carried Boone all the way back to camp? "Pure adrenaline," Locke responded. Sayid asked

Locke had been the one who had earlier knocked out Sayid and destroyed his transceiver. Sayid was incensed but John recalled Sayid's own lie when he tried to keep the French woman's transmission secret. Sayid reluctantly concluded John was telling the truth and Boone's death was a tragic accident.

But things took a dangerous turn when Jack awoke and realized the key to the gun case was gone. He suspected Locke—until Sayid recalled Shannon's desire to see Locke dead. Jack, Kate and Sayid headed to Locke's personal area in the jungle, arriving to see Shannon aiming one of the guns at Locke. She probably would have killed him if Sayid had not knocked her down as she fired, the bullet just grazing Locke's temple.

Sayid realizes Locke is our best hope for survival and finally demanded the truth. And so Locke has taken Sayid to the hatch.

Things Locke said about survival and what was in everyone's best interest turned Sayid's thoughts to the recent time, before the crash, when he learned his beloved Nadia was alive. Sayid had been on the move for seven years when the CIA caught up with him and proposed that they would reveal Nadia's whereabouts in exchange for his helping locate 300 pounds of C–4 explosives stolen by terrorists from an army base outside Melbourne. One of the suspects was Essam Tazir, an old college friend, whose wife had been killed in a bombing. Sayid went to Sydney, infiltrated the cell, and discovered his friend was scheduled to be a suicide bomber. But Essam was reluctant to take innocent lives, even for "a greater good." Sayid accomplished his mission, leading the CIA to the explosives, but lost his friend— Essam, shocked when Sayid revealed he was working for the CIA, shot himself.

The CIA kept their part of the bargain, telling Sayid that Nadia lived in Irvine, California, and they had him booked on an Oceanic Airlines flight to LAX that was leaving in two hours. Sayid, determined to claim his friend's body and properly bury him, demanded they arrange a flight for the next day. It was the doomed Oceanic Flight #815.

why Locke lied about the plane. Locke admitted he was afraid and made a mistake.

Sayid wasn't ready for Locke's big revelation—

BORN TO RUN
EPISODE 120

STORY BY
JAVIER GRILLO-
MARXUACH

TELEPLAY BY
EDWARD KITSIS
AND ADAM
HOROWITZ

DIRECTOR OF
PHOTOGRAPHY
JOHN BARTLEY

DIRECTED BY
TUCKER GATES

To this island of mystery, we survivors have brought our secret lives. Today the secret life of one of the most respected among us was shockingly revealed.

It began when Dr. Arzt, a science teacher, explained that monsoon season was nearly upon us. Michael had to launch his raft immediately or wait months for the southerly monsoon winds to shift back to the north and the direction of well-traveled shipping lanes. But Michael and Jin have built a veritable boat and Michael announced he was prepared to launch by tomorrow. The four-person crew was set: Michael, Walt, Jin and Sawyer, because of materials he provided for the first raft. Kate was lobbying to replace Sawyer but Michael told her a deal was a deal. There the matter seemed to end—until Michael drank poisoned water.

Meanwhile, Sayid took Jack to the hatch where Locke was waiting. Sayid, troubled that the hatch seems designed to open from the *inside*, wanted to bury it. (News of the hatch has since spread, and a terrified Walt has begged Locke not to open it.)

When Jack returned to camp he was called to attend to a gravely ill Michael. It was easy to deduce someone had poisoned him—the water bottle Michael drank from had a pasty residue of the substance, which has walloped him with terrible

stomach pains. Jack suspected Kate poisoned Michael. Michael is still determined to launch, but was convinced Sawyer poisoned him and told him Kate would get his seat on the raft. But Sawyer had earlier seen Kate doctoring the passport photo of one of our casualties, Joanne, the woman who drowned. He knew she was the prisoner of the U.S. marshal and that she wanted to get off the island before a rescue team arrives with authorities looking for her. Sawyer revealed *all* of this, exposing Kate in front of a group witnessing the scene.

Kate, cornered, admitted that *yes*, she was a wanted criminal on the run, and *yes* she thought the raft was her only hope. But she had not poisoned Michael. The last point was small consolation as everyone walked away, upset to learn the truth about the woman who has had everyone's respect.

Kate's secret, which no one knows except Jack (and he only vaguely), was how she had killed the man she loved. It happened when she returned

The two had kissed, then drove off in Tom's car to see Kate's mother. What they did not expect was Kate's mother *screaming* for help at the sight of her fugitive daughter. Outside, Kate took the wheel of Tom's car and ordered him to get out. They wasted enough time, with Tom begging Kate to give herself up, that a policeman who was already in position got a good opportunity to fire on the car, killing Tom.

Other secrets have been revealed on the island today, as Walt confessed to his dad that he burned the first raft.

Jack solved another mystery when he got Sun to admit she had tried to poison Jin to keep her husband from the dangerous sea voyage. Jack promised he would not reveal Sun's secret.

What Jack doesn't know is that Kate put Sun up to it! Jack was good at keeping secrets, Kate told Sun, as the two women sat together, lost in their thoughts.

FAR LEFT: **DR. ARZT LECTURES MICHAEL ABOUT LAUNCHING THE RAFT BEFORE MONSOON SEASON STRIKES.** LEFT: **MICHAEL IS FELLED BY A MYSTERIOUS AILMENT ON THE EVE OF THE LAUNCH.** ABOVE: **JACK AND LOCKE DISCOVER MICHAEL HAS BEEN POISONED.**

EXODUS: PART ONE
EPISODE 121

WRITTEN BY	DIRECTOR OF	DIRECTED BY
DAMON LINDELOF AND CARLTON CUSE	PHOTOGRAPHY MICHAEL BONVILLAIN	JACK BENDER

home to Iowa to see her dying mother. As a wanted fugitive, Kate enlisted the help of Tom, her old sweetheart, now a doctor with a family. His wife and infant son were away on a trip, so he was free to help.

During their brief reunion, Kate and Tom revisited their past—and that aching place of lost dreams—by digging up a "time capsule" lunch pail of favorite things they had buried on August 15, 1989. Their treasures included the DC–3 model plane Tom's grandfather had once given him, the very model Kate went to so much trouble to get from the U.S. marshal's case.

Today has been a watershed day on the island—the raft has launched! But it did not happen without incident, and the raft set sail with both our camps under a shadow of terror.

It began before dawn when Walt saw a stranger exploring the beach camp. He woke his dad, whose shouts got everyone rolling out of their tents and shelters. Sayid calmed people down—it was Danielle Rousseau, the French woman.

She told us how her ship ran aground sixteen years ago and how there had been six on her team, all dead by the time she was seven months pregnant. She delivered her baby boy, Alex, alone. A week later, she saw black smoke rising five kilometers inland and that night "they" came and took her baby. And now, she warned, the Others are coming for us. She gave us three choices: "Run. Hide. Or die."

"She's not playing with a full deck," Jack said to Locke afterwards. Despite Rousseau's dire warning, Jack got everyone motivated to help launch the raft. A huge group tried to push it down the rails and into the water, but it slid off, causing considerable damage. And worse was to come: Walt was the first to spot a pillar of black smoke rising from the jungle—the sign of the Others.

Run, die—or hide. Jack and Locke both gravitated to the hatch as the perfect hiding place and even showed it to Rousseau. It's as much a mystery to her as it is to us. The immediate question was how to open it, and Locke asked Rousseau about her cache of dynamite. She agreed to lead a team to the explosives kept at the Black Rock, deep in what she calls the Dark Territory. Back at the beach, Jack announced they were going into the jungle to get "supplies" and everyone should help Michael and Jin repair the raft for another launch and then head to the caves and wait.

Rousseau took Jack, Locke, Hurley, Kate and Dr. Arzt into the Dark Territory. Their hurried good-byes with the raft's crew were poignant, since they knew that by the time they returned the raft might have launched. Kate didn't get to see Sawyer, who had gone off in the jungle by himself to build a new bamboo mast. Jack saw him, though, to hand him one of the guns from the Halliburton case to take on the sea voyage, "just in case." Sawyer finally told Jack about that time in a Sydney saloon when he met Jack's father, who had spoken with regret for not having the strength to tell his son how proud he was of him, how much he loved him. Jack held back his tears but was grateful to hear this. "Good luck, Jack," Sawyer called out as Jack headed off for the Dark Territory.

Their journey has been fraught with peril, including a near–miss encounter with the monster, which Rousseau inscrutably reveals is the island's "security

system." The group has headed deeper into the mystery of the island and has reached the mysterious "Black Rock," which turned out to be an old sailing ship, inexplicably lodged deep in the jungle!

Meanwhile, back on the beach Michael and Jin quickly repaired the raft with an unexpected assist from Sawyer, who triumphantly brought over the sturdy sailing mast he had built. Sayid provided a radar transmitter and monitor for detecting ships up to twenty–five miles away, and a flare gun with a single flare. Many have contributed notes and messages for a bottle that will be taken away on the raft.

Walt, ready for his great adventure, unselfishly gave his beloved dog Vincent to Shannon for her protection. Sawyer, looking for Kate, realized she was gone and there would be no goodbye. The most poignant parting came when Sun finally confronted Jin to press into his hands a phonetic Korean/English dictionary she had prepared for him. In their brief moment of kisses and tears, a chastened Jin promised he was leaving to save her

and confessed he was full of sorrow for the pain he had caused her. "I love you," was Sun's reply.

A final round of hugs and handshakes and the raft was pushed down the rails, this time smoothly landing in the water. Jin hoisted the sail and the wind caught it.

As the raft began moving, Michael, Walt, Jin and Sawyer waved to the crowd. The beach swiftly receded from view. On the starboard side was the rugged coastline, ahead the beckoning blue of the ocean.

But on the island, that ominous pillar of smoke still rises into the air.

EXODUS: PART TWO
EPISODE 122

WRITTEN BY
DAMON
LINDELOF
AND CARLTON
CUSE

DIRECTOR OF
PHOTOGRAPHY
MICHAEL
BONVILLAIN

DIRECTED BY
JACK BENDER

Since the last diary entry, the beach camp has been in a frenzy trying to relocate to the caves before nightfall and the coming of the Others.

Rousseau led Jack's group into the Dark Territory and to the massive old sailing ship carved with the name the *Black Rock*, a ship inexplicably lodged deep in the jungle, although Dr. Arzt noted a tsunami probably deposited it there. Rousseau then disappeared back into the jungle. While Hurley and Arzt waited outside, Jack, Locke and Kate entered the dark ship and discovered a row of chained skeletons—the *Black Rock* was a slave ship. They also found the promised dynamite. Jack and Locke were bringing out a case when Arzt shouted for them to put it down very carefully. Dynamite in heat and humidity becomes unstable, it becomes nitroglycerin, he explained. How unstable became shockingly evident when Arzt, while handling one of the sticks, was blown up.

Meanwhile, on the beach, smoke from the Others could be seen in the distance. Charlie was helping Claire carry her infant when Rousseau suddenly appeared in a panic, asking for Sayid. Charlie ran off to get him but they returned to the awful scene of a dazed and bloodied Claire, her baby stolen by Rousseau. Sayid, convinced Rousseau was headed for the black smoke to trade Claire's child for the child the Others once took from her, headed after her with a vengeful Charlie close behind. Claire had shouted after Charlie to bring back her baby and blurted out the infant's name—Aaron (a vast improvement over the "Turnip-Head" nickname Charlie had bestowed).

Back at the *Black Rock*, the foursome had carefully taken six sticks of dynamite, dividing them between two backpacks, as a failsafe should one pack explode. Jack was adamant that Kate not carry any of the packs, but at Locke's suggestion they drew straws. Kate and Locke "won" and everyone headed for the hatch. But Jack switched packs and was shouldering the explosives when the monster suddenly reappeared, revealing glimpses of strange tendrils of black smoke that almost dragged Locke down a hole. Jack ditched his pack to hold onto Locke who kept *begging* for Jack to let him go. Jack called out for Kate to take one of the dynamite sticks from his pack and toss it into the hole and the resulting explosion freed Locke.

Sayid and Charlie's pursuit of Rousseau led them past the airplane where Boone was mortally wounded. Sayid, not knowing of Charlie's addiction, noted the Virgin Mary statues crammed with heroin — a junky godsend that was irresistible as Charlie

surreptitiously took a statue. They pushed on, surviving a Rousseau booby-trap that rained rocks down on Charlie's head, his bleeding halted by Sayid with a battlefield treatment of bullet gunpowder lit

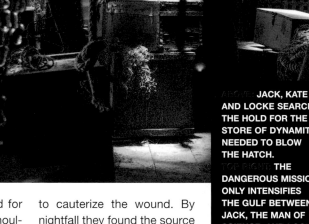

ABOVE: **JACK, KATE AND LOCKE SEARCH THE HOLD FOR THE STORE OF DYNAMITE NEEDED TO BLOW THE HATCH.** TOP RIGHT: **THE DANGEROUS MISSION ONLY INTENSIFIES THE GULF BETWEEN JACK, THE MAN OF SCIENCE, AND LOCKE, THE MAN OF FAITH.** BOTTOM RIGHT: **THE BLACK ROCK—IN REALITY AN OLD SLAVE SHIP INEXPLICABLY GROUNDED IN THE JUNGLE.**

to cauterize the wound. By nightfall they found the source of the smoke but no sign of the Others—Rousseau had seemingly set the fire herself. She appeared with her rifle slung over her shoulder and the baby in her arms, weeping that the Others weren't there. She had just wanted her Alex back. Charlie was furious—he believed she made up the whole story of the Others. Rousseau relinquished the child and Charlie had the supreme satisfaction of returning to the caves and safely delivering Aaron to Claire.

Meanwhile, the raft was in the open ocean and

That night Michael told Sawyer he was either a hero or had a death wish. Sawyer noted he was no hero, but their revealing exchange was interrupted as the radar screen showed an object coming towards them. The flare gun had only one precious flare but it seemed time to use it and Michael fired. Then, off the starboard side, came a blinding searchlight, the welcome form of a motorboat, and the silhouette of a crew. But the crew *wanted the boy*. Things happened quickly: Before Sawyer could draw his gun, somebody fired at him, knocking him into the water—Jin dove in to rescue him, the men boarded and took Walt, an explosive was dropped into the raft and it exploded. The boat sailed off into the darkness and Walt's screams for his father were answered by a shocked Michael who was bobbing in the water.

It was night when Jack's team arrived at the hatch. Locke's willingness to let the monstrous smoke tendrils drag him into a hole has given Jack pause. Locke said that he's a man of faith and Jack a man of science but destiny brought them all to the island. Jack feels Locke is a fanatic and he pulled Kate aside to confess his concerns. She has agreed to watch Jack's back in the event of any future "Locke problem."

Locke seems correct about one thing—the path we've all been on ends at the hatch. It was wired with the explosives, the fuse set. Hurley then saw the numbers on the hatch—the cursed numbers: 4 8 15 16 23 42—and tried to stomp out the burning fuse, lest they blow the lid off a Pandora's Box. Jack restrained him and the explosion allowed the busted hatch to be pulled off the cylinder.

Torches were brought over. Jack approached with apprehension, Locke with anticipation. They gazed down into a vertical shaft where only a few metal rungs of a ladder built into the wall remained, leaving a sheer drop into darkness, into the mystery of ...

the crew had settled into their respective tasks, including surveying the radar screen that would show if the radio transmitter was picking up any vessels as they approached the shipping lanes. Michael was letting Walt work the tiller when they hit a submerged log that ripped off the rudder. Disaster was averted when Sawyer dove into the ocean and with the aid of a rope tossed to him by Michael, pulled the rudder in.

WARRIORS
OF

THE MAKING OF AN EPISODE

Lost unit photographer Mario Perez calls it "the monster" and when the monster is ready, it takes over. The "monster" is not the creature lurking in the jungle of the show's mythical island—it's the production itself. Some call a production "the circus" and when a production

rolls into a location, with equipment trucks and vans and trailers, it does seem like the circus has come to town.

On *Lost*, the production circus might set up anywhere on Oahu, from the streets of Honolulu to interior rain forests. If it's a daytime shoot, the circus is usually ready before dawn. On location, "base camp" is where the circus is parked and the commissary tent and tables set up for serving main meals. A shooting location is usually a short walk from base camp, but sometimes it can be enough of a distance that the transportation department is kept busy just shuttling cast and crew back and forth for lunch.

This production circus is an ephemeral thing. An amalgamation of disparate talents and personalities meld into one unit to make a little magic and when a production ends, whether it's principal photography for a movie or the final episode of a television series, that talent disperses to the winds, each one moving on to a new project, a new city or maybe even some exotic and remote region of the planet. It's been called a "gypsy" culture, but *Lost* director of photography John Bartley recalls once talking with someone in the business who came up with the phrase that perfectly summed up their wandering life, with all its adventure, tedium, hard work and glory: "Warriors of the Wilderness."

Warriors of the Wilderness! To Bartley, that says it all. His own career is an example of its deepest meaning. His work has taken him around the world and he counts as one of his most exotic experiences some docudrama work in Saudi Arabia, where he and a small crew traveled the alien desert, living in tents. The life itself is an itinerant one and a true Warrior must be ready to jump to the next assignment at a moment's notice. Bartley recalls he had just finished as second-unit director of photography for the 2004 release *The Chronicles of Riddick* and was heading into the weekend, when he got a telephone call asking if he could be in Miami on Sunday to shoot a TV pilot. "Yeah, sure," he instantly replied.

"You get on a plane and when you land someone either picks you up at the airport or you get a rental car, go to the production office and start work. But you go to different cities, you meet new crew people, you get friends all over the place. I love the excitement of finishing a project and not knowing what the next project, the next challenge, will be."

Lost assembled its own Warriors of the Wilderness in Oahu. The production's designated hotel, where some of the crew were ensconced and where rooms could be arranged for set visitors or guest actors, was the Renaissance Ilikai Hotel in Honolulu, just off the Waikiki beachfront strip. The show's first season saw two main beach sets, the summertime site of Mokuleia, where the original pilot and early episodes were filmed, and the wintertime locale of Police Beach, both about an hour's drive away on the north shore, where legendary waves made for a surfer's paradise. And there were those remote jungles

NAVEEN ANDREWS WAITS FOR THE CALL WHILE JOSH HOLLOWAY GETS A LITTLE TOUCH–UP FROM JAY WEJEBE (MAKEUP ARTIST) BEFORE A SHOT. FAR RIGHT: CAST AND CREW SURVEY THE "POLAR BEAR" SAWYER HAS JUST GUNNED DOWN.

and valleys and other location places that recalled the "People of Old" and the island kings and culture that had once flourished in Hawaii.

The following documents a production visit made by the author from January 9 to 16, 2005, during the filming of episode 115, " … In Translation." The episode, featuring the troubled young Korean couple Jin and Sun, was directed by Tucker Gates, a veteran television director who also helmed the *Lost* episode "Confidence Man." Heading up camera work for " … In Translation" was DP Michael Bonvillain.

The episode already had a few days of filming completed by the time of this production visit. Although the normal work week was five days, deadline pressures sometimes dictated a six–day work week—and this was one of those weeks. The marathon began at dawn of the first day and didn't come to a close until the clock was near to tolling midnight of the sixth day.

MONDAY, JANUARY 10 KUALOA FISH POND AND KUALOA RANCH

It's the pre–dawn darkness at Kualoa Fish Pond, an 800–year–old pond that was once the province of ancient island kings. The base camp, with lights illuminating the circus of equipment trucks and production trailers, has been set up on a rough patch of ground a short walk away. DP Michael Bonvillain, who consumes seemingly endless cups of green tea over the course of a workday, is already into his third cup as he sits around the well–lit meal area at a table that includes episode director Tucker Gates, gaffer Jim Grce, key grip Chuck Smallwood and other production principals. Assistant locations manager Mathias "Scratch" Wessinger is already here, as location manager Jim Triplett's department is charged with securing this and every other location on the shooting schedule.

Filming is scheduled to begin at 7:30 a.m. and B–camera operator and Steadicam ace Gary Camp, and A–camera operator Paul Edwards—the veteran operator Camp hails as "the glue" of the photography department—have just arrived by van from the Ilikai hotel, along with John Shin, a San Francisco actor. Shin will play Mr. Kwon, a fisherman and father to Daniel Dae Kim's character, Jin, in a flashback scene where the ambitious Jin, so ashamed of his humble background he has told people his father was dead, arrives at his father's fishing pier for an attempt at reconciliation.

At dawn, the contours of the surrounding green mountains and jungle are revealed as the darkness wanes to a clear blue sky. The vast fish pond itself is one of the last functioning ancient Hawaiian fish ponds. The rising sun sets off diamond sparkles of light glittering from the horizon line to the camera view of a pier redressed as a Korean fishing village, with a thatched roof façade erected under the heavy branches of an old jungle tree, stacks of storage boxes, hanging lanterns and a steaming cauldron whose smoke billows

from a hidden smoking unit. At the far end of the dock, out in the sunshine, poles and fishing nets and fish have been set up. For background action, two extras man a junk that sails in line with the rising sun.

As set dressers Michael Gilday and John Lee attend to the details of the set, behind the old tree shading the dock Patti Dalzell, the script supervisor, settles into a folding chair at "Video Village." Here monitors display the feed from the cameras, allowing a director to see exactly what the camera eye is seeing (some crew also have "clam shells," portable monitors that get the same wireless feed). Right behind Video Village is the craft service that Nancy James keeps stocked with fruit drinks, soft drinks, bottled water, cookies and chips and power bars, bowls of fruit and other munchies.

Cameras are set up on the shore and on a boat just off the pier, while crew people communicate via radio with each other. "Let's go, while we've got that sun," Bonvillain calls. First assistant director Allen DiGioia calls out, "picture's up" or "quiet on the set" and then director Tucker Gates calls, "Action!"

Daniel Dae Kim drives Jin's car close to where the dock begins, gets out and pauses, surveying the tree canopy above him. He's dressed in a fine suit and slips off his dark glasses before striding out of the shade

FIRST ASSISTANT DIRECTOR ALLEN DIGIOIA CALLS OUT, "PICTURE'S UP" OR "QUIET ON THE SET" AND THEN DIRECTOR TUCKER GATES CALLS, "ACTION!"

and into the sunlight, walking to the boat where his father is among the fishermen working the morning haul. On the monitors at Video Village, Shin shows tenderness

to his "son." Although this morning is the first time he has met Kim, as a professional actor Shin must encompass the emotions of a father happy to embrace his prodigal son.

"I'm just trying to bring a little warmth to the character," Shin explains as he takes a drag from a cigarette between takes. "Since I live in San Francisco, the chance of working in Hollywood productions is rare. Not many casting directors in Los Angeles know about my work. But I thought I could find my niche looking for Korean characters."

At Video Village, Dalzell, a veteran of the business who laughingly calls herself the "den mother," notes every take and pertinent data on the episode's master script. Since keeping track of continuity is a must for episodic television, particularly with specific *Lost* flashback scenes often spread out over several episodes, she also prepares "Continuity Notes" prior to this and other episode productions.

Out on the water, the junk is discovered to have a slow leak and the extras bail between takes. The sun is higher now and the cameras get tighter on the father and son reunion.

Gary Camp is taking a break between setups. His big goal is to become an A–camera operator, the position that handles all the big shots and works closely with a director of photography. He notes he has taken up the Steadicam as another skill that might lead to his becoming an A–camera operator. Not everyone can buckle on the harness and attach the free–floating eighty–pound camera and then move up or down stairs, over rough terrain, get into the thick of a scene and record everything beautifully and naturally. Camp has the tough, rangy build to carry the weight, but he still estimates that in the five years he's strapped on the Steadicam he's lost about an inch, down to around six and a half feet. But he has no complaints. "I'm living my dream," he says.

─────

After lunch, the script pages shift from the flashback to the lost island, which takes the production up the ocean–facing Kamehameha Highway to rugged Kualoa Ranch. It's not the entire circus, but a few key trucks and vans and personnel have come to this primordial setting, with its deep valley surrounded by towering green mountains. *Jurassic Park*, *Godzilla*, *Windtalkers* and other features have been shot here and it's clear this is a valley of dreams. For now, this stunning spot is the site of the golf course Hurley built.

Scenes are usually shot out of the scripted continuity for reasons of scheduling and logistics, so this afternoon's work includes scene 7, featuring Jin venting frustrations by swatting rocks when Hurley approaches with fishing rods in an overture of friendship. Next comes scene 21, in which Jin, suspected of burning the raft Michael has been working on to leave the island, is captured by Sawyer and marched back to the beach.

Integral to the setups are Mike Shower, a regular

stand–in for Josh Holloway, and Tony Natoli, a designated "utility" stand–in. Shower once had a business in Japan and had bought a house not far from the Kualoa Ranch, drawn to life in Oahu because of the great surfing. Being an extra is a great gig but today, looking past the valley entrance towards the blue sky and ocean directly across the way, he wistfully murmurs, "It's a good day for surfing."

But he and Natoli take their jobs seriously. "We're part of the crew," Natoli says. "Before the actors get to the set, while they're getting made up or miked, we help

the set get lit, the cameras to get set up and focused. It's a nice dance."

One of the dancers—an ex–Broadway dancer, actually—is Klair Ethridge, who both handles the boom mike and hides the tiny wireless microphones on the actors. The boom itself is a microphone on the end of a long handle, which an operator dips into a scene. Meanwhile, sound man Michael Moore sits at his controls, recording all the microphones and making sure no outside sounds, such as low–flying planes, ruin the deserted island illusion and force actors to later "loop" dialogue voice–overs. Ultimately, Moore explains, a scene requires five separate "performances" happening simultaneously while he's recording: actors doing their scenes, a dolly grip getting a camera into position, the main camera operator working, first assistant camera adjusting focus and the boom operator picking up the dialogue.

LEFT: JIN'S ORDEAL IS REFLECTED IN THE BLOODY EFFECTS PROVIDED BY THE MAKEUP ARTISTS. ABOVE: DURING A BREAK IN THE FIGHT SCENE, PERRINEAU AND KIM PRACTICE THEIR MOVES.

For the scene of Sawyer capturing Jin, Daniel Dae Kim sits in a folding chair in the open air as incriminating burn marks are applied by makeup–department head Steve LaPorte and assistant makeup artist Mark Sanchez. The burns are from Jin having tried to put out the fire, but despite his innocence he'll be brought back to the beach to suffer.

Kim is asked if it's hard playing a character who is constantly on edge. "It can be," he says as the makeup artists work. "There's always a lot boiling under the exterior, so you've got to do your homework and make sure it's not an empty coldness. As you play any scene, you have to keep in mind your character's history and the circumstances he might be in at the moment, what the character really wants in not only the particular scene but in general."

Kim recalls that when he auditioned for the pilot, the script was not yet ready, so it had been "a leap of faith" to decide to do the show. He was still making that leap of faith since he, like the other actors, had no idea where the creators and writers were taking their characters. "There's a lot of information we don't have, but it's a lot like life that way," Kim smiles.

He reflected on the character of Mr. Paik, Sun's father and Jin's boss, the formidable man with whom Jin will have a dramatic confrontation in the course of this episode. "If you took MicroSoft, doubled their market share, and had them making cars and trucks, dishwashers and electronic equipment, then you'd get an idea of the size of his company. Those kinds of companies have their hands in everything, from government to the economy to possible ties to the underground. My character was asked to do whatever the boss wants, so I don't know what I'm getting myself in for when I say, 'Yes.'"

In minutes, the makeup artists have finished, giving black–and–blue burn marks to Kim's arms. "This is nothing compared to what's going to happen," he says before stepping off the chair to get into his scene with Josh Holloway. "Tomorrow I get a real beating."

Near where the makeup crew is gathered is Susan Schuler, hair–department head, and assistant hairstylist James Sartain. Each department has its own responsibility, she explains, but makeup and hair naturally go together, so both departments share a production trailer. One of her concerns is continuity. They have to trim hair to specific lengths because, while many months have gone by in the life of the production, in the *Lost* universe, where each episode represents only a few days at most, only a few weeks have passed. "We've also talked to the production about having more scenes of the characters cutting their hair and beards," Schuler adds. "The actors want that, too. Every department wants to make things as authentic as possible."

In the rough scene that follows, Kim has his arms tied as Holloway roughly pushes him along the rim of the grassy hill, with Tucker Gates and the cameraman filming from the slope below. A few takes and the company heads to the waiting trucks and vans to drive into the surrounding hills for another scene, rushing to catch the sun.

Josh Holloway is still standing atop the ridge as he contemplates his own "overnight" success story, which has been years in the making. "I was eight and a half years in the trenches in L.A. trying to get a frigging break in acting," Holloway says, biting down on the toothpick languidly hanging on his lips. "I did seven independent movies and four or five TV spots but I was just busting my ass, four or five readings a week to get close to something only to hear, 'Thank you, we gave it to a name.' So, weren't no easy road for me! I quit and started again and quit and started again so many times. I finally decided I had to do something for my sanity and had just gotten my real estate license when *this* happened!"

Holloway recalls that when he was called to read for *Lost* it was clear this was a big chance. Instead of the process of reading for the casting director's assistant, then the casting director and then a producer, he would be reading for series creators J.J. Abrams and Damon Lindelof. "You know that means it's happening soon," Holloway says, snapping his fingers, "so you only got a couple of shots. I'm Southern and I know how to lose the accent and supposedly this guy [Sawyer] was from Buffalo, New York, so in my reading I did it without an accent and really practiced that because I didn't want to lose the job."

Holloway recalls being halfway through his monologue, the confession of a confidence man's scams and lost loves, when he "got stuck." Instead of getting flustered, he kicked a chair across the room and his lines came back to him, an explosive outburst he feels helped get the people in the room thinking of him as Sawyer.

"That first day of work [on the pilot], J.J. comes up to me and says, 'It sounds like you're trying to articulate everything just right, like you're not trying to speak with your accent.' I said, '*Absolutely*, I'm trying not to!' J.J. said, 'No, man. That was before we booked you. Be free, be free! Be Southern.' And that truly set me free. For eight and a half years I'd been hearing people in L.A. say I'd never work with that accent. Sawyer is actually one of the first roles for a Southern man since Rhett Butler that isn't demeaning, where the guy isn't super dumb or a psycho. Sawyer's a bit of an ass, but he's smart and there's some weight to him, which is rare."

That evening, Holloway would join his series mates at a *People* magazine reception and photo op. But Holloway had too many battle scars from his years in the trenches to be blinded by the sudden, golden glare of his *Lost* celebrity. "I'm a little gun–shy ... But I'm just

happy that as an artist I get to work. I've had all this built up in me—I'm *ready* to work! I'm *lovin'* this, are you kidding me?! It's just weird when people recognize you everywhere. I like my privacy, but I will sacrifice that to get to the next level as an artist."

And what is the next level?

"Big, *cool–ass movies*, man!"

Holloway grins, exuberantly throwing his arms wide against the primordial valley where Godzilla and the *Jurassic* dinosaurs once roamed. The air is cool and the sky still blue but the sun is setting behind the mountains. Holloway looks around and he's alone. Most of the crew has jumped into trucks and vans and left to catch the light for the last scene. At the bottom of the ridge is a waiting van that'll take him to the location, but Holloway is enjoying this brief idyll, his dreams as expansive as the sky.

"I want to do beautiful character work and have choices and bring back westerns, I want to write and direct—I want to do *everything*! That was all a faraway dream and it's still a dream. But now it's a possibility. But this [*Lost*] is fine, it's just fine ... And we're all getting of," he smiles, while his van mates debate the merits of fatherhood.

It turned out that Camp, Grce and Edwards had all been together on a film project in Kazakhstan, which gets votes as one of the strangest places they had worked around the planet. Camp talked about the national game in which riders on horseback engage in a violent keep–away game that uses the head of a goat. It was an interesting place, Camp added, but he had no desire to go back. It was true "warriors of the wilderness" talk that took them all home into the city.

TUESDAY, JANUARY 11 POLICE BEACH, HALELWA

It's another early day, with shooting to start at 7:00 a.m. The production is back along a stretch of Police Beach, which represents the new beach settlement after the first beach eroded. The first scheduled scene on the call sheet (the bible of the day's work schedule), is at the charred remains of Michael's raft. Harold Perrineau vents Michael's anger, but simmers down when his son approaches, and they vow to build a new raft. Since young Malcolm David Kelley is here to play Walt, it means studio teacher Suzy Salerno is on set. Although a series regular, Kelley still has to do his schooling, which amounts to three or four hours a day and covers a full curriculum from algebra and science to world history and literature, health and physical education.

To get the shot of the ruined raft, a track has been laid on the sand upon which the main camera setup, with a seat for camera operator Paul Edwards, will be pushed along. Some twenty yards back from the sandy beach towards the dirt trail and brush, sound man Michael Moore sits at his station. This includes his mixing board, a small video–fed monitor and a spot where the day's script pages (the "sides") are pasted in view. The setup includes cables connecting to remote radio receivers, with radio antennas picking up the sounds from the wireless microphones. "We're recording onto DVDs that are designed for video cameras and simultaneously onto hard drive, which gives me a lot of protection," Moore says.

into our rhythm. That feeling of 'island fever'—that's gone. Now I don't want to leave."

It's twilight, at the end of a long day, as one of the production vans is taking crew back into Honolulu, a group that includes Gary Camp, Paul Edwards, Chuck Smallwood, Jim Grce and Chuck Askerneese, the assistant prop master. Askerneese says he's forty–five years old and he and his wife have just had their first child. He pulls out a picture of his one–year–old daughter, Zoe, and passes it around. "You're always thinking of yourself and now you have a new life to take care

The recorded tracks include the boom mike and body mikes. "I try to keep only one mike open at a time," Moore explains. "I'm concerned about each player leaking into the other player because since both actors are wearing mikes and [the dialogue of one actor] is going into the other mike as well, although arriving at a different time. Wireless mikes have been around more than thirty years, but they've become smaller and more efficient—I have two and a half times the range of what they had before. Antennas, which used to be about one and a half feet, are now like three or four inches."

Sitting and watching the work and morning unfold is producer Jack Bender, who keeps watch on the overall production's creative side as the script pages come to life each episode. Also behind the camera is producer Jean Higgins, who handles the purse strings. Higgins came to *Lost* with a resume that included commercials, documentaries and low-budget features—"I was the queen of chop-socky for quite a while," she grins.

But Higgins feels her work making corporate-sponsored documentary films, which requires thinking on one's feet on location and making a meager budget look like a million, was the best preparation for *Lost*. "For me, it was, 'Join the movie business, see the world.' It's probably easier to say where I haven't been." Memorable adventures include shooting a documentary for NATO that took her to the eternal daylight of the Norwegian Alps, where a military helicopter set her down upon a rocky mountaintop where ancient Vikings once lit their signal fires. Then there was the airstrip in Zaire where she encountered a "cargo cult," native peoples who know nothing of aviation technology, only that a downed cargo plane is like manna from heaven. "I will never forget a cargo cult living at the edge of this runway in Zaire, with an encampment not dissimilar to ours [on *Lost*]."

Higgins looks up the beachfront to a bend in the coastline about a fifteen-minute drive away—Mokuleia beach, site of the show's original crash site. The strategy for the story, as the season evolved, was that the

survivors would burn the fuselage because of the dead bodies inside. Eventually, it would make sense for them to move to another stretch of beach, away from the burnt-out metal hulk. There was also a practical concern to having the survivors relocate, as the original location was a narrow beach and the winter surf would wash away the fuselage.

"We're on the north shore of Hawaii and there's a reason the north shore is legendary for the size of the waves and intensity of the surf," Higgins says, still staring at the distant point. "I was telling the writers that by the middle of October we'd have to get rid of the

LOCKE ENDS THE FIGHTING BY DECLARING THAT THEY HAVE TO STOP FIGHTING AMONG THEMSELVES. THE REAL ENEMY IS OUT THERE, IN THE JUNGLE, LOCKE WARNS: "WE'RE NOT THE ONLY PEOPLE ON THIS ISLAND AND WE ALL KNOW IT!"

fuselage. It was early November and I knew our luck was running out, the winter surf was coming."

The weather held and the episode was filmed of the fuselage being burned and the survivors moving up the beach. The production had rented the location from the state and cleared away the wreckage and officially signed off that the beach had been completely cleaned up. "That same week the state signed us off we got a fifty-foot surf, the biggest since 1988! The water was not only over the beach, but on the other

himself at home. Before his scene where Locke makes his dramatic entrance, O'Quinn walks up from the beach towards the forested beachfront, where trees are spaced apart and the ground is soft. He calls it "the sacred grove." He sits down, leaning against a tree, and stretches out his legs.

O'Quinn is asked about the earlier episode when Locke looked into the eye of the mysterious thing lurking in the jungle. What did Locke see?

"I don't know, honestly. I actually asked Damon, 'Something is approaching me, I look up, what do I see?' He said, 'How about, and I hope this is enough, that you're seeing the most beautiful thing you've ever seen in your life?' I said, 'That's enough. I'll play that.'"

So, what is the most beautiful thing O'Quinn has seen in his life?

O'Quinn pauses. He smiles. "Probably my sons when they were little, my wife. The ball that I shot going in as the buzzer went off. There are moments, as insignificant as they may seem, that you'll remember on your deathbed, I'm sure. I really didn't have to think about anything in particular. Actors draw on their personal experience. I didn't always do that because I didn't have enough personal experience. Now that I'm in my fifties, I've got a lot of personal experience. And there's been plenty of sadness in my life to draw upon ... things that come into your head at night when you're trying to go to sleep that you don't want in there. So, you might as well be able to call on them when you want them, because you often get them when you don't." Locke himself has struggled with his own pain. But the island seems a chance at redemption, a miracle, a gift beyond his wildest dreams. "Locke says to Shannon at one point, 'Everybody gets a new life when they come to this island,'" O'Quinn smiles. "That gift of perception he has, what Locke sees in people—I don't know if he had that before, that might be a certain clarity that was given to him [when they crashed]. He was convinced destiny had spoken to him, sent him to go on a walkabout. But actually the voice wanted him to get on the plane. Consequently, he welcomes everything that happens to him here, maybe more so than anybody else. He figures it's all part of his destiny."

Most of all, the veteran character actor has surrendered himself to the character. "I've played a lot of uniforms and suits and ties, like CIA and FBI men, so this whole job is a wonderful opportunity to explore the

side of the road! I had moved it out *just* in time and thank God, otherwise I'd still be doing the EPA cleanup salvage operation right now!"

In the call sheet, scene 33 is written: "EXT–BEACH Michael Beats up Jin—Sun Speaks English." Then, shooting in rare continuity, came scene 34: "Everyone Shocked Sun Speaks English—Locke Defends Jin."

It's going to be a long day in the sun, with practically the entire cast assembled as Michael will pound Jin, certain he burned his raft. But Jin refuses to hit back. His wife's dramatic plea on his behalf ends the fighting. The sequence would end with Locke appearing and telling everyone the problem was out there, in the jungle: "We're not the only people on this island, *and we all know it!*"

The production has been shooting on Police Beach for about a month since relocating from the original crash–site location, but Terry O'Quinn has already made subtleties of acting. Here's a character who has deep thoughts and doesn't go by the book—he's writing his own book! I believe most of us have a color wheel but even as performers we don't get to touch upon some of our colors. Locke, simply because of how he's been written and how they've allowed me to play him, gets to bring in a lot of colors, which is very exciting. This experience has allowed me to blossom a little. Maybe there are seasons as an actor. You're out of work for a year and you fade; you get something good and you bloom."

O'Quinn himself lives the vigorous life that Locke leads on his own island. O'Quinn lives in a house in a wooded area of the north shore, five miles from Police Beach, and when the production is shooting here he walks to work in the morning and walks home at night. Indeed, at lunchtime, when vans pick up cast and crew for the mile–long ride to base camp, O'Quinn walks the dusty trail that cuts through the forest and curves out into the open view of the ocean, flipping his knife as he strides along—like Locke, he's never without a knife. O'Quinn has been mastering handling knives, throwing knives (although he later points out the scar on his hand he got from "playing").

In a strange way, it seems Terry O'Quinn *is* John Locke.

"For most actors, the work obsesses them, if it's a good part. This job never leaves, I guess, because it's a series. I can also equate my personal experience here in Hawaii with Locke's experience, I don't have any trouble relating. In making this character my own, there are certain attitudes we both share. It's not like I had to dig, dig, dig. I simply wormed my way into his clothes and feel quite comfortable in them."

O'Quinn had so settled into the island life that it was quite a jarring adjustment during the several weeks of Christmas break when he went back home to Maryland. It had been a welcome break for most of the cast and crew, who had been working hard since the pilot, but O'Quinn had the strange feeling that Locke's phantom presence was dissipating on the mainland. "I'd get up in the morning and go into the bathroom and when I looked in the mirror I could see that as my [tan] color faded, I could see my character fading! I felt I was losing all that edge that was Locke.

There was something magical that was happening here—how brilliant the writing was, how fortunate I was to get this character, how I'm trying to do him justice. I only now feel like I've gotten my stride back ...

"I don't have any theories about Locke. As long as they [the creators and writers] keep me wondering, the happier I'll be. I believe in the empirical evidence—we've crashed, we're on this island and I can walk! My thinking has cleared up, I can see a direction—which may

WE'VE CRASHED, WE'RE ON THIS ISLAND AND I CAN WALK! MY THINKING HAS CLEARED UP, I CAN SEE A DIRECTION—WHICH MAY MAKE LOCKE DANGEROUS.

make Locke dangerous. But what he's sure of is that this isn't just an island, it's a magical island. The island is a spirit or maybe the island has become his god, I don't know. But this is where it [Locke's destiny] was meant to happen. That's what he's sure of."

Jorge Garcia is on the beach and getting ready for the big fight scene between Michael and Jin. He's also anticipating his character's first big flashback story, which unfolds when the new episode begins shooting the following Tuesday. "Hurley has won $156 million in the Lotto with numbers he got from a guy in a mental institution," Garcia explains. "What triggers this flashback is they're the same numbers that the French woman had in her papers! Somehow, people who use those numbers are cursed and bad things happen to people who use them. I win all that money, but all this bad stuff starts happening around me. I actually blame myself for the plane going down.

"This [insight] is also based on my sneaking a peek of the treatment, which I wasn't supposed to do," Garcia smiles sheepishly. "I haven't read the script yet, although a lot of the crew has it already. But when I go to visit my friend at this mental institution, where apparently I'd also been a patient at one point, my friend is reciting those numbers and freaks out when I tell him I used the numbers. He says he got the numbers in Australia, which is what sends me to Australia, that's how I got on the plane from Sydney to Los Angeles."

Practically the entire *Lost* cast has now assembled for the big fight scene: Matthew Fox and Evangeline Lilly, Dominic Monaghan, Naveen Andrews, O'Quinn and Garcia, Josh Holloway, Harold Perrineau, Malcolm David Kelley, Yunjin Kim and Daniel Dae Kim. The winter waves are crashing against the shore, which will make the perfect tumultuous backdrop. It not only promises to be an exhausting scene for the actors, but a challenge for the camera and lighting crew, with Paul Edwards and Gary Camp in the sand to get all the coverage with handheld cameras.

Walking along the beach, checking the lighting setups, is gaffer Jim Grce. "I have a crew on this show that ranges from five to fifteen people. We design the lighting, put up the lights and take 'em down. When you're on the island, if anything looks good, it's OK. But the look at night is basically people lit by fires and we have little machines that duplicate a fire look with lights, making them randomly flicker, and we put gels on the lights to match the color of the fire. We'll have a bit of moonlight effect that plays in the background.

"My favorite thing is the flashbacks because we get to do anything we want," Grce adds. "We're in all sorts of cities all over the world, but they tend to be shot in Chinatown here [Honolulu]. In the 'Outlaws' episode, Sawyer's second piece, we had a really nice bar scene that was supposed to be a back–alley hole in Sydney. The lighting figures into the emotions of the scene, the way we cut the light. We might have a very strong piece of light that might not hit the character or a little slash of light if it's dark, so you can see what's going on in their eyes."

LEFT AND ABOVE:
A CLASSIC EXAMPLE OF ATMOSPHERIC *LOST* LIGHTING IS THIS MOODY "OUTLAWS" BAR SCENE SET IN SYDNEY (BUT STAGED IN HONOLULU'S CHINATOWN).

Grce surveys the beach, which presents a very different kind of challenge: shooting outdoors. "We have done a lot of lighting on the beach. A lot of times we'll bring in big lights and soften them [the actors] up to try to make them look as natural as possible. But for this particular scene we can't spend the time to actually light it because it basically has every character and there are so many pages [of scripted action and dialogue] to cover. What we do is try to balance some of the keys and background with the characters. This will basically be both cameras, handheld, running around. It's documentary–style—just do it!"

Steve LaPorte is preparing a cotton roll to put into Daniel Dae Kim's mouth to make him puffy from the pummeling. He also has a blood capsule for the actor to chomp down on for the added touch of bloody drool. "It's a brutal moment in the show," LaPorte says.

The action starts as Michael runs down the beach, headed like a missile for Jin to confront him about burning his raft. Michael cannot be restrained by Jack and Hurley but even Jack finally backs off when Sawyer tells him it isn't his business. The circle of survivors widens to watch the two men settle things with their fists. But with every punch from Michael, Jin defiantly yells back in Korean. The scene culminates with Sun screaming in English, "Stop it! *Leave him alone!*"

The scene plays out in the sun and against the breaking waves, take after take—some twenty takes or more, someone estimates—as the handheld cameras capture various angles. When one take ends, the next one usually starts at the top, beginning with the call for quiet on the set, then director Gates yelling, "Action."

Among those watching up on the beach, under the shade from the forest, are stand–in Jim Mazzarella and John Ludwig, one of the background extras whose presence adds to the illusion of a survivor population beyond the main cast members. Both came to Hawaii years ago and fell in love with the islands. Mazzarella grins that he recently visited the mainland and all he wanted to do was get on a plane and fly back. Mazzarella then notices a giant turtle disappear below the froth of the waves and scans the horizon for signs of migrating whales.

Also watching the big scene is Rand Wilson, a utility stand–in who also stands in for Harold Perrineau. He had asked to try stunts and it's "so far so good," he grins, as he has been put in the way of wild boars,

doubled for Perrineau and done a stunt rollover for a car that hits Michael during a flashback scene.

During a break in the action, the stunt coordinator himself, a big, brawny man in a black T–shirt, is down in the surf having Josh Holloway bring down a knife and then, slowly and deliberately, showing how to block the downward stroke and apply a wrist lock. It's not a piece of stunt action for the scene, just Michael Vendrell showing one of the stars a little martial arts technique.

Vendrell lives on the Big Island and has a nice commute to Oahu for the work week. He explains he's been in the stunt business for thirty years and has concentrated on television, although he worked with

Arnold Schwarzenegger on his early films and with the late Brandon Lee on his movies, and he trained Sean Connery for *The Rock*.

Vendrell is a martial arts master and his is a "soft" style, meaning emphasis is not on overpowering kicks and blocks but channeling energy to effortlessly focus and release power. "Everyone has their own way of moving. I teach people to get in touch with a way of moving that's most natural and fulfilling to them ... Each person is an artist and they develop their own art. I try to lock in on that mastery and make it come forward as a martial art."

Vendrell's history is the stuff of martial arts legend. He was growing up in California, in Orange County, when he was taken under the wing of his martial arts master at the age of three and raised in the system of Yee Shuan Tao, emerging many years later as the eighty–eighth master of the system.

The regimen included physical training and instruction in Chinese healing and energy arts. His master, Sifu John Leong, was eighty years old when they started, but always spry. He loved and nurtured Vendrell as if he were his lost son. "As I got older, I realized what an honor it was to have someone like that always at my disposal, who was anxious to teach me. There never was a time where he said, 'Now, we're taking a lesson.' I didn't even know I was studying a martial art, I just

DURING A BREAK IN THE BEACH FIGHT, STUNT COORDINATOR MICHAEL VENDRELL HAS JOSH HOLLOWAY PRACTICE PARRYING A KNIFE ATTACK.

thought everyone had a Chinese master who showed them how to move like a tiger and climb trees like a monkey. Then, when I was about ten years old, one of the bullies in my school attacked me and I threw the guy. I'd never been taught to throw during my drills, it just instinctively happened. I told my teacher about it and asked what happened and he said, 'Oh, you got in touch with your *feelings*!' I thought that was great and he started showing me more fighting techniques and it was probably fifty/fifty, learning healing and martial arts."

Then, when he was sixteen, Vendrell got into a street fight and afterwards a bystander pulled him aside and asked, 'Hey, kid, want to make some money?' For the next three years, Vendrell became a weekend warrior, as that bystander became his manager in the underground world of cage fighting, arranging bouts in warehouses, bars, meat–packing plants and even churches all over the United States for "The Kung–Fu Kid," Vendrell's fighting name.

Vendrell finally called it quits, afraid of the bloodlust consuming him that was against the moral principles of a true martial artist. His last bout was at a ranch outside Las Vegas in a sunken cage surrounded by bleachers crowded with high rollers dressed in tuxedos—unbeknownst to Vendrell it was a to–the–death match. But the Kung–Fu Kid unleashed a special strike that stopped his opponent's heart for a few minutes, long enough for his manager to collect the winnings and before his opponent revived from being seemingly dead. "My manager said to split up and meet back in L.A. I never saw him again, and not a dime of the $250,000 [purse]. But I got out of there and never looked back."

Suddenly, Terry O'Quinn leans in with his guitar, playing and singing, "Sweet Mary Lou, I'm still in love with you."

"Have you tried a ukulele yet?" Vendrell grins.

"No!" O'Quinn laughs, spinning away and strumming his chords.

———

Scenes 33 and 34 have taken all day to shoot, with seemingly dozens of separate takes, virtually all from the top. The fight had played out, Sun had screamed for them to stop, and Locke had entered to declare that instead of fighting among themselves they should start worrying about those who seemed to be out there, in the jungle. The survivors have listened, chastened and emotionally drained. In the day's script pages for scene 34, what happens next is described: "And this is one of those KICK–ASS SHOTS which will define the episode—if not the show—because … "

And, one by one, the group peels away and silently walks off the beach, each going their separate way, leaving Sun standing alone.

With the final take, Matthew Fox heads up to stand in the welcome shade. For him it's been a long and winding road to *Lost*.

Fox was one year old when his father moved his mom and older brother from Philadelphia to Wyoming, where his father started a new life as a rancher and outfitter. "The ranch wasn't an old family, generational thing," Fox explains. "My dad was kind of running away from an old money family in Philadelphia, he didn't want any part of that sort of thing. So he started his own thing out west."

The ranch had longhorn cattle, they raised barley for Coor's beer, and provided outfitting for elk and deer hunting. As Fox grew up, his responsibilities on the ranch grew. Feeding livestock was always a big part of the day and so was irrigating the crops, driving heavy equipment and the ritual of harvest time. "Ranching is a great world, it's too bad it's so hard to make a living at it, especially the small guys these days. But it is an amazingly healthy and challenging way of living life. I have a lot of respect for people who give their lives to it."

Fox had been a standout wide receiver for his high school football team and was recruited to play for the Columbia University Lions in New York City. But Fox wasn't there just to play football and he graduated with a degree in economics, fully expecting to be working on Wall Street. But Columbia had been expensive and to make a little extra spending money Fox started modeling and doing television commercials. He hadn't taken it seriously, but upon graduation he became inexorably drawn into acting as the agent getting him

those commercial gigs began encouraging him to go for acting jobs.

"I started studying acting and I bounced around New York until I found a place, The Atlantic Theater Company, founded by Bill Macy and David Mamet, that made

J.J. ABRAMS DIRECTS MATTHEW FOX IN THE PILOT EPISODE. THE SERIES CREATORS ORIGINALLY PLANNED TO HAVE THE JUNGLE MONSTER KILL OFF JACK AND LEAVE HIS BLOODY—AND HEAD-LESS—BODY IN A TREE.

sense to me. I studied there for a year. I'd always been a big fan of Mamet, who has an amazing ability to boil something very complicated down into something very concise. The mechanics of acting are sort of vague and mysterious, but the simplest way of explaining it is if you can make yourself want what your character wants in specific moments, then on the grand, philosophical scale, you become the character. Now, actually doing that in a way that's natural, believable, committed and lived–in is the real challenge." Fox is asked if his ranching background and training as a college football player helped make him a disciplined actor.

"I think hard work is part of my DNA. I do have a pretty intense work ethic and bring a high intensity level to each take. Not to say that every take I did today was as good as I wanted them to be. But I was still giving as

much as I could. If I go home after a day's work and feel there might have been two or three takes where I wasn't giving 100 percent, that would make me feel like crap." During his original *Lost* audition, Fox also read for the part of Sawyer, but was happy he was ultimately cast as Jack. "Jack is such an incredibly cool guy to play. He's a hero but he's also complicated, he has a dark side and a lot on his shoulders ... Damon likes to say that Sawyer and Jack could have been twins separated at birth and raised in different environments. I couldn't agree with him more. In their essence, I think they're similar types, real guys of action and go–getters and very intense. Jack was raised in a world of pursuing surgery and under the umbrella of his father's legacy and all the things he rebelled from, but he also lived in a socioeconomic status where he didn't have to worry about the things that Sawyer did. I think Sawyer, while a similar soul, has had to scratch and scrape and con and front his way through everything he ever got. On the island these two guys butt heads on everything. Jack essentially feels Sawyer is useless and self–centered and he's not good for much on this island. I feel Jack, deep down inside, is standing up for human dignity in this situation and feels people [on the island] need to step up."

The subject of the notorious torture episode comes up, the time Jack and Sayid captured Sawyer in the mistaken belief he was hoarding Shannon's asthma inhalers. Jack had looked on, complicit, as Sayid tortured Sawyer. The scene was shocking, Fox admits, but totally in keeping with Jack's character.

"For someone looking for 'Hero,' in quotes, that was not something you'd expect from Jack. But Jack was still serving a bigger, overriding good—he was trying to save a girl's life! I can totally see the rationalization for his going that step. He's the character with the strongest sense of a moral compass, but that's going to be whittled away over time. Sometimes he's going to have to play dirty to get something done on a bigger scale of good ... I dig that here's a guy who's crash–landed on this island and who's come out of hospitals—clean, white, sterile environments—and suddenly he's got to learn the street! Characters like Sawyer are going to teach him the street and he's going to learn quick and be able to play that game with them as good or better."

As Fox talks, he gazes off down the beach, as if at a fixed point. As he gets deeper into musing about the soul of Jack, he talks faster, more forcefully, as if he's getting his second wind. He then realizes the beach set is practically deserted, that almost everyone has walked up to the trail to catch the vans back to base camp.

"I think we're heading home," he says.

It has been an exhausting day, but Fox has the satisfied glow of an athlete who gave his all on every play.

FOX WAS ONE YEAR OLD WHEN HIS FATHER MOVED HIS MOM AND OLDER BROTHER FROM PHILADELPHIA TO WYOMING, WHERE HIS FATHER STARTED A NEW LIFE AS A RANCHER AND OUTFITTER.

"People ask me what it's like to shoot in Hawaii and I often say it's wonderful, but being out in the elements for hours and playing really physical and emotional material takes a lot out of you. It's hard work, but very, very gratifying."

WEDNESDAY, JANUARY 12   POLICE BEACH

Today's shoot begins at 9:00 a.m., with Yunjin Kim in a bikini and braving the waves. The water is rough, but she wades in as far as possible. In the story, a scandalized Jin rushes forward to throw a towel over his wife and Michael, seeing him treating her roughly rushes to protect her—and gets a surprising slap on his face from Sun, who walks off with Jin.

Watching the action is Chuck Askerneese, who supplies the "action props," all the axes, guns, rings, watches, backpacks, wallets and whatever else the actors physically handle. Today's props include bamboo and an ax for Michael to make his raft. "Doug [Madison], the prop master, is already in meetings with the new director for the next episode, talking about what we'll need," Chuck explains. "We get stuff at hardware stores, and have stuff flown in from a mainland prop house that makes everything from license plates to fake fish, and rubber axes to match real ones in case there's going to be a stunt."

Askerneese joined the show in January, but has been in the entertainment business a long time. In the 1980s, he was front–man singer for a ska band called the Untouchables. "But when I got out, about fifteen years ago, I felt ninety years old. It was the partying, the rock–and–roll lifestyle. I started doing set construction and then got into doing set dressing. I liked it and fell into it."

Like most of the steady crew working on the show, he has relocated to Honolulu, although his family is still back home in Burbank. He brightens when he mentions his wife and one–year–old daughter will be arriving this week for a visit. "When my daughter looks up to me and says, 'Daddy, daddy … ' I don't know how to describe the feeling. You just want to melt inside. I never thought it was going to happen to me [having a child]. It's just amazing.

"The crew here is great. You fall in with a bunch of guys who are caring and all get along good. We're like carnies, a group of people who go from set to set and location to location. It was just like when I was in a band, although we were a small pack. Now it's a big group of people. It's kind of a family, you know."

Meanwhile, out in the surf, Paul Edwards is demonstrating to Daniel Kim the best way to grab Yunjin and throw a towel over her for the camera. One of the crew nods towards Edwards and gaffer Jim Grce and pays them the ultimate compliment: "We couldn't do this [the show] without them. They're geniuses … "

"A little more violent with these motions," Edwards drawls, as he directs Yunjin to slap Harold Perrineau.

During a break, boom operator Klair Ethridge explains that wiring the actors, her other task, is an art in making sure wires aren't visible and don't generate clothing and environmental noises. "The wireless [radio microphones] are fine, but the boom is just a better sound–recording device, it makes a richer sound. On television, we use radio mikes much more frequently than on a feature because of the [faster] pace. On films you have so much more time. But here we're shooting seven, eight, sometimes nine pages a day."

The boom mike itself is sixteen feet when extended and the operator has to lean over to angle it just right above the performers. The dance requires knowing what size camera lens is being used for a scene, how not to dip the boom into frame or cast a telltale shadow.

But what does it take to keep the boom mike held high for hours on end?

"Strength," Ethridge deadpans, then laughs.

Also up on the beach is set dresser Michael Gilday. "Nobody calls me Michael, everybody calls me Gilday, my last name," he grins. "Being an on–set dresser is quite a glamorous position. Basically, we're paid furniture movers, heavy–airplane lifters and sand shovelers. Seriously, everything has to get tweaked to camera to create an image and facilitate the action, so we're pulling stuff out and pushing stuff in, lifting stuff all the time. Everything that's on camera that the actors aren't interacting with, is pretty much us. If we're out in the jungle, there's greens with the Greens Department."

WHEN SUN WADES INTO THE SURF IN A BIKINI IT'S NOT MERELY AN ACT OF DEFIANCE AGAINST HER DOMINEERING HUSBAND—IT'S AN ACT OF INDEPENDENCE.

Gilday started on *Lost* as a production assistant on the pilot after answering a job announcement posted on a Web site. The pilot was a rough shoot, he recalls. "The whole thing was on location and it was five weeks of six–day work weeks. For me, it was eighteen hours a day, because as a PA, I was the first one in and the last one out. I'd show up in the mornings and load everyone into the vans and go to the sets, be there all day, then go to the office and hand out the call sheets around the hotel because everything changed every day and we had to hand out revised call sheets. It was a lot of blood, sweat and tears. It's actually easier now, in wintertime, than when we were at the original [beach set location] at Mokuleia in the hot, hot summer sun for twelve hours, with no shade, and running on the sand all day long."

Back then, in the pilot and early episodes, the on–set dressing involved moving airplane parts around on the beach. "That's all we did all day long, John Lee and me. We'd get help from the grips for some of the pieces. These were real parts from a plane chopped up by a construction crew on the direction of the art department. The ironic thing was some of the pieces that looked really light would be really, really heavy and pieces that looked heavy were really light. You never knew until you went to pick them up.

"Actually, I don't know how we did it. We probably completed three or four episodes before we went to air. There was also a lot of pressure on Jack Bender to match up to the pilot, which had so much energy and talent and money put into it. He did an amazing job, but it was definitely pressure for everyone involved, the DP's, the gaffers. By November the days were shorter and the weather better and things were running smoother. But everything felt just as hard because we all felt so burnt out. We started going into six–day weeks and everybody was just tired. We'd given it our all. But seeing the show and its success propelled people, I think, because we all felt like we were fighting for something really good. But it was just hard. But everyone got recharged [at the Christmas break]. People think it's great to shoot in Hawaii, but it always rains here, we might spend all day in mud. But we keep coming back every Monday and starting all over again."

———

Emilie de Ravin, who plays Claire, is on set today to play a scene with Dominic Monaghan. She's trussed up with a foam shell to simulate Claire's pregnancy. Like her character, she hails from Australia. In high school she had dedicated herself to ballet, but at the crossroads of making that a career, decided to explore acting as an option. "One way or other, performing arts has always been my forte. I'd never really explored acting and it was just time to step away from dancing and see what would happen. But I just loved creating a completely different entity within yourself. It was so interesting, to do all the research and put yourself into someone else's shoes and try to make something become real. I got a job very quickly in a show that was being shot in Australia and I've stayed with it ever since."

Ravin pats her belly. "I am *not* pregnant," she chuckles. "I don't understand how people could think I could be pregnant, seriously—the baby would be out by now!

I haven't been pregnant myself, but I'm trying to be as true to the situation as I can. I have two older sisters I'm quite close to who have each had children, and I remember everything about their pregnancies. Having said that, everyone is different. Not every pregnant woman acts exactly the same. But you do have to move a little more gingerly and take into consideration that you can't sleep the same way, you need to have support when you sit down, there's a lot of things to consider when you're moving."

She recalls how her character arrived on the island because the psychic had foreseen her Los Angeles–bound plane would crash. "[The psychic] knew the plane would crash and I'd be on this island, he wants Claire to be forced to raise her child. I personally don't believe in psychics, but that episode kind of creeped me out."

So … what is it about this child Claire is carrying?

"I think there's going to be something a little different about the child, there almost has to be, whether it'll be known immediately or not. It could be normal or maybe it won't be normal. I don't know, I'm just guessing. As far as what the island means and whatever it is on the island, I have no idea and I quite like it that way. When we [the actors] read the next script, it's the same [sense of surprise] as a viewer watching the next episode."

It's just before lunch when Harold Perrineau pauses by the trail that runs through from the beachfront to base camp. He recalls the previous day's big scene on the beach, with him in the thick of things, confronting Kim's character. "We work as a group and are really respectful of each other and the process. We knew it was going to be a long day, so we had to pace ourselves. I think when you get any group of people together they sort of play off each other's energies. Like the scenes where we've been golfing, the energy is light and we're all laughing and joking. But this [the scene on the beach] was such tension, which is really hard on your body. On a day like yesterday it was so physical that when you walk away you're sort of drained. You play what your character could

be thinking. Where is he going, what is he doing, what's happened before, what's happening now? You try to keep all that rolling and not pay attention to the camera and the people around. It's actually quite interesting what goes on. Our brains are really fascinating."

Perrineau is one of the veteran performers on the show with both movie and TV experience, but his love is the stage. "I'm actually more of a theater guy, I'm solid on my feet there. I know where I'm going."

Prior to *Lost*, Perrineau was performing on stage in *Topdog/Underdog*, a Pulitzer Prize–winning play by Suzan Lori Parks, when he got a call that J.J. Abrams was planning to do a new show in Hawaii. It seemed a missed opportunity but he got another call, a few weeks later—the start dates for Abrams' show had been pushed back and they were still interested in him. "Everybody is always saying they're interested in seeing you and when you get there they're like, 'Who are you, again?'" Perrineau chuckles. "But I get the sides and I go in expecting to see the regular Hollywood guys and I find these guys who are really passionate and they start giving me some tight background of who [Michael] is. I go, 'Wow, you guys are serious, you aren't play-ing!' They told me this guy is a father and there's a plane crash and he has his son with him and they don't really know each other. After that meeting, I was excited to do it and they were excited about me. Fortunately, it just worked out. My play was closing and I had a day to pack. The next day I was on a plane to Hawaii and here I am."

In addition to the storyline of a father and young son who were strangers to each other and stranded on an island with strangers, Perrineau was intrigued with the larger notion of starting a civilization from scratch. "Many years ago, I used to wonder what it would be like if there were no books, no recordings of history, no lines to follow— what would we do? I thought it was a really interesting idea, to be totally in the present."

Back on the beach the wind is blowing off the surf and Dominic Monaghan is stretched out under a tree in a hooded sweatshirt and dark glasses, waiting for the call to play Charlie. Earlier this morning, he had curled up for a quick nap under one of the makeshift shelters at the beach location set—he wasn't sleeping off a hard night, just conserving energy, Monaghan explains, a lesson he learned while working on *The Lord of the Rings* trilogy. "I'm someone who doesn't sleep when I'm not working, but when I'm working I'll try to get twenty minutes to sleep [here and there during a day] because you have to be ready to go when you get the call.

"I did go into the pilot partying and trying to be the last man standing and having fun because I was playing a straight–out drug addict who thought he was going to be rescued from the island within thirty–six hours. But I turned a little corner with the part of Charlie, who's a little bit more in the shadows now, he isn't necessarily the party boy all the time. So, I've kind of backed away a little bit, made a decision not to socialize as much as I normally would. Anytime it's my [flashback] episode, I

RAVIN PATS HER BELLY. "I AM *NOT* PREGNANT," SHE CHUCKLES. "I DON'T UNDERSTAND HOW PEOPLE COULD THINK I COULD BE PREGNANT, SERIOUSLY—THE BABY WOULD BE OUT BY NOW!

tend not to see anyone at all. It takes about eight or nine days to film your own episode so I'll just back away into myself. I'll tend to stay in, read the script a lot, go to bed early … "

Monaghan feels a defining aspect of Charlie is he's "hugely self–analytical." He's also terribly insecure, a former rock star who had a taste of fame and is forever hoping he'll be recognized. "It's fun to play someone who reveals his insecurities so easily, yet has a darkness to him. I'd been searching for a character that had a few more issues than the parts I'm usually thrown, which make people think I'm good at playing happy–go–lucky, cheeky, non–issue, non–threatening types of characters. My main struggle as an actor is to consistently scare and challenge myself and, hopefully, the audience.

"Playing a rock star is great because you can get into that rock star cliché, those rock–and–roll moments where you're on stage and wearing nail polish and makeup. But behind that façade is a human being trying to make sense of his place. Charlie thinks he can defend himself against the world because he's holding a guitar and singing into a microphone. When you take all those things away, you realize here's a guy who needs to be loved and clearly needs therapy."

Monaghan also acknowledges that his own fame—*Lord of the Rings* made him familiar to an international audience—echoed Charlie's own predicament. "I'm treading on thin ice a bit—I could very well have been that guy and could still very well be that guy, someone who's had a certain amount of success and then disappears into obscurity. A fantastic musician I really admire is Eminem, and he's talked about fame a lot in his music. There's a line in one of his songs where he goes, 'What do I think about fame? It *sucks*!' You still have the same problems as everyone else, none of that goes away ... I still worry about my family, my friends, I worry about money, I worry about whether I'm doing the right thing, am I as happy as I could be, is this what I should be doing, should I be saving the whales or throw all this away and go live in a hut somewhere and write the great American novel? More than anything else, I worry about what this decision means for me as an actor—why I chose Charlie, why Charlie chose me."

Monaghan will soon be called to walk onto the beach for his scene, but he has a final burst of personal insight, which he finishes precisely the moment before he gets the call.

"I was a small amount of Charlie when I went into that initial audition and they saw a small amount of Charlie in me. I embraced Charlie after that. But it means there was something in me that was growing and becoming

more and more Charlie. If I play Charlie for the next four years, ultimately I'll be able to play someone who is more insecure than I am personally, who is less sure about life and more emotionally unstable. I, as Dom, will learn something from the gift of playing that character."

Because of the relatively late start, the lunch break comes later in the afternoon. It's a long night ahead, with scenes turning on the triangle of Shannon, Sayid and Boone. Michael Bonvillain is taking his lunch under the tent at base camp and recalls his earlier work on J.J. Abrams' *Alias* series, in which the illusion of far–flung world locales usually had to be created in exotic Burbank. *Lost* has a whole island to explore for their own mythic island and Honolulu was practically made to order for flashback settings. "We found that Honolulu's Chinatown is a very diverse source of locations," Bonvillain notes. "It actually looks like New Orleans, in a way. It has this Edward Hopper quality, with beautiful old two–story brick buildings."

But shooting on an island and working on location, isn't a breeze. Bonvillain notes the challenges for camera can vary dramatically, including the "documentary style" approach to the previous day's fight on the beach. "That scene had about fourteen principals on an open beach, which is ridiculous. There's no way to get a construction crane in or put up hundred–foot silks over them and we couldn't afford to wait for cloud cover and we couldn't light every shot separately because of constraints of time, budget and access.

"Having actor's squinting [in the sun] is a huge problem. On Mokuleia, the first beach set where the airplane wreckage was, the trade winds were always blowing in at fifteen to twenty miles an hour. So, if you wanted to fly anything big, like an eight– by eight–foot silk or diffusion frame to take the harshness out of the sunlight, the actors either couldn't move very far or they

had to step into a close–up, which is static and this show is all about movement. The trade–off is we'd bring in a bounce card to give a little light in their eyes, but that made it even worse on the squinting. So, it can be a little frustrating when you spend time on a nice wide–shot and when it's cut they use a lot of the close–ups. It's an uphill battle and it's all a trade–off."

Bonvillain estimates that one of the vagaries of shooting on location is the travel time. The typical daily two–hour round–trip to locations amounted to sixteen hours over the course of an eight–day production schedule, more than an entire working day lost traveling. "The writers are starting to understand our situation because now, with winter, the days are shorter and by

4:30 or 5:00 in the afternoon it gets too dark to shoot. So, they're writing a few night scenes so we can go from day to night and get our twelve hours of shooting and make the page count."

He recalls that earlier in the season, people got burned out from long hours and working a lot of Saturdays, but Christmas break recharged everyone. Bonvillain adds it wasn't as hard on him, because the DP position rotated, allowing each DP to prep their next episode. In the meantime, he keeps his energy going with copious cups of green tea—and the fun of it. To him, it's a kick to try to duplicate for a new generation the enjoyment he recalls as a kid watching *Mannix*, *Hawaii 5–O*, and other classic TV shows.

"I come from a big family and we always used to fight over our favorite chair to watch those shows. You remember watching these shows as a kid, they make an incredible impression. I always think about the kids who might be watching and how, when they're forty, they'll go, 'Yeah, that show *Lost*, we used to sit down and watch as a family and it was so cool!' So whenever you get a little ragged or burnt out, what keeps you going is that this is going to go on forever, now in DVDs, but more so in people's memories.

"This show is really great. Basically, we try to live up to the quality of the writing. There are positive lessons, like Charlie kicking heroin and the idea of self–sufficiency and working together. There's all this biblical stuff, too, like the resurrection of Charlie after he was hung in the tree, the prodigal son stuff we shot on the dock where Jin meets his father.

"My pet idea is they find a herd of wild horses that Locke tames, so when the Others emerge, in, like, season three, they've got this mounted army on horses and have armor and lances and we stage this big set piece in the Kualoa Valley. That's one big set piece I'd love to do. I emailed the idea to J.J. and he said, 'Great idea.' But he says that no matter what I say."

———

After lunch, the work shifts to an area just up from the surf, where the beach meets the trees of the surrounding forest. The "shelter area," as it is known, is the set for the beach encampment, with temporary dwellings constructed of bamboos and branches, salvaged pieces of wreckage and tarps. In the scene, Shannon struggles while stretching a white tarp between two poles. When Sayid comes over she asks him to help her. When Gates calls "Action," the "background people," as the extras are called, fill out the frame as Grace and Naveen Andrews perform in front of the camera Paul Edwards is operating.

As the various takes are shot, Jim Grce checks the light as some ominous clouds threaten to obscure the setting sun. "The sun's good," urges first assistant director Allen DiGioia. "We should strike."

Dusk arrives and the shelter area campfires are going. The fires, however, are manufactured. Clarence Logan, special effects foreman on the crew of special effects coordinator Archie Ahuna, sits quietly in a folding chair like an Hawaiian Buddha, watching everything with an easy air. "What's interesting about special effects is we do so many different things every day," Logan explains. "We have fires, we're burning rafts and airplanes, we have explosions, we get to 'shoot' people and get paid for it. And we always have to make sure the company is safe. How big our group is depends on how big is the show. We had eighteen people on the pilot, all skilled union people."

Logan notes he's pulled one man off to go help with the second unit work, as Jack Bender directs a sunset scene a stone's throw away of Charlie and Claire walking the beach. "You need to understand that we've only been trained by one man and that's Archie Ahuna. He's the man. There's one way and that's the Ahuna way, which is the right way. I was trained by him about 1983. He comes out of Hawaii and I'm a local guy, too. I grew up down the road. My family are fishermen and farmers and my dad was a welder."

Fires, such as the campfires burning in the shelter area, are usually done with propane using setups like a T–burner, Logan explains. "A T–burner is a burner on a quarter–inch galvanized pipe that looks like a 'T' and you can use it to control the height of the burn. But any damn fool can burn anything. The idea is to be able to control it, *that's* the talent. We have an operator who sets the height, and he's a registered technician who has the skill."

By night, the main campfire—a mixture of cement logs and real wood—is blazing, providing a torrid backdrop to a romantic interlude where Sayid and Shannon share a passionate kiss, and a scene where Sayid gives

A ROMANCE KINDLES BETWEEN SAYID AND SHANNON.

Boone the courtesy of asking his permission to woo Shannon. The latter scene, always scripted as a night scene but originally planned to have Boone picking fruit when Sayid approaches, seems all the more intense with Boone tending a roaring fire.

The entire beach area is lit up by a lighting crane that sends light streaming through the forest, illuminating the billowing campfire smoke that rises into the night sky like windblown fog …

THURSDAY, JANUARY 13 TECH SCOUT AROUND OAHU

Today, director Tucker Gates' unit continues through more script pages for " … In Translation," with scenes set at a private residence meant to be the home of one Byung Han, an environmental safety official who has closed a Paik factory. The scheduled work included Jin delivering a message from Mr. Paik and a dramatic scene of Jin beating up Han to ensure his compliance and save him from a dapper assassin dressed in white, "White Suit," as he's called in the call sheet and sides.

Meanwhile, the tech scout for episode #116, "Numbers"—dubbed "Hurley's episode"—was ranging across Oahu, checking locations for the show, which was scheduled to begin shooting on Tuesday. The morning found some nine production people in the Kaneoha area, gathered in a muddy jungle setting. Jack Bender is here, along with episode director Dan Attias, DP John Bartley, first assistant director Craig West, unit production manager Pat Churchill, special effects man Archie Ahuna, stunt coordinator Michael Vendrell, production designer Stephen Storer, and location manager Jim Triplett.

In "Numbers," Hurley is convinced the numbers he used to win the lottery are cursed. He's shocked to find the same numbers in the French woman's papers that Sayid had taken, and has plunged into the jungle to find her and get some answers. It's overcast here at the location, with a light rain drizzling down from the thick jungle canopy. This area is the French woman's territory, the spot where Naveen Andrews' Sayid was first caught in her trap.

The scout team discuss a scene where Hurley and Charlie will encounter the French woman and run from her rifle fire. As they talk, Ahuna uses colored strips to mark off trees where the wild bullet hits will be set.

Off to one side, hands in his pockets, DP Bartley gazes up at the towering trees, seeming to take it all in. When asked about his resume, he notes he has done shows like *The X–Files* and now here he was on the *Lost* island. "I get the weird shit," he smiles.

Vendrell was off by himself, checking out the mighty banyan trees. In this grove, Hurley will trip a trap in which a massive log swings down and the big guy has to jump out of the way. There would be a real wood log for any camera close–ups (the "hero" log), but the actual pendulum swing would utilize a full–scale foam substitute log built by Ahuna's team, while Vendrell would have a stunt double executing the main move, with a soft pad set up for shots using Jorge Garcia.

The night before, Vendrell notes, *Lost* had aired "Shannon and Boone's story" in the USA and he had taken it as a point of pride that his wife had watched the episode and declared there were no stunts. "That was the best compliment she could give me, because there was Locke fighting with Boone, Boone getting tied up, there was a scene where the monster grabs Shannon and lifts her up in the air. By saying there were no stunts, that meant they integrated perfectly. The key to a good stunt is not making people aware it's a 'stunt,' they just consider that what is happening is part of the action, the story."

"It seems that each episode melds into the next one," smiles Craig West, a twenty–two–year veteran in the business, as the group heads on down the trail. "We work on all of the episodes, except for the guest director, who is supposed to come in and prep eight days and shoot eight days. But we're so ambitious that we don't do it in eight days because it's too much work. The studio would like us to do it in eight days but the scripts are telling us to do it in ten or eleven for the quality of the show. So we have second units and splinters for the actual shooting, people working two units, people shooting when they're supposed to be prepping. We just scramble to accommodate all the work that needs to be done. It keeps us all real busy. Sometimes we get an additional scene or something that has to be shot Monday to air on Wednesday and that gets a little tight. Jack [Bender] has led the way with us, so all the other directors try to follow suit."

The group jumps into their vehicles for the drive out to the main location set at Police Beach. On the way, Storer and Attias discuss a scene in which a rope bridge is supposed to break when Charlie steps onto it. Storer excitedly works up a sketch in which one side of the bridge falls in a trapdoor effect, avoiding the movie cliché in which two ropes holding up a bridge always seem to snap simultaneously.

A stop just up the road from Police Beach provides another hike into an area of thick jungle—"Locke's area," someone notes. Bender looks up at a break in the canopy—it's almost noon but today the sky is dark and cloudy, leaving the jungle shrouded in gloom. "One of the challenges of the show is it gets dark so early," Bender sighs. But he's excited about Hurley's episode: "A lot of the mythology of the show is in this episode."

There's only a brief stop at the Police Beach set as sheets of wind–whipped rain blow through the deserted beach and location, shaking the makeshift shelters. Some in the production have said the show has been lucky with the weather, and this seems an example, as the previous night's campfire scenes in this shelter area missed this sudden storm.

West keeps the scout rolling with the call, "Let's move on, next location." Triplett also notes the tight schedule for appointments he has set up with office managers and home-owners back in Honolulu.

The flashback scenes for "Hurley's episode" includes Hurley visiting the mental hospital and the patient from whom he got the cursed numbers. Doubling for the mental institution will be the downtown Honolulu YWCA, a classic example of Beaux–Arts architecture designed by Julia Morgan, who also designed fabled Hearst Castle in California. The production envisions the ground–floor reception area for the asylum's

main entrance, while a separate "kid's room" is seen as the patients' common room where Hurley visits his old friend. Some wide–eyed kids look up as a YWCA rep ushers the scout group in to survey the room that'll be the setting for the madman with the cursed numbers. "Are you going to buy this place?" one little kid asks.

West calls out that it's time to keep moving and it's back in the vans and off to a residential area of Honolulu where, someone says, "We're heading for Australia and L.A." Indeed, the scout stops at a house that looks

ABOVE: FOR "HURLEY'S EPISODE," THE CREW SETS UP THE SCENE OF HURLEY FOLLOWING THE CABLE TO THE FRENCH WOMAN'S LAIR. ABOVE RIGHT: HURLEY AND CHARLIE INVADE ROUSSEAU'S TERRITORY.

straight out of L.A.'s Boyle Heights district and which will be Hurley's home, while a smaller rear house will double as a house in the Australian outback. One of the production persons who joins this leg of the scout is Ivan Hayden, co–visual effects supervisor who will see that the "outback" house has greenscreen set-ups. "I handle the prep and shoot the plates, take the measurements, make sure the [actor's] eye lines work," Hayden explains. "For this shot, we'll replace the greenscreen with the vast expanse of the Australian outback."

"The challenge of filming in Hawaii is to make Hawaii look like other places," Attias remarks as he walks down the driveway to the street. "It's all an act of illusion but you have to be selective about the details. Less is more."

FRIDAY, JANUARY 14
ILIKAI HOTEL, HONOLULU

It's a 9:00 a.m. shooting call at the Ilikai, where scenes for two episodes will be filming. As Craig West noted, the show's grand ambitions often result in production for different episodes overlapping. Today is a perfect example, with Jack Bender scheduled to borrow the main crew for a big scene for episode #114, "Outlaws," a Sawyer story he's directing. Then the crew will shift back to Tucker Gates and " … In Translation." Both directors are working out of separate suites directly across a narrow hallway from each other. The atmosphere of each would be, figuratively, a world apart: The "Outlaws" scene features a seedy motel room in which Sawyer and a mystery man from his past discuss revenge on the man who ruined Sawyer's life, while the "Translation" scene is ostensibly set in Korea at the home of Sun's father on Sun and Jin's wedding day.

The "Outlaws" shooting hasn't begun, but the hallway is bustling with crew as both adjoining suites are prepared. It's a tight space, but the circus of production today has the advantage of paved streets outside the hotel to park the equipment trailers, while just down the hall production gear can be safely stored and Nancy James has a comfortable room to set up the craft service refreshments.

Things seem under control and first assistant director Allen DiGioia is grabbing a rare moment's respite. "My job is to run the set, recognizing all union rules, and I'm responsible for seeing the work allotment scheduled for each day is accomplished," explains DiGioia, a veteran of twenty years of television. "I plan the day with the amount of hours that we're supposed to shoot and allot so many hours for each scene, for which the director can shoot three cuts, six cuts. But everything depends on the shot and a lot of variables, like the performances, equipment breakdowns, the elements when you're on an outdoor location. What's fascinating about what we do is every day is different. Every day presents new directions and new challenges and that gives us all a high, I think."

DiGioia adds that they're all on weekly contracts— "In this business, as the saying goes, 'You're only as good as yesterday's dailies.'" But he is an enthusiastic advocate for television work. "I do like the pace of TV. It's more my style because I'm naturally hyper and intense. Feature films you have time and work with huge people, which is wonderful stuff. But a lot of times, people in film will have this ego. But in TV we're using the same elements, the same equipment and cameras. In my opinion, take a movie person out of their slower pace and put them in our fast world and they'll be a fish out of water. But take someone out of TV and put them in a movie production, it's like: 'Hey guys, I got two hours to set background! Holy Mackerel!' In TV it's such a challenge to make something good with less time and less money. We have to execute each day and we have a fabulous crew that works like a Swiss clock."

As if to echo DiGioia's sentiment, set decorator Rick Romer is busy preparing a floral arrangement to put in the adjacent Diamond Head Suite, next to Sun's wedding gown. He's working with South American roses, baby's breath and white orchids, the special flower Jin will hand Sun as a token of their love.

"Today, we're doing three different sets here in the hotel," Romer explains. "We're doing a pickup for a hotel room scene for episode 114 ["Outlaws"]; we're doing a scene that's supposed to be Sun's father's house where she is removing her wedding gown, which is the next-door room here, where we've built a wall and completely redressed the room to look Korean; and a third set is the Harbor Suite, which we shot in last August, which is the apartment of Sun and Jin but this time we've added a dining room, where she's prepared a lavish meal for her husband."

The room in Mr. Paik's house is a mix of Old World European and Korean, while Sun and Jin's apartment (on the call sheet schedule to be shot that night) would reflect a younger, contemporary feel emphasizing leather furniture and glass with traditional Asian ornaments. "Unfortunately, we've not been able to be as authentic as we like to be, we've actually mixed in a lot of Chinese and Japanese things with a few things we know to be Korean, like magazines and paintings," Romer says. "But, historically, there is a link between China and Korea, so we're not that far off. The problem is we don't have prop houses in Hawaii so we wind up making deals with stores to rent their items. It helps that we're a huge hit and we've been on the air for a while. When we were starting, all we got was, 'Oh, that plane crash show.' It's always fun to find out what different environment we get to create each week. It'd be a bit easier to find some of the things we need if we were in L.A., but they haven't stumped me yet!"

The flashbacks, Romer explains, provide a fresh challenge each week, such as Monday's Korean fishing village, for which they rented authentic fishing gear. The junk that sailed in the background, however, was a little more made up on the run. "A leaky rowboat is what it was," Romer laughs. "We put two guys in it and one guy's job was to bale and the other guy's job was to throw the net. We had that sail made by an awning company and to age it we put it on the dock and walked on it for about six hours. The funniest thing about that set on Monday was the fish we used we couldn't hang up the day before, it had to be the day of shooting, when they were still frozen. So that morning my crew had their cordless drills out on the dock and were drilling holes through frozen squid by flashlight at six in the morning. So, you never know what you're going to do."

With that, Romer finishes the floral arrangement, the flowers radiating out in layers so the camera can visually "read" the arrangement. Instead of a florist charging the production an exorbitant fee and perhaps packing the flowers too tightly together, Romer has it completed and camera–ready within fifteen minutes.

"Hopefully, audiences won't notice that it's the same carpeting in all three sets," he laughs as he carries the

vase into the wedding suite. "But we did add a rug here. Like I always say, if they're showing the floor we've got other problems."

Across the hall, the crew was transforming the Kolo Head Suite into a motel room for the hard–boiled scene where Sawyer brings a girl he's trying to lay and con and where he'll discover Hibbs, the con man from his past, waiting for him.

There's a rehearsal with Josh Holloway, the woman he's trying to con, played by Brittany Perrineau (Harold's wife), and Hibbs, played by guest star Robert Patrick, whose roles have included the virtually unstoppable T–1000 Terminator in *Terminator 2: Judgment Day* and special agent John Doggett for two seasons of *The X–Files*. The rehearsal takes it from the top: Sawyer making out with the woman in the hallway, pushing into the room and falling on the bed when a light is flicked on

by Patrick's icy character, Sawyer escorting the woman out before pushing Hibbs up against the wall, then settling down while Hibbs calmly walks around to the bar, fixes himself a drink, and a deadly deal goes down.

After the rehearsal, the crew goes to work. Small strips are laid on the carpet for where the actors will hit their marks in the complex choreography that has to take place within the small confines. Klair Ethridge is in the room, loosening her wrists and "getting ready for the day," noting her job requires not only upper body strength but supple wrists for angling the boom. Gaffer Jim Grce and key grip Chuck Smallwood are in with their crews, setting up lights, putting up black cloth outside the window—because of a scheduling quirk, this seedy scene that should be shot in the dead of night is being filmed on a bright Hawaii morning.

Also in the room is Casey Alicino, A–camera dolly grip who will be the right-hand man for Paul Edwards as he shoots the scene. "Paul is high energy. Especially since the DPs alternate on the show, Paul helps keep things consistent, so we're all on the same page, the choreography of it all. I take care of Paul. I spot him when he's doing handheld, or I'll move the dolly."

Off to the side, watching the preparations with a quizzical eye, is "Outlaws" DP John Bartley. "This room shouldn't be this room," Bartley shrugs. "For various reasons, we've had to make this room work, but [the walls] should be darker and not a white hotel room. We're going to run the scene through as far as we can. So it has to be lit dimly and interestingly enough. It's day outside but it's supposed to be night, so we're blackening the windows. It's quite an action scene."

The lights, Bartley explains, are all strategically

THE FLASHBACKS, ROMER EXPLAINS, PROVIDE A FRESH CHALLENGE EACH WEEK, SUCH AS MONDAY'S KOREAN FISHING VILLAGE, FOR WHICH THEY RENTED AUTHENTIC FISHING GEAR.

IN HAPPIER TIMES, JIN PRESENTS SUN WITH A WEDDING RING. BUT TO GAIN SUN'S HAND, JIN HAS HAD TO FORGE A FAUSTIAN BARGAIN WITH SUN'S POWERFUL FATHER.

placed to highlight where the actors will be. The trick will be for Edwards to catch the continuous movement from the wild entrance and fumbling on the bed to when Hibbs turns on the light, then he has to follow the girl out the door, get Sawyer's rough stuff with Hibbs, and catch the con artist as he moves around to the bar to pour a drink. "I want to keep the scene going as long as they can go, so Paul is going to go in handheld, then he's going to whip through with these guys and try to avoid the lights. It'll be dim, it's got to be dim. We don't want to see these white walls. If we were in the third season or something like that and had a swing stage with a whole bunch of flats and a set sitting around we'd probably do this in the studio. But this show is still young, it's still a baby."

The talk of dark hotel rooms is a reminder of Bartley's comment during the tech scout that he likes things "weird." "You get a reputation for being dark and it's hard to get [lighter material] ... But I do like weird and I do like dark. I love film noir, it's one of my favorite things, and we try to incorporate a little bit of that whenever we get a chance."

Out in the narrow hall, makeup man Steve LaPorte explains he got an unexpected note on Thursday asking him to make it appear that Patrick's character was missing most of his left ring finger. So he has taped the actor's finger back and put a prosthetic over it to make it look like Hibbs' finger is missing. "Another rabbit out of the hat," he smiles.

"We're good, we're smoking," someone calls as Jack Bender takes up his seat inside the room to direct the action. The crowded and cramped room is cleared of all unnecessary personnel, and Josh Holloway and Brittany Perrineau take their station outside the hotel door for their big entrance. "Quiet" is called, people stop moving in the hallway, conversation ceases. From within the room there's the call to "Action" and Holloway pushes open the door and he and the woman he wants to con stumble into the room and close the door behind them.

Out in the hallway is set costumer Susan Zaguirre who not only has to make sure the actors are in proper costume but that continuity is maintained—if a jacket is buttoned in one scene, it has to be buttoned in all successive scenes. "Billy Ray McKenna, the costume designer, chooses the costumes by what the character is, what the other characters are going to be wearing, what the period is and what the set is going to be," she explains.

Although the costume department will make specific outfits, because of episodic television's quick turn-arounds, the job usually involves "a lot of shopping," Zaguirre says, although McKenna did have the traditional Korean dress that Yunjin Kim will be wearing specially made.

The costuming for flashback scenes is vastly different from the jungle sequences, Zaguirre adds. "For the island, we have to age a lot of stuff, put stains on the clothes or whatever. Their clothes on the beach and in the jungle can't look like you just bought them, they have to be washed and aged down. Because they might do a stunt, they'll have three or four different [versions] of a shirt. But they all have to look alike. If you have a hole in a shirt you have to match that."

During a break, Robert Patrick heads to the craft room for some refreshment. He recalls it was before Christmas that he got the call to play the part of Hibbs. "What's cool is you don't know how Sawyer is going to react to my character being there and that's when the audience will find out they have a history together. During the scene it's revealed I'm aware something went sour and I'm here to make up for it and give Sawyer information I know he's going to want. The real dark side to all this is I'm actually using him to go kill somebody for me.

"I can say that being hired to fly down to Hawaii and do one scene makes you feel like you're on some sort of secret mission," Patrick chuckles. "It's a neat way to make a living."

Patrick, a veteran of the movies, admits he used to look down on television. But after he did *The Sopranos*, which led to his stint on *The X–Files*, his eyes were opened. "What's appealing to a lot of actors who are making the jump to television, especially in my age group, is the quality now, good shows with very good writing. J.J. Abrams knows what he's doing, I'm telling ya. Television is so fragmented now, with 900 channels, that to catch anybody's eye, a show has to be classy and well written. I think audiences are smart and they won't hang with you if you don't have something that will hook them in some way."

Outside the hotel, near the circus of equipment trucks and trailers, is the camera truck and inside Gary Camp is getting his equipment ready. "It's such a demanding show," he says, recalling the big beach scene and fight between Michael and Jin, when he and Paul Edwards did hours of hand-held camera work, covering many script pages. "At the end of the day, your shoulder is throbbing. But when you're doing any scene with a lot of energy, you want to use handheld. If you want the nice floating, fluid look, or you're on uneven terrain and can't set up a dolly track, you go to Steadicam because it takes out all the erratical movements."

His Steadicam is what Camp hopes will be his ticket

to an A–camera operator position. It is mounted in place in the truck and when it's time for work, it operates like a mechanical appendage, with a gimbal system allowing for the floating camera effect. A built–in monitor provides real–time reference for what the camera sees and whether a shot is on the level. The Steadicam requires strength to carry and grace in the fluid movements with which the operator must move with a scene. The job itself is a workout, but Camp takes it further and since he lives at the Ilikai, he keeps in fighting trim, even after an exhausting work day, with regular weightlifting and workouts in the hotel's twenty–four–hour fitness room.

Around the corner from the camera truck is a tent in a parking lot that has been reserved for the production's commissary. It's lunchtime and Chuck Askerneese, a very proud father, shows up with his wife and baby Zoe, who have flown in from California for a visit.

Tucker Gates is at a nearby table, and during his lunch break contemplates the work of an episodic television director. "I always go into a scene hoping it'll be taken a little further than what I thought it would be. Maybe an actor will take it somewhere, or the director of photography will elevate it somehow, or someone else on set. It's an interesting game. It's funny, I've found that the more experience I have and the more opinionated I am about what I like or don't like, the looser I've gotten about letting people run with things. In my earlier years I was very shot–oriented, trying to make great–looking shots and very involved with the camera. Now, I'm more interested in actors and their performances because the most unexpected things can come from that. The trick is to make everything seem believable."

Tucker gives credit to A–camera operator Paul Edwards, who's a constant presence from episode to episode. "Paul is an essential driving force on the show and he kind of keeps things moving. That's become his role and it's great. It takes a lot of pressure off of me, and again, that's a case of letting it go because it's going someplace that's greater than you ever imagined. This whole process is so collaborative."

Gates echoes Robert Patrick's comments about how TV has changed. "I think television has gotten more sophisticated as audiences have gotten more sophisticated. Some shows have very strict rules about how to shoot things, what's expected in terms of coverage, how scenes are approached. *Lost* seems to be more film–oriented in its style, that's something J.J. and Jack [Bender] have instilled in the show. Being on a soundstage can get a little old after a while, so it's fun that this

LOST SEEMS TO BE MORE FILM-ORIENTED IN ITS STYLE, THAT'S SOMETHING J.J. AND JACK [BENDER] HAVE INSTILLED IN THE SHOW.

show has the dynamic of being outside and dealing with the elements. I love being on the beach and battling the wind and surf and sun and losing the light.

"It's so much fun being here in Hawaii. The first week I was here prepping for this episode, a huge swell came in and they had all these surfers from around the world and they surf this contest called the Eddie Aikau [the "Big Wave International"] at Waimea Bay, which hasn't broken in like four or five years, it only breaks on a certain type of big swell. Well, it went off and the whole island was electric! It was amazing. We went out at six in the morning, before work, and watched for a couple of hours. There were already like 2,000 people out there watching. It was just great because I'd wanted to see this ever since I was a little kid watching surf movies."

Gates is asked whether the big waves were the perfect omen with which to begin his *Lost* episode.

Gates smiles and nods. "Maybe it was a good omen."

In the afternoon, with the "Outlaws" pickups completed, Gates and the crew move into the suite that has been redesigned as a room in the home of Sun's father. Sun and Jin have just been married and the script calls for Sun to be changing into a new dress for the reception, with the traditional wedding dress on a mannequin stand by the lavish floral arrangement Rick Romer whipped up that morning. A best girlfriend is helping Sun change when there's a knock at the door and Jin appears, asking for a moment alone with his wife.

Jin is about to tell his bride he wants to delay their honeymoon to focus on management training for his new role in her father's company. He will give his love a flower, but in the full flush of the romantic moment, neither realizes this is the first sign that Jin has made a Faustian bargain, that Sun's father will gradually pull her husband away from her and into his orbit.

"Be sure to register the tenderness between you," Gates directs Yunjin Kim and Daniel Dae Kim. In the scene, Sun's best friend is played by Tess Yong, a former bodybuilder, personal trainer and sometime actress, who goes through various takes as she gives her friend a knowing glance and exits the room to leave the lovers alone. Off in a corner, behind the camera, makeup man Mark Sanchez and hair stylist Susan Schuler wait to come in between takes to touch up Yunjin Kim.

It's a tender, poignant scene and a marked contrast to the morning's boozy atmosphere of rough sex and cons. But, ironically, the switch in the shooting schedule has this daytime scene with Sun and Jin fighting the light. The sun begins to set and by six o'clock shooting is interrupted to wait out the conch shells blowing outside, which signal the hotel's traditional lighting of the torches at dusk.

That night the crew moves to another floor and a new hotel suite for the scene set in Sun and Jin's apartment. The call sheet notes the focus of the scene: "Jin reflects on what he has become."

SATURDAY, JANUARY 15 FIRST HAWAIIAN BANK, HONOLULU

It's the sixth day and the production will not rest until the seventh day—Tucker Gates explains they've had to play "catch-up," one of the costs of making a weekly TV show look like a movie.

On the day's schedule is a shoot at the First Hawaiian bank at Bishop and King streets, not far from Chinatown, which is not open to the public today. The workday is set to begin at a reasonable hour—the morning sun is actually high in the sky, it's not the usual pre-dawn darkness—and Paul Edwards waits outside the Ilikai for the production van that will take him and other crew members to the downtown location. During the week he's literally been in the center of the action, often directing actors in where and how to move for his camera. "I don't know if it's normal, I'm fairly aggressive at it," Edwards shrugs, talking about his being in the thick of things. "Basically, since the directors and DPs rotate, I'm the consistency on the set, I'm the one who's there every day. I know the actors and they know when I move them around it's for the benefit of the shot. I don't like to sit around."

Edwards has been in the business for twenty years. Like the rest of the band of gypsies, Edwards is well traveled—he singles out Kazakhstan as one of the weirdest places he'd been as a cameraman, a location shoot he shared with Grce and Camp. "We're all location specialists," Edwards says of the *Lost* crew. "A lot of guys do television because they don't like to leave town. Most of it [episodic television] is shot in a centralized area in L.A. or Vancouver."

One of "the carrots" that got him on *Lost*, he says, is the chance he might get to direct in the show's second season. "It's a gift to be on a high-quality show where this opportunity has arisen. I came to Hollywood in 1980 and started in low-budget films when there was still independent, non-union feature filmmaking going on. It's pretty much nonexistent now. I guess the only way to get your chops now is to do rock videos or the odd low-budget film."

Although the production this week has made virtually all its days, getting in all the scripted pages on the daily call sheet is unusual, says Edwards, adding that second unit work had recently been started because most episodes weren't being finished within the regular shooting schedule. "But that's just the nature of the show. Initially, the schedule was supposed to be four days in the studio and four days on location. But that has never happened. We do in eight days to get an hour, what a feature will take months to do. Technically, the job is

A–CAMERA OPERATOR PAUL EDWARDS SHOULDERS HIS CAMERA ON THE POLICE BEACH SET.

getting men and equipment moved around a beach with 700-pound dollies and 300-pound tracks. The show is difficult because just the nature of being on a deserted island makes things difficult to get to. But one of the charms of this show is you actually see water and beach and jungle—it's not a *Gilligan's Island* set. There's definite production value being here in Hawaii, they're getting a lot of bang for their buck. The nature is spectacular, it's hard to find a bad angle on the island. And

WHEN I FIRST READ THE PILOT SCRIPT, TO BE FRANK, I THOUGHT THESE TWO KOREAN CHARACTERS WERE VERY STEREOTYPED.

whenever we get tired of shooting one place, we have the flashbacks that allow us to recreate a lot of stuff in Hawaii that doesn't exist here."

———

It's "skirt day" and some of the crew, including DP Michael Bonvillain, have shown up with island skirts tied around their waists. On the bank's second floor is a spacious area with a high ceiling and vaulting glass walls already dressed out as the high–tech office of Mr. Paik. Stand–in Mike Shower is seated at a table, playing the role of Mr. Paik, and Tony Natoli stands before him as Jin. As the lighting and camera crews set the shot up, Tucker Gates is on the other side of a wall, in an area of office desks where Video Village has been set up and where Patti Dalzell is seated with her production bible. Nearby, Michael Moore has his headphones on and is at the controls of his sound board while John Mumper, another integral member of the sound department, is getting equipment ready.

Gates is seated at one of the office desks with his " … In Translation" script. It's a working document and to help think through a shot he does rough, stick–figure storyboards that he won't refer to on set but which are basically "notes to myself," a mental rehearsal that etches a scene in his mind.

At Video Village, Gates and Dalzell are joined by Jeong Hyeok Park, a Korean dialect coach who can't speak English, and Yunjin Kim, who's come in on her day off to act as a go–between for the translation work.

Even though Daniel Dae Kim and Byron Chung, who plays Mr. Paik, speak Korean, they aren't fluent in various dialects, so Park and Kim work together to make sure the two actors affect the proper pronunciations. It's a touch that's vital to the authenticity of the scene and an example of the production's attention to detail.

During a break for another setup, Yunjin Kim walks to a far end of the floor and another deserted office area where production equipment has been temporarily stored. Kim curls up in a chair and recalls how she came to *Lost*.

"When I first read the pilot script, to be frank, I thought these two Korean characters [Sun and Jin] were very stereotyped and I had a problem with that. The idea of Sun as the typically submissive housewife—I don't know any Korean women who are like that in 2005. I called J.J. and after a two–hour conversation he convinced me why the characters had been developed

TONY NAGY WATCHES THE CAMERA AS IT ZEROES IN ON GARCIA, FOX AND MONAGHAN. NOTE THE CAMERA BOOM DIPPING IN FROM TOP OF PICTURE.

that way, that he wanted to make a point by exaggerating the characters' faults. He told me how my character was going to be developed, that Sun has a great knowledge of eastern medicine so when the western medicine runs out she's going to be helping Jack heal people."

Ultimately, the rift between Sun and Jin at the heart of " … In Translation" is a heartbreaker. "After I read the script for this episode I wrote a note to Damon Lindelof and said, 'The characters of Sun and Jin are so Chekhovian, like in *The Three Sisters*.' The three sisters know they want to go to Moscow and all they have to do is get up and go, but because of who they are they can never do that. That's how I feel about Sun and Jin—If only they could just *talk* to each other! But they can't communicate because of their character faults. To me they're more tragic than the other characters on this island."

Kim's big break had come with her starring role as an undercover North Korean assassin in *Shiri*, a made-in-Korea film done in the American action-thriller mode, which began production with a ceremony that prayed that all the gods of the movie business smile upon their film. The gods answered the prayers as *Shiri* became an international hit and raised the profile of the Korean film industry. Kim's own high-profile role led to her being named a Korean ambassador for the 2002 World Cup. It was also a "Friendship Year" between Korea and Japan, with famous actresses from the respective countries involved in cultural exchanges, and Kim represented Korea for some twenty trips to Japan, including meeting the emperor and empress.

But despite her success in Korea and in Asia, Yunjin Kim has always had a foot in both East and West. "I came to America when I was ten years old and I had been living in New York City all my life. Being famous in Korea and throughout Asia was never in my master plan. I know it sounds silly and shallow, but my dream, ever since I was a kid, was to 'make it' in Hollywood as an Asian-American actress. I wasn't attracted by the idea of fame, it was more about identity. I came to America not knowing how to speak English and I wanted to find my voice and the stage was the only place where I felt, strangely enough, more comfortable than my everyday life. It wasn't a racial issue, no one made fun of me because I was an Asian girl, but I was always on the outside because I couldn't speak English very well."

In seventh grade, Kim played one of the singing extras in the school's production of *My Fair Lady*. Then, in eighth grade, in a play about the life of famed New York Mayor Fiorello La Guardia, she won a major role in the part of Thea, La Guardia's wife. "When I found myself singing out loud in English in *My Fair Lady*, I was loving that I was part of something, that I wasn't an outsider. Then, when I got the role of Thea, it was just liberating. Before that I was almost nonexistent and then, all of a sudden, I was this important person in school, the most popular girl. I thought, 'That's really strange. Just because you get to act on stage they care about you! What is that?'

"But I loved just being part of something. I was

LEFT TO RIGHT:
PRODUCERS JAVIER
GRILLO-MARXUACH,
SARAH CAPLAN AND
BRYAN BURK, SERIES
CO-CREATOR DAMON
LINDELOF AND
MALCOLM DAVID KELLY,
IAN SOMERHALDER
AND DANIEL DAE KIM.

always attracted to talented people and wanted to be among them. One of my best friends knew how to play the piano like you wouldn't believe. I would sit and watch her play and it seemed she was in a different world, a different reality. It's like with talented actors who get so involved in a scene they forget a camera is shooting them, that the other person is another actor pretending to be a character. You really see this on stage. When you're an actor you feel that heightened level of reality and the audience watching you forgets, even for a few seconds, that they're watching you on a stage with actors and props. They're really believing and you're sort of lifted off your seat."

It's night outside the wall–sized glass windows of the downtown bank. Daniel Dae Kim and Byron Chung have been doing takes of a dramatic confrontation — the warning that Mr. Paik has asked Jin to give Byung Han, the Secretary for Environmental Safety, has gone unheeded. Han has closed down one of his factories and Paik is furious. The actor raises his voice, slams his palm on a table, which echoes in the vast room. Off to a side is the ominous presence of White Suit, the cool killer played by Chil Kong.

story, Jin will be driving White Suit to the final rendezvous with Byung Han, a scene that will come before the sequence shot done on Thursday, in which Jin beat the man to win obedience to Mr. Paik and keep White Suit's gun holstered.

Outside the bank it's a breezy, pleasant night. There's a dinner break, with a sushi bar set up in the plaza outside the bank building. On–set dresser John Lee is celebrating a birthday and in the bank's ground–floor reception area a birthday cake is sliced up and there's talk of drinks later at the Buddha Bar in Waikiki.

Meanwhile, the "dark sedan" is rigged with cameras. Some of the crew sits around and watches. There's Richard "Udee" Dahl, the transportation co–captain who's always keeping an eye on the logistics of moving the production around, there's set medic Michael Broady, who's always on call, but for the moment can indulge in a sushi dinner.

BUT THEN COMES THE RADIO MESSAGE FROM GATES' CAR—THEY'VE DECIDED THEY DON'T NEED TO SHOOT THE CAR-TO-CAR STUFF. FINALLY, MARTINI TIME HAS COME.

The next scene to be shot is in script continuity on the call sheet: "Dark Sedan Driving Thru Traffic." In the

It'll be cramped in the camera and "hero" car, with Bonvillain and Gates riding along and the actors alternating for respective cuts of Kim at the wheel and Kong in the backseat. But it's going to be particularly cramped

feed—White Suit is on the little screen, coolly screwing a silencer on his gun as streaks of neon and headlights stream outside his car window.

By 11:00 the end of the work week is tantalizingly close and with not much to do but follow the camera car, conversation picks up and soon the group is joking and swapping stories. Talk turns to *Lost* "fall downs"—literally the spills taken during work, and there's a roar of approval when Ethridge describes the time she tripped over a branch and fell but managed to still keep her boom held high! And then Grce and Smallwood begin talking about "the martini" and everyone nods—the phrase is classic Hollywood parlance for the last shot of the day.

But the workday seems destined to go past the midnight hour. The plan is to get a series of complex "car-to-car" shots that will require a camera car running alongside the hero car where Daniel Dae Kim will be at the wheel.

But then comes the radio message from Gates' car—they've decided they don't need to shoot the car-to-car stuff. Finally, martini time has come.

for sound man Michael Moore, who will be secured with his equipment in the car's trunk. The best way to do this scene, Jim Grce and Chuck Smallwood explain, is to have motorcycle cops as escorts and use an "insert car" for filming. The production will be getting an insert car soon, someone says, but tonight it's down and dirty.

A police officer has shown up for the shoot, which involves the lead car and several crew vans merging into traffic and circling a planned circuit of downtown streets so the camera can record the actors in the car with neon and streetlights and traffic headlights flashing.

While they start with filming Kong in the backseat, Daniel Dae Kim gets into the "follow van" that carries Grce, Smallwood, Klair Ethridge and Allen DiGioia. The vehicles leave the bank and head out into downtown Honolulu traffic. While DiGioia keeps in radio communication with the lead camera car, Smallwood holds up a handheld wireless monitor that's getting the camera

The vehicles return to the bank, where Michael Moore gingerly extricates himself from the trunk, none the worse for wear. Dahl is still there, waiting to see that all the transportation department vehicles get everyone home.

Some of the *Lost* crew, already having wrapped work, have headed to the Buddha Bar in Waikiki, others are unwinding in their apartments or hotel rooms, some run late–night errands. Sunday beckons, a welcome respite after the long work week, a chance to escape the lost island.

But it's a brief rest for the *Lost* crew. Monday's final shooting for " … In Translation" is scheduled for the cave set and then the work week will turn to Hurley's story and that mysterious sequence of cursed numbers. It all begins on Monday with a 7:00 a.m. call, a few minutes before dawn officially breaks. That's when the Warriors of the Wilderness will reassemble and get back to the business of making dreams.

US ACKNOWLEDGMENTS

Thanks to J.J. Abrams and Hyperion for letting me get "lost." On the Hyperion side, there was the expert guidance and good humor of editor Gretchen Young, with a tip of the hat and a low bow to her assistant, Zareen Jaffery.

On the ABC side, my thanks to Bruce Gersh. Melissa Harling was wonderful, as usual, in handling logistics and all incoming questions and requests. My appreciation also to Jason Hoffman, for access to the voluminous photo archives.

Bryan Burk was extremely helpful in providing Lost background and general help, while his executive assistant, Samantha Thomas, expertly handled the various requests that came her way. My thanks as well to Athena Wickham, J.J.'s assistant, for her help and good grace, and to Claudette Waddle for coordinating time with Sarah Caplan.

My appreciation to Damon Lindelof, Carlton Cuse and all the geniuses in the Writer's Room. A special thanks to Matt Ragghianti for fact-checking help— dude, you get "carte blanche" for any of Sawyer's cool stuff!

My thanks to Jack Bender and Jean Higgins for every courtesy on the island and for Kaleen Yamase for all her help on the island and off. My deep appreciation to Tucker Gates and all the cast and crew on " … In Translation" for letting me watch them at work and to Kris Krengel for getting me started. And I'm not getting out of here without a salute to Anthony Shields, Megan Hirokawa, Nancy James and "Udee" Dahl.

Special thanks to the entire crew at Madison Press Books, which worked with Hyperion on the book's editorial and production challenges. Charis Cotter provided superb editorial guidance and coordinated production between Madison, the author and Hyperion. A grateful thanks to the rest of the Madison crew, including Christopher Jackson for his leadership and Claire Dawson of Underline Studio for her exciting design.

To my brother Peter, who helped get me a guest spot on the San Francisco "Morning Show" radio program to discuss this Lost world—thanks, bro.

Thank you, one and all! May you all find what you're looking for on the island.
—M.C.V.

Hyperion

Thanks to everyone at Hyperion for their support and enthusiasm for this project, especially Bob Miller, Ellen Archer and Will Schwalbe; Gretchen Young and Zareen Jaffery in editorial; Dan Taylor for the front-cover design; Linda Prather and Navorn Johnson in production; and Deirdre Smerillo in contracts.

Madison Press Books

The Lost Chronicles was produced by Madison Press Books for Hyperion
Project Editor: Charis Cotter
Assistant Editor: Shima Aoki
Book Design: Underline Studio
Director, Business Development:
    Christopher Jackson

About the Author

Mark Cotta Vaz is the author of twenty-one books, including several *New York Times* bestsellers and the award-winning *The Invisible Art: The Legends of Movie Matte Painting* (co-authored with Craig Barron). His recent titles include the biographical work, *Living Dangerously: The Adventures of Merian C. Cooper, Creator of King Kong*. In addition to *The Lost Chronicles*, his other television series "companion book" is *Alias: Declassified*.

PHOTO BY BRUCE WALTERS

LOST CREW

Created By:
Jeffrey Lieber and J.J. Abrams &
Damon Lindelof

Executive Producers:
J.J. Abrams, Damon Lindelof,
Bryan Burk, Jack Bender, Carlton Cuse

Co–Executive Producers:
David Fury, Jesse Alexander

Supervising Producers:
Javier Grillo–Marxuach, Christian Taylor

Consulting Producer:
Lynn Litt

Executive Consultants:
Jesse Alexander, Jeff Pinkner

Producers:
Leonard Dick, Eddy Kitsis,
Adam Horowitz

Co–Producer:
Jennifer Johnson

Story Editor:
Paul Dini

Staff Writer:
Monica Macer

Producers:
Sarah Caplan, Jean Higgins

Co–Producer:
Ra'uf Glasgow

Directors (in alphabetical order):
J.J. Abrams, Daniel Attias, Jack Bender,
Tucker Gates, Marita Grabiak, David
Grossman, Rod Holcomb, Kevin Hooks,
Robert Mandel, Stephen Williams,
Greg Yaitanes, Michael Zinberg

Cast: (Series Regulars in alphabetical order)
Naveen Andrews, Emilie de Ravin,
Matthew Fox, Jorge Garcia, Maggie
Grace, Josh Holloway, Malcolm David
Kelley, Daniel Dae Kim, Yunjin Kim,
Evangeline Lilly, Dominic Monaghan,
Terry O'Quinn, Harold Perrineau,
Ian Somerhalder

Guests and Co–starring Cast (in order of appearance):
Fredric Lane, L. Scott Caldwell, Kimberley
Joseph, John Dixon, Michelle Arthur,
Dale Radomski, Geoff Heise, Barbara
Vidinha, Nick Tate, Billy Ray Gallion,
Stephen J. Rafferty, John Simon Jones,
John O'Hara, John Terry, Sev Palmer,
Veronica Hamel, Andy Trask, Sora Jung,
Meilinda Soerjoko, Neil Hopkins, Glenn
Cannon, Christian Bowman, Richard
MacPherson, Dustin Watchman, Kristin
Richardson, Michael DeLuise,
Billy Mayo, Jim Woitas, William Mapother,
Jenny Chang, Nick Jameson, Keir
O'Donnell, Barry Whitfield, Lisa Fraser,
Andrea Gabriel, Scott Paulin, Mira Furlan,
Navid Negahban, Xavier Alaniz,
Jackie Maraya, Matt Moore, Mark Stitham,
Michael Adamshick, Tim Halligan, Victor
Brown, Achilles Gacis, Dezmond Gilla,
Michael Vendrell, Kelly Rice, Charles
Mesure, Adam Leadbeater, Tamara Taylor,
Monica Garcia, David Starzyk, Natasha
Goss, Darren Richardson, Sally Strecker,
Jim Piddock, Eric Griffith, Gordon
Hardie, Susse Budde, Brittany Perrineau,
Jeff Perry, Robert Patrick, Stewart
Finlay–McLennan, Alex Mason, Byron
Chung, John Choi, Joey Yu, Chil Kong,
John Shin, Angelica Perreira, Tess Young,
Kiya Lee, Lillian Hurst, Archie Ahuna,
Derrick Bulatao, Joy Minaai, Ron Marasco,
Dann Seki, Maya Pruett, Ron Bottitta,
Jayne Taini, Swoosie Kurtz, Kevin Tighe,
Tyler Burns Laudowicz, George O'Hanlon,
Lawrence A. Mandley, Julie Ow,
Zack Ward, John Tilton, Julie Bowen,
Clarence Logan, Jenny Gago, David
Patterson, Donnie Keshawarz, Dariush
Kashani, Ali Shaheed Amini, Warren
Kundis, Anosh Yagoob, Daniel Roebuck,
Tamara Lynch, Mackenzie Astin,
Beth Broderick, Michelle Rodriguez,
Kevin E. West, Chard Hayward, Ruz
Rusden, Kylie Dragna, Wendy Braun,
Robert Frederick, John Walcutt, Terasa
Livingstone, Suzanne Turner, Mark "Kiwi"
Kalaugher, Mary Ann Taheny, M.C. Gainey

Production Staff:
Pat Churchill, Steve Cainas, Jack Philbrick,
Day Permuy, Melinka Thompson–Godoy,
Dustin Gomes, Shelley Stevens,
Adam Courier, Jason Skweres, Oliver
Coke, Kaleen Yamase, Nicole Andersen,
Claudette Waddle, Athena Wickham,
Marybeth Sprows, Samantha
Thomas, John Kapral, Sean Gerace

Accounting Staff:
Jon Cohoe, Leah Estes, Dianne
Mapp–Cheek, Chad McQuay, Trey
Sullivan, Julie Bernards, Faye Baker,
Mele Locey, Anne Marie Feldman

Art Department:
Mark Worthington, Christina Wilson,
Carlos Barbosa, Tim Beach, Stephen
Storer, Mimi Gramatky, Ron Yates,
Ray Yamagata, Lynette Wich, Michelle
Coleman, Christopher Tandon,
Mynette Louie

Assistant Directors:
Craig West, Allen DiGioia, Kris Krengel,
Ric Groenendal, Lon Takiguchi, Mary
Ellen Woods, Sally Sue Beisel–Lander,
Hope Garrison, Bobbie Blyle, Bernadette
Axelrod, Joyce McCarthy, Ken Wada,
Brenda Lyn Richards

Set PAs:
Michele Cusick, Mandy Yaeger, Luke Pearsal, Lillian Awa, Matt Sivaborvorn, Michael Iwamasa, Rich Linke, Hera Guillano

Camera:
Lawrence Fong, Michael Bonvillain, John Bartley, Paul Edwards, Ric Tiedeman, Neal Norton, Phil Carr–Forster, Gregory Lundsgaard, Doug Oliveras, Tony Nagy, Mary Stankiewicz, Don Duffield, Jr., Serge Nofield, Andy Sydney, Rick Brock, Matthew Berner, Torry Tukuafu, Jim Cobb, Mario Perez, Darren Necessary, Joaquin Castillo, Guy Lorio, Paul Gentry, Mark Connolly, Chris Toll, Jeff Pelton, Alan Jacoby

Casting:
April Webster, Veronica Collins, Mandy Sherman, Alyssa Weisberg, Scott David (LA) & Anna Fishburn, Rachel Whitley, Julie Carlson (Hawaii), Jerry Franks (Hawaii)

Catering:
Moumen El Haji, Darren Sato, Susan Gilhooley, Brian Market

Construction:
Dale Destefani, Curtis Crowe, Jeff Passanante, William Gideon, Brian Barnhart, Jim Davis, John Leone, Bob Decourt, Philip A. Coffman, Tim Vierra, Brian Walker, Troy Bourguignon, Cliff Bergman, Mariano Fernandez, Mokuahi Ribuca, Cory Tomimatsu, Derrick Kaupiko, William Risso, Paul Heatherly, John Quincy Adams, Timothy Cullen, A'ne Tranetzki, Damon Darchuck, Kanoa Dahlin, Barry Jones, Michael Bomar, John Michael Hull, Robert 'Dante' Denne, Garry McEvok, David Cambra, Jonathan Kamaka, Lucius Lau

Costumes:
Kathryn Morrison–Pahua, Billy Ray McKenna, Roland Sanchez, Keawe Thurston, Susan Zaguirre, Dallas Dornan, Mel Pang, Ivy Rowan, Steven Stitt–Bergh, Steve Adams, Sloane Perry Torne, Artemio Carpio, Robert Steward, Olga Ishkhanova, Toni Kehaulani Reed, Robyn Zucker, Thomas Morrison, Judith Matsumoto, Charlie Kaeo, Priscila Coronel

Craft Service:
Jeff Tapert, Jon Gardner, Donovan Ahuna, John Cambra, Jr., Dayne Ahuna, Nancy James, Jason Skaggs, Dana Sato, Bernard "Bulli" Lam Ho

Editors:
Mary Jo Markey, Steve Semel, Mark Goldman;
Assistants: Lucy Wojciechowski, Lance Stubblefield

Electric:
Jim Grce, Mark "Kiwi" Kalaugher, Kevin Kersting, Paul Santos, Lucas Seno, Stan Tandal, Henry Fordam, Charles Kramer, Zachary Kim, Ishmail Hill, Adam House, Jeff Zucker, Kieran Waugh, Jeff Barco, Andy Huber, Damon Marcellino, Florentino Jimenez, Rene Jiminez, Kevin Lang, Steve Hastings, David Dubois, Brewnt Studler, Joshua Sinkoski, Mark Hadland, Gomidas Semerjian, Brian Vollert, Shawn Christiensen, Jeff Levy, Bruce Sharp, Andre Williams, Steve Bentley, Jon Munson

Grip:
Chuck Smallwood, Jeff Miller, Casey Alicino, George Gregory, Jessie Martin, Jimmy Thurston, Austin Fraser, Bert "Kolo" Barber, Shane White, Glenn Grimes, Edward "Ted" Tunney, Lee Kaneakua, Keoki Smith, Keith Talley, Eric Kamakaole, Jeff Day, Nathan Sharp, David Ahuna, Gregg Norton, Steve Hoch, Jerry Kim, Christopher Reed, Jeffrey Brown, William Hewson, Paul Rychlec, Steve Savage, Walter Byrnes, Keola Jones, James Levy, Harland Kanahele, Vincent Mossman, Willliam Uale, Tony Marra, James Walsh, Bob Preston, Hector Miranda, Tim Nash, Steve Allessi, Marshall Valentine, Matt Barden

Greens:
Troy Araki, Koa Sua, Kamron Kamauoha, Nainoa Glover, Matthew A. Kekoa, Wallace Wong, Keli'l Correa, Keith Frank, Daryl Tachibana, C. Liloa Wong, Kelii Correa, Isaia Robins, Walter Thuener, Louis Freitas

Locations:
Jim Triplett, Randy Spangler, Michael Haro, George Larson, Mathias "Scratch" Wessinger, Miki Yasufuku, Linda "Sam" Glynn, Donnie Darnell, Sean Hallock, Ryan Hoke, Robert Potter, Brent Wloczewski, Alex Reed

Makeup and Hair:
Steve LaPorte, Mark Sanchez, Kate Shorter, Jay Wejebe, Keith Hall, Veronica Lorenz, Karen Preiser, Bryan Furer, Laine Rykes, Tania Kahale–Taylor, Christine Lillo–Haunga, Mary Ann Changg, Matthew W. Mungle, Susan Schuler, James Sartain, Rita Troy, JoAnn Stafford–Chaney, Laurel Kelly, Tyler Ely, Paulette Crammond, Chantal Boom'la

Medic:
Michael Broady, Oliver Kunia, David Dever, Harry Tam Alu

Music Composer:
Michael Giacchino

Music Editing:
Steve Davis, Alex Levy

Photographers:
Mario Perez, Carin Baer, Steve Fenn

Postproduction:
Tamara Isaac, Amanda Lencioni, Kyle Pennington

Property:
Doug Madison, Mike Carrillo, Chuck Askerneese, Shawn Gray, Jennings Fowler, Peter Clarke, Michael Gastaldo, David Saltzman, Andrew Swan, Zachery Corteau, Scott Ejercito, David Dever

Script Supervisor:
Dawn Gilliam, Patti Dalzell, Summer Banner

Set Dressing:
Rick Romer, Gary Brewer, Derrick Kaupiko, Byron Jeremiah, Alvin "Budge" Akiu, John Lee, Michael Gilday, Robert Greenfield, John Maxwell, Cythia LaJeunnesse, Sean Ginevan, Cameron Mathison, Russell Maki, Michael Kaahanui, Jonah Chang, John Marrano

Sound Mixing:
Production: David Barr–Yaffe, C.A.S.,
Richard Lightstone, Michael Moore,
Robert Joe Michalski, Dan Lipe,
Klair Ethridge, John Mumper, Tanya Peel
Post Production: Scott Weber,
Frank Marrone

Sound Editing and Effects:
Tom deGorter, Trevor Jolly, Marc
Glassman, Maciek Malish, Chris Reeves,
Dana Olsefsky, Gary Wilkes

Special Effects:
Archie Ahuna, Clarence Logan, Gary W.
McEnroe, Sr., Charles Raymond, Fern
Ahuna, Michael L.K. Sua, Nash Lyons,
Kahi "Easter" Logan, Jay B. King,
Alan Kiriu, Bo K. Ulii, Ralph Kawakami,
Ronald Goldstein, Matthew Leong,
Alvin B. Akiu, Keith Frank, James Murphy,
Auwae Noa Kepoikai, Rick Crumb,
Paul Heatherly, Dana Olsefsky

Stand–Ins:
Eyal Zimet, Claudia Cox, Tony Natoli,
Rand Wilson, Mike Shower, Dustin
Geiger, Joah Bailey, Paul Rosenthal,
Jen Sheridan, John Yee, Aaron Gold

Storyboards:
Todd Robertson, Eric Ramsey

Studio Teachers:
Susan Salerno, Missy Simms

Stunt Coordinator:
Michael Vendrell, Gregg Smrz, Colin Fong

Technical Advisor:
Tommy Fisher

Transportation:
Jeff Gowing, Jeff Couch, Marlo Hellerstein,
Myles Kawakami, Jeff Eggleston, Michael
Menapace, Richard "Udee" Dahl, John
Rodrigues, Bill Hannah, Kim Magruder,
Lyle Yashuhara, Andrew Pangkee, Harold
"Bunny" Ahuna, Alex "Lance" Teixeira,
Shane Soares, Anna Camenson,
Patti Patterson, Joseph Tavares, Stuart
Soosman, Darren Dacosin, Mike Hipa,
Nathaniel Dearmore, Bill Hernandez,

Shyrome Pahia, Carl Bertelman, Keoua
Kauhi, Sr., Fredrick Kaluna, Ekepati
"Masa" Niko, Mike Gueso, Alfred "Sonny"
Lum, Alber Saddler, Stace Kawakami,
Vernon Dautenhahn, Jalmes Jones,
Galo Diaz De Tuesta, Clinton Taylor, Jesse
Parton, Gregory Hoslet, Michael Moss,
J. Larry Michael, Lance Lee, Devin
Donohue, Douglas A. Farias, William
Keamohuli, Chad Kawakami, Raliegh
Otineru, Abraham Hall, John Cambra,
Keoni Nakanelue, David Su'a, Clinton
Yoshikawa, Robert Suka, Keoua Kauhi,
Jesse Duarte, William Duarte, Blaine
Kaakimaka, Wade Nagata, Mike Young

Visual Effects:
Kevin Blank, Mitch Suskin, Ivan Hayden,
Armen Kevorkian

Script Coordinator:
Brent Fletcher

Writers' Assistants:
Rachel Mellon, Dawn Kelly,
Matt Ragghianti

Animal Wrangler:
Kim Stahl

"Vincent":
Madison

Second Unit

Camera:
Phil Carr–Forster, Don King, Ron Condon,
Mark Gerasimenko, Paul Atkins Scott
Ronnow, Rick Brock, Jimmy Cobb, Jal
Mansson, Brian Matsumura

Sound:
John Reynolds, John Fielden, Leu
Maddox, Christopher Wiecking

Transportation:
John "Sudee" Dahl, Clinton Yoshikawa,
Gerald Mito

Water Safety:
Brian Keaulana, Terry Ahue

Boat Coordinators:
Victor Lozano, Leah Warshawski

Water Unit

Assistant Director:
Stephen Buck

Set PA:
William Hyde

Camera:
Pete Romano, Peter Lee

Catering:
Jose Elmer Flores, Elmer Oceda

Costume:
Tim Wegman

Electric:
David Maddux

Grip:
Jason Poteek, John Miller, Curt Siverts

Locations:
George Larsen

Makeup and Hair:
Mark Landon

Stunt Coordinator:
Tim Trella

Special Effects:
Gary D'Amico, Philip Bartko

Transportation:
Mario Hellerstein, Rudy Herrera,
James Neilan, Vernon Deutenhahn,
John Huskins, Don Levinski

Bad Robot Productions:
Thom Sherman, President